BOOK SOLD
NO LONGER R.H.P.L.
PROPERTY

RICHMOND HILL
PUBLIC LIBRARY

MAY 3 1 2013

CENTRAL LIBRARY
905-884-9288

PHILOSOPHICAL PEARLS OF THE SHAKESPEAREAN DEEP

Rembrandt van Rijn, *Aristotle with Bust of Homer*, 1653.
Oil on canvas. Courtesy of the Metropolitan Museum of Art.

PHILOSOPHICAL PEARLS OF THE SHAKESPEAREAN DEEP

Farhang Zabeeh

Prometheus Books
59 John Glenn Drive
Amherst, New York 14228–2119

Published 2013 by Humanity Books, an imprint of Prometheus Books

Philosophical Pearls of the Shakespearean Deep. Copyright © 2013 by Farhang Zabeeh All rights reserved. No part of this publication may be reproduced, stored in a retrieval system, or transmitted in any form or by any means, digital, electronic, mechanical, photocopying, recording, or otherwise, or conveyed via the Internet or a website without prior written permission of the publisher, except in the case of brief quotations embodied in critical articles and reviews.

Inquiries should be addressed to
Humanity Books
59 John Glenn Drive
Amherst, New York 14228–2119
VOICE: 716–691–0133
FAX: 716–691–0137
WWW.PROMETHEUSBOOKS.COM

17 16 15 14 13   5 4 3 2 1

Library of Congress Cataloging-in-Publication Data

Zabeeh, Farhang.
 Philosophical pearls of the Shakespearean deep / by Farhang Zabeeh.
  p. cm.
 Includes bibliographical references and index.
 ISBN 978-1-61614-652-8 (hardcover)
 ISBN 978-1-61614-653-5 (ebook)
 1. Shakespeare, William, 1564-1616—Philosophy. 2. Philosophy in literature. I. Title.

PR3001.Z326 2013
822.3'3—dc23

2012027545

Printed in the United States of America on acid-free paper

For Irma B. Jaffe

"'Fair, kind, and true,' is all my argument.
'Fair, kind, and true,' have often lived alone,
Which three till now, never kept seat in one."
—Shakespeare (SON 105)

"Poetry is something more philosophic and of graver import than history, since its statements are of the nature of universals, whereas those of history are singular."
—Aristotle, *Poetics*

CONTENTS

AUTHOR'S NOTE		9
ABBREVIATIONS OF SHAKESPEAREAN TITLES		10
PREFACE		11
INTRODUCTION		15
Chapter One:	Philosophy and Poetry	31
	The Historical Setting	31
	Socrates on Poetry	33
Chapter Two:	Falstaff: A Parody of Socrates	55
	Plato's *Phaedo*; Aristophanes' *The Clouds*	55
Chapter Three:	Plato's Voice	81
	The Real and the Shadow	83
	Self-Knowledge: The Mirror Metaphor	95
	On Autonomy and Bondage	98
	On Death and Intimations of Immortality	114
Chapter Four:	Aristotle: Poetry and History	131
	The Universal and the Particular	131
	The Presence of Aristotle's Ethics	140

Chapter Five:	On Thinking and Speaking	151
	The Semantic Ascent	157
	On Metaphor	171
	The Magic of Names	195
Chapter Six:	Subjectivity	209
	Inwardness or Consciousness	209
	Conscience or Moral Awareness	217
	Knowledge of Other Minds	219
Chapter Seven:	The Pragmatic Dimension: Shakespeare's Presentation of Political and Moral Values	223
	Virtue and Vice	223
	Justice and Mercy	236

NOTES 257

SELECTED BIBLIOGRAPHY 267

INDEX 271

AUTHOR'S NOTE

My introduction to Shakespeare was through *Macbeth*, which I read in a Persian translation in 1934 when I was a sixteen-year-old student in Tehran, my native city. Excited, I found in our school library other plays by this author in English, which I read nonstop over and over again. However, at the University of California at Berkeley, where I arrived fourteen years later, studied philosophy, and eventually received a PhD, my studies and my academic career left little time to read outside of my field (the most frequent of academic complaints!) until as a professor of philosophy at Roosevelt University in Chicago I was able to offer a course in the philosophy of literature. Thus, Shakespeare came back into my life and I have been absorbed in the plays and poems ever since.

I wish to thank my dear friend Professor Irma B. Jaffe for her tireless efforts in editing my book, and Steven L. Mitchell, editor in chief of Prometheus Books, for his constructive criticism.

ABBREVIATIONS OF SHAKESPEAREAN TITLES

ADO	*Much Ado about Nothing*	MND	*A Midsummer Night's Dream*
ANT	*Antony and Cleopatra*		
AWW	*All's Well that Ends Well*	MV	*The Merchant of Venice*
AYL	*As You Like It*	OTH	*Othello*
COR	*Coriolanus*	PER	*Pericles*
CYM	*Cymbeline*	PHT	*The Phoenix and the Turtle*
ERR	*The Comedy of Errors*	PP	*The Passionate Pilgrim*
F1	*First Folio ed. (1623)*	Q	*Quarto ed.*
F2	*Second Folio ed. (1632)*	R2	*Richard II*
HAM	*Hamlet*	R3	*Richard III*
1H4	*Henry IV, Part 1*	ROM	*Romeo and Juliet*
2H4	*Henry IV, Part 2*	SHR	*The Taming of the Shrew*
H5	*Henry V*	SON	*Sonnets*
1H6	*Henry VI, Part 1*	TGV	*Two Gentlemen of Verona*
2H6	*Henry VI, Part 2*	TIM	*Timon of Athens*
3H6	*Henry VI, Part 3*	TIT	*Titus Andronicus*
H8	*Henry VIII*	TMP	*The Tempest*
JC	*Julius Caesar*	TN	*Twelfth Night*
JN	*King John*	TNK	*The Two Noble Kinsmen*
LC	*A Lover's Complaint*	TRO	*Troilus and Cressida*
LLL	*Love's Labour Lost*	VEN	*Venus and Adonis*
LR	*King Lear*	WIV	*The Merry Wives of Windsor*
LUC	*The Rape of Lucrece*		
MAC	*Macbeth*	WT	*The Winter's Tale*
MM	*Measure for Measure*		

PREFACE

The presence of philosophical thought in Shakespeare has been acknowledged by many literary critics from William Richardson, *A Philosophical Analysis of Shakespeare* (1774); W. J. Birch, *An Inquiry into the Philosophy and Religions of Shakespeare* (1848); and K. J. Spalding, *The Philosophy of Shakespeare* (1963); to Wyndham Lewis, *The Lion and the Fox. The Role of the Hero in the Plays of Shakespeare* (1930). However, this aspect of Shakespeare's plays and poems has been denied by a number of writers including Bernard Shaw, *Epistle Didactory to Man and Superman* (1903); André Gide, *Letters-Preface* (the translation of *Hamlet*); George Santayana, *Interpretation of Poetry and Religion* (1900); and T. S. Eliot, *Selected Essays* (1964). In recent times the issue has been revived largely due to the linguistic turn in philosophy by literary critics such as A. D. Nuttall in his *Shakespeare the Thinker* and by Colin McGinn, a philosopher by profession who discusses six plays in his *Shakespeare's Philosophy* in the context of his perception that doubt and uncertainty are evident in the characters throughout the plays. Those critics have contributed valuable insights in their investigations of philosophy in Shakespeare's works.

Like McGinn, I am also a philosopher by profession. My aim in this book is to reveal Shakespeare's use of the heritage of rich thoughts he acquired and expanded upon, not in a few quotations, as others have done, but to string the many philosophical pearls, the conceptual inventions, from the Shakespearean deep on strands of the *philosophical issues* that have preoccupied Western philosophy since ancient times so as to present to the reader a necklace of rare beauty.

Thus, I have considered philosophy in the Bard's works through the use of such philosophical issues as universals and particulars; time: objective, subjective, and personal; reason, will, and passion; sign, sense, and denotation (semantics); and moral and political values (pragmatics) as they appear throughout his entire oeuvre rather than point them out as they are found in various plays.[1]

My approach reveals the clear and evident relationship of Shakespeare's thought, as expressed through the characters in the plays as well as by the speaker of the sonnets, to the expression of similar ideas found in the writings of the ancient classical philosophers and the Renaissance humanists. We may take as examples, among many, Hamlet's eulogy of the human being as a paragon of animals compared with Pico della Mirandola's oration on the dignity of man, which we quote in chapter 1, and Richard III, for whom, as for Thrasymachus in the *Republic,* justice is in the interest of the stronger. "Conscience is but a word that cowards use devised at first to keep the strong in awe. Our strong arm be our conscience, sword, or laws." In the *Prince* Machiavelli argues that the prince may violate all moral principles in the interest of the state.

The presence of these philosophical concepts, the detailed depiction of the glories and miseries of humankind, the "invention of the human" (according to Harold Bloom), the conception of art, and the exultation of nature as God all speak of Shakespeare as a secular humanist. He was a humanist such as were his contemporaries Erasmus, Thomas More, and Francis Bacon, the notable figures of the northern Renaissance, which followed the Italian Renaissance minus its religious context; his philosophical views resemble particularly the naturalistic ideas of Bacon. Shakespeare was aware of the writing of some Italian Renaissance writers such as Pico della Mirandola and Castiglione, and shared their antischolastic views although not their Neo-Platonism.

Shakespeare's erudition is celebrated in a Latin inscription on the monument at his grave site: JUDICIO PYLUM, GENIO SOCRATUM ARTE MARONNEM, TERRA TEGIT, POPULUS MAERET, OLYMPUS HABET (A Nestor in judgment, a Socrates in intellect, a Virgil in art: the earth covers him, the people mourn him, and Olympus has him). Readers of this book will doubtless be surprised and delighted, as I was, when I first encountered the extraordinary echoes from Homer, Socrates, Plato, Aristotle, Lucretius, Ovid, Horace, Virgil, and from Dante to Machiavelli, Montaigne, Erasmus, and others, most of which have never been discussed heretofore.

I hope that this book will delight, inform, and enrich its readers as it provides the clasp that holds together the pearls that make the necklace—Shakespeare's gift, which, with his substantial heritage, he has bequeathed to "ages hence . . . and states unborn." It has been said that each age discovers something new in the great works of art of the past unrecognized by previous generations.

As M. M. Bakhtin observed of the Bard, "He has grown because of that which actually has been and continues to be found in his work but that neither himself nor his contemporaries could consciously perceive and evaluate in the context of the culture of their epoch."[2]

Let us, then, not lose sight of the philosophical pearls of the Shakespearian deep while we are still under the spell of the poet's enchanting songs and the wonder of his stage.

INTRODUCTION

> "Poetry is more philosophic and of graver import than history."
>
> —Aristotle, *Poetics*

According to Cicero, Socrates "brought down from heaven to the cities and homes of men" the enduring philosophical issues that, acknowledged or not, determine human behavior. These are the issues that drive the actions of the characters in Shakespeare's plays and their presence in the plays doubtless explains why audiences as well as scholars and general readers have for centuries and over vast continents continue to meditate and ponder over what they see and hear and read in his works.[1]

A cursory look at the folio and the poems reveals without question the Bard's keen awareness of the vast literature of philosophical thought that was available in Elizabethan culture, both in the original texts and in translations. Shakespeare's treatment of various philosophical issues is drawn from many sources, beginning with Socrates' conversation in the *Apology,* the *Ion,* and the *Phaedo* (the "Socratic dialogues"), in which Plato records his master's voice, and to Plato's dialogues, in particular the *Republic* and the *Symposium.* Plato's dialogues constitute one of the main sources of philosophical ideas in this book. Consider the following examples:

On beauty, the good, and truth:
   "Fair, kind, and true is all my argument."
On love and lust:

"O, powerful love! that in some respects make a beast a man and in some others make a man a beast."
On art mirroring nature:
"There is an art which in their piedness shares with great creating nature."
On seeing in the same light the lunatic, the lover and the poet:
"[they] are of imagination all compact and dissimilar in their words and actions."
On time—objective, subjective, and personal:
"Time's thievish progress to eternity"
On time:
"that goes slow and swift and short in folly and in sport."
On time that "must have a stop by death"
On intimations of immortality:
"the dread of something after death, the undiscovered country."
On pricks of conscience:
"this deity in my bosom."
On inwardness:
"I have that within which passeth the show."
On the problem of others' minds:
"There's no art to find the mind's construction in theface."
On the role of reason:
"as physician to love, not his counselor."
On values: "what is aught but as 'tis valu'd."
On language:
"They have been at great feat of languages."
On words:
"Words are very rascals since bonds disgrace them."
On the ideal of the commonwealth—the Republic:
"I would with such perfection govern
To excel the golden age."

Aristotle, it hardly has to be said, was another highly important source for Shakespeare, especially his *Poetics* on the concept of tragedy and the tragic hero as universal persona as well as his *Nicomachean Ethics* on virtue, happiness, and on the contrasting values of active and contemplative ways of life.

The inquiry into the nature of language is an ancient philosophical enterprise. Socrates begins his critical inquiry into the ordinary language used by the common folk about such concepts as justice, piety, and beauty, and ends with his demand for a precise definition of words that convey such values. Shakespeare, too, like Socrates, sharpened our awareness of words, as A. J. Austin observed, to sharpen our perception of the phenomena. The poet indeed is an alchemist who, like the poet in *Timon of Athens*, has turned the base metal of the world into his golden words. We are reminded of Nietzsche who thanked Socrates for casting enough light to make his own thoughts visible. That saying *mutatis mutandis* applies to Shakespeare. Although the Socratic concern was purely philosophical and his method was dialectical, the outcome was similar. The philosopher and the poet both sharpen our perception of the world, so we may rise above it, unlike the animals that exist only in the world according to their perceptions, as Schopenhauer observed.

Shakespeare knew intuitively what the Stoic philosophers had written theoretically about the nature of language. The Stoics' views on signs, denotation, sense, and connotations that were recently discovered[2] are reflected often in connection with the meaning of words and the black magic of names (Romeo and Juliet, Clarence, Rosalind, and Cinna). One player (Biondella) complains that "his master has left [him] behind to expound the meaning and the morals of his signs and tokens"; another (Juliet), laments, "'Tis but thy name that is my enemy; O! be some other name. What's in a name?"[3]

Stoic cosmology, which places the microhuman within the macrouniverse, and its moral prescription of the triumph of the will on facing death and disasters, along with the semantics of the old Stoics, appears in many of Shakespeare's plays and poems, as well as Epicurean materialism with its belief in pleasure as the ultimate good, and on death as utter annihilation. There are allusions to Pyrrhonic skepticism that "modest doubt [is] the beacon of the wise"; to Machiavellian power politics, "policy sits above conscience"; to egocentric psychology; to Montaigne's prescriptivism and his criticism of rational theology and to moral absolutism; and Erasmus's humanism in *Praise of Folly* and his rejection of slavery.

We hear the mockery of mediaeval beliefs in miracles; of judicial astrology; of the efficacy of final causes—that barren vestal virgin of natural philosophy—of mystics of titles, names, and numerals; of the divine right of anointed kings and the laws of primogeniture. We hear one player (clown) saying, "I say there is no darkness but ignorance, in which thou art more puzzled than the Egyptians in their fog." Here Shakespeare repeats the second line of the character Machiavelli in Marlowe's *The Jew of Malta,* "I count religion but a childish toy . . . and hold there's no sin but ignorance," but cautiously changes "sin" to "darkness." In *The Merchant of Venice,* Bassano says, "The world is still deceived with ornament . . . in religion, what damned error but some sober brow will bless it and approve it with text, hiding the grossness with fair ornament." In *Love's Labour's Lost,* we hear Berowne's skeptical remarks about reading and learning "from base authority," and other books, and his mockery of astrology:

> These earthly godfathers of heaven's lights
> That give a name to every fixed star
> Have no more profit of their shining nights
> Than those that walk and wo't not what they are.

The "base authority from others' books" is an allusion to Aristotle whose authority was constantly invoked by the scholastics. The very criticism appears in a poem by John Dryden (1631–1700) who, after mocking scholasticism, then expressed his admiration for Columbus "who was the first who shook Aristotle's throne," and boasts of the English contributions to science such as Francis Bacon who explained that heat is caused by motion, and Robert Boyle's contribution to chemistry, William Harvey's discovery of the circulation of the blood, and William Gilbert's explanation of magnetic power. John Dryden's poem "His Learned and Useful Words" is dedicated to his learned friend Dr. Charleton. Dryden wrote,

> The longest tyranny that ever sway'd
> Was that wherein our ancestors betrayed
> Their free-born reason to the Stagirete,
> And made his torch their universal light.[4]

The same admirer of science and new discoveries and debunker of scholasticism speaks of Shakespeare as "The man who of all modern and perhaps ancient poets had the largest and most comprehensive soul." Dryden, who became the poet laureate of King Charles II and was an erudite scholar and poet, defends Shakespeare against the charge of lacking classical education, "small Latin and less Greek" with his sharp remark that "He needed not the spectacles of Books to read Nature."

Francis Bacon (1561–1626), who is called by Percy Bysshe Shelley (1792–1822) "the poet of science," sharply criticized the scholastic education at Oxford, where he studied. Thus he argued that education at Oxford was a waste whereas the study of natural philosophy is of the greatest benefit to humankind. He proposed that students should use their "sovereign reason" in search of efficient causes of events and read the Book of Nature. Bacon held that new discoveries and recent inventions in Europe such as the printing press, gunpowder, and the compass had changed the course of civilization. In his book *Novum Organum* he writes of "the Idols of Theater," that is, the uncritical acceptance of the received systems of thought.[5] Idols are his symbols of scholastic dogma, and there are many kinds of idols. He argues that knowledge is power not only over ourselves, as in Socrates' injunction "Know thyself," but also over nature. He compared natural philosophers to King Solomon in his great quest for truth—as if God were playing hide and seek with man. "Solomon the king although he excelled in the glory of treasure and magnificent building—yet he maketh no claim to any of these glories, but only to the glory of inquiring after truth, for he saith expressly 'the glory of God is to conceal a thing but the glory of the king is to find it out,' as if according to the innocent play of children, the Divine Majesty took delight in hiding his secrets to the end of having them find them out."[6]

Shakespeare used almost the same metaphor when in *King Lear*, Lear says,

> so we'll live, And pray, and sing, and tell old tales, and laugh at gilded butterflies . . .
> And take upon's the mystery of things
> As if we were God's spies. (LR,V:3)

In *Antony and Cleopatra* the same metaphor is expressed by Charmian:

> Cha.: "Is this the man? Is't you sir that knows things?"

The Soothsayer answers,

> "in nature's infinite book of secrecy/
> A little I can read." (ANT, I:2)

Note the revolutionary Baconian ideas expressed by Lafeu in *All's Well that Ends Well*:

> They say miracles are past;
> and we have our philosophical persons,
> to make modern and familiar, things
> supernatural and causeless.

> Par.: Why 'tis the rarest argument of wonder that hath shot out in our latter times.
> Laf.: To be relinquished of the artists, of all learned and authentic fellows?
> Par.: Right, so I say.
> Laf.: I may truly say it is a novelty to the world. (AWW, II:3)

Shakespeare makes frequent references to mathematics and to science, which in his time was called Natural Philosophy. These references reveal his deep knowledge of the beliefs, predilections, and understandings of his contemporaries.[7] In *Troilus and Cressida* Ulysses refers to the parallel axiom,

> That's done; —as near as the extremest ends.
> Of parallels (TRO, I:3)

In *King Lear* the Fool tells Lear,

> Thou wast a pretty fellow . . . now thou art an O without
> a figure . . . thou art nothing [zero]. (LR, I:4)

In *Two Gentlemen of Verona* a player reveals the progress in popular knowledge when he refers to his earlier belief in the Ptolemaic universe saying,

> At first I did adore a twinkling star
> But now I worship a celestial sun. (TGV, III:6)

In *Troilus and Cressida* Ulysses makes an analogy between the solar system and the early kingdom ruled by a king.

> And therefore is the glorious planet Sol
> In noble eminence enthron'd and spher'd
> Amidst the others; whose medicinal eye
> Corrects the ill aspects of planets evil,
> And posts, like the commandments of a king
> Sans check, to good and bad. (TRO, I:3)

In *Midsummer Night's Dream* a player refers to the moon's gravity, "The moon, the governor of floods" (MND, II:3) and in *Hamlet* Horatio speaks of the eclipses of the sun that occurred in Rome before the mighty Julius fell (HAM, I:1). Shakespeare's admiration for science is evident where he lets the enlightened Duke of Burgundy in *Henry V* speak of the importance of science in the education of children who were acting like savages.

> And as our vineyards, fallows, meads, and hedges,
> Defective in their natures, grow to wildness,
> Even so our houses and ourselves and children

> Have lost, or do not learn for want of time,
> The sciences that should become our country
> But grow like savages,— (H5, V:2)

In *All's Well that Ends Well* the king of France is presented as somewhat of a fool who believes in the magical power of his ring as superior to the science of medicine.

> Plutus himself
> That knows the tinct and multiplying medicine,
> Hath not in nature's mystery more science
> Than I have in this ring (AWW, V:3)

Again, in *Love's Labour's Lost* there are certain allusions to the virtue of knowledge, and the importance of language and philosophy, albeit with a caveat that there is no true learning without true love. When the king of Navarre in imitation of the Renaissance practice of establishing academies for the pursuit of knowledge says,

> Navarre shall be the wonder of the world;
> Our court shall be a little academe
> Still and contemplative in living art.

Dumaine (one of the king's councilors), speaks like a Stoic philosopher:

> My loving lord, Dumaine is mortified;
> The grosser manner of these world's delights
> He throws upon the gross world's baser slaves:
> To wealth, to wealth, to pomp, I pine and die;
> With all those living in philosophy. (LLL, I:1)

However, Browne qualifies the king's command for pursuit of knowledge without love saying,

> From women's eyes this doctrine I derive:
> They sparkle still the right Promethean fire.
> They are the books, the arts, the academes
> That show, contain and nourish all the world. (LLL, IV:3)

There are other references to "academe," cultural institutions that developed in Italy beginning in the fifteenth century, called such after Plato's academy, which was located in the sacred grove of the demigod Academus outside the walls of Athens.

Shakespeare's command of language and his creative power of imagination have been extolled by many writers. Nietzsche admired Shakespeare's evident knowledge and intellectual imagination when he alludes to Hamlet's comment:

> There are more things in Heaven and earth, Horatio,
> Than are dreamt of in your philosophy. (HAM, I:5)

In *Thus Spoke Zarathustra*, the speaker says, "Alas, there are so many things between heaven and earth, of which only the poets have dreamed."[8] It is not Shakespeare's imagination alone that Nietzsche admired, but the overwhelming power of his language that served his imagination. The Bard's love for his native language is well known and evident in his use of a vast vocabulary. "There is no other writer like Shakespeare for condensing ideas and feelings into memorable words and phrases," wrote Jonathan Bate in *The Genius of Shakespeare*.[9]

Ben Jonson, his most rigorous critic and admirer, is not alone in eulogizing the poet. Printed on the first page of Jonson's First Folio he wrote:

> Sweet swan of Avon! Soul of the Age!
> The applause! Delight! The wonder of our stage.[10]

The poet himself makes insightful predictions about the significance of his artistic achievement and the future performance of his play. He lets Cassius speak for him:

> How many ages hence
> Shall this our lofty scene be acted o'er
> In states unborn and accents yet unknown! (JC, III:4)

So, too, says the Speaker of the sonnets:

> So long as men can breathe or eyes can see
> So long live this and this gives life to thee (SON 18)

and

> When tyrant's crests and tombs of brass are spent
> And thou in this shall find thy monument. (SON 1-7)

Shakespeare's astonishing prediction about performances of his play through the ages in states unborn and accents yet unknown (for example America and India) was as accurate as the predictions of his contemporary natural scientists (Galileo, who was born in the same year)—astonishing because there is more predictability in the course of heavenly bodies than there is within the cultural world.

The richness of Shakespeare's tragedies has been compared by some critics to the simplicity of his comedies; however, the seeming simplicity of those compressed ideas in his comedies and the brief philosophical utterances of the players and the speaker of the sonnets are deceptive: "But all noble things," as Spinoza reworded Plato, "are as difficult as they are rare." Shakespeare's most difficult and intended paradoxical and enigmatic language and oblique allusions to antiquity and the biblical literature were a challenge to his audience, the courtiers, lawyers, and university fellows and have continued to be through the centuries; in our own times Helen Vendler, Stephen Greenblatt, and other Shakespeare scholars have commented on certain difficulties in the language.

There were also common folk among the audience who were familiar with their legends and morality plays and who were rewarded by merely watching the plays while standing through the performance. Hamlet, who directs the players in the "mouse-trap," referred to those "groundlings" when he says, "to split the ears of groundlings who for the most part are capable of nothing but inexplicable dumb shows and noise." Coriolanus's mother, Volumnia, says the same thing about the ignorant citizens: "action is eloquent, and the eyes of the ignorant more learned than their ears "(COR, III:2). The ears of groundlings hearing less and the eyes of the ignorant learning more tells us something about the presence of theater-loving, ordinary English citizens.

Notwithstanding the presence of philosophical thoughts and the humanist ideas and values of the English Renaissance in the text, we shall avoid making unwarranted assumptions that turn the Bard into a philosophical or theological poet such as the Epicurean Lucretius, the Catholic Dante, the Puritan Milton, or Goethe—a poet who is justly praised for his self-conscious detachment and his "divine impersonality"—or for his various philosophical references into old categories of the history of ideas, or by making him a hidden Catholic, or an unabashed atheist like his admired fellow-playwright Marlow. There are no textual or biographical supports as yet for such claims.

George Santayana in his essay "The Absence of Religion in Shakespeare" speaks of the underlying positivism of Shakespeare's thinking, while writing that among the greatest poets, Shakespeare is notable for being without philosophy and without religion. In his "Three Philosophical Poets" he was accurate as he presented Lucretius, Dante, and Goethe as great Western philosophical poets.[11] That he did not include the Bard among them is understandable, though his indifference to Shakespeare's thought is not. There is as much philosophy in Hamlet, as there is in Goethe's *Faust*. To be sure, the Bard to his credit is neither a philosophical poet (given that amorphous category) nor a disguised preacher as Johnson, Tolstoy, and Elliot wish him to be. Nonetheless, the claim that "There is no philosophy in Shakespeare," which is the opinion of many literary critics such as George Bernard Shaw and T. S. Eliot and even Jan Kott, a modern critic who writes "Shakespeare did not know philosophy," shall be falsified by digging deeper into the poet's texts, which reveal the reverse.[12]

A. C. Bradley, for example, states categorically that "Shakespeare nowhere shows, like Chaucer, any interest in speculative problems concerning foreknowledge, predestination, and freedom."[13] The famous Shakespearean scholar seems to be oblivious of many examples in the Folio alone: his defense of man's freedom, the mockery of predestination as by inheritance or by the course of original sin, and contrasting views on fatalism and autonomy and moral responsibility, as they were spoken by players such as Hamlet, Brutus, Cassius, Edmund, Gloucester, and the Earl of Kent.

Our primary focus is on the Bard's philosophical thoughts that he inherited from many sources and were incorporated within his art. We shall avoid talking about the author and his cultural surroundings or the pragmatic dimension of the text, unless it is relevant (such as in discussions of politics and ethics in *Troilus and*

Cressida), or viewing the stage as a Platonic Academy, or as a pulpit for Shakespeare's beliefs, or separating thought from the content of thought by committing the fallacy of paraphrasing.

Of all Shakespeare's works it is the Speaker of the sonnets, in particular the "Will" sonnets, and Prospero in *The Tempest* that may speak for the author, who remains almost hidden in the pages of his plays and poems. In Henry James's story, "The Birthplace," a visitor to the birthplace speaks of a man who "covers his tracks as no other human has ever done." The Speaker and his company were visiting "the early home of the supreme poet—the Mecca of the English-speaking race," in the hope that "the more we know Him, the more we shall love him." When that knowledge is denied to them one of the visitors pronounces with regret, "This man isn't everywhere—I defy you to catch him." And then said the husband to his wife, "the play's the thing" and "let the author alone."[14]

It is reasonable to believe, as some scholars do, that Prospero represents Shakespeare himself. An obvious clue lies in the love of books, which he shares with that magician. On the island he is well supplied with books, as he remarks, "Knowing that I love my books he [Gonzalo] furnished me from his own library with volumes," and he is said to spend all his time reading. Surely the man who could conjure up a world with a few actors on a stage could think of his art as magic. Prospero is endowed with magical power over Ariel, the spirit, and Caliban, the devil, but although he flourishes the appurtenances of magic, his robe and his wand (TMP, I:2), his real power comes from his books. Caliban, the savage slave, is not fooled. He recognizes that his master's power depends on his books, "Remember! First to possess His books for without them He is but a sot as I am—Burn but his books" (TMP, III:2).

At the end, Prospero breaks his wand, drowns his books, and returns to Milan, "Where every third thought shall be my grave."

Although the similarities between Shakespeare and Prospero are strong, we shall avoid the temptation to take all the speeches of the player as expressing the playwright's belief. The scrupulous use of quotation marks that is called by logicians the "use-mention distinction" is a semantic device for a conspicuous representation of linguistic symbols. Thus, if we write "Shakespeare says, 'there was a Prince of Denmark called Hamlet' and Hamlet says 'frailty, thy name is woman,'" the last quoted phrase within the larger quotes should not be taken as the author's expressed belief.

Another way to avoid mistaken inferences about an author's beliefs, such as pointing an accusing finger at the author for sexism in Hamlet's speech, is to consider different utterances of other players on the same subject. For example, in contrast to Hamlet's cynical comment, Emilia (Desdemona's maid) protests that the word "frailty" applies to the moral weakness of both men and women.

> And have we not affections, desires for
> Sport and *frailty* as men have?
> Then let them use us well, else let them
> Know, the ills we do their ills instruct us so. (OTH, IV:3)

Shakespeare has been accused not only of sexism but also of racial prejudice, most famously in his characterizations of Othello, the African Venetian, and Shylock, a Jew. Such criticism should be rejected since Shakespeare shows both Shylock and Othello are themselves *victims* of prejudice.

In *Romeo and Juliet* we note the similarity of Emilia's protest against sexism and Shylock's protest against religious bigotry. Behind these specific protests lies the ancient Stoic moral perception of such notable figures as Epictetus, Cicero, and Seneca that all humans are equal and therefore must be treated equally. "*Homo* is a common name for all men," says Thomas Gargrave (1H4, II:1).

Shakespeare probably read the protest against slavery by Erasmus (1466–1536), the humanist who wrote, "Tyrants hold their subjects in the same state as the average man considers his horse or his ass. For men take care of their animals but all the care they give them is judged from the advantages to themselves and not to the animal."[15] We believe we hear an echo from Erasmus when Shylock protests against the Venetian treatment of slaves.

> You have among you many a purchased slave,
> Which like your asses and your dogs and mules
> You use in abject and in slavish parts
> Because you bought them: shall I say to you
> Let them be free, marry them to your heirs? (MV, 4:1)

Leaving aside possible unwarranted inferences from the text to the author, there is still a pragmatic aspect of inquiry concerning the relation of the author to his culture that falls within the domain of the cultural historian. There are recognizable Stoic moral prescriptions, such as the Renaissance view of the human as the paragon of animals as well as Baconian anti-Scholastic voices in the Bard's presentation of various "Forms of life" within the "language games" of drama (Wittgenstein). He expresses his overall outlook and reveals his streaming thoughts and the influence of those philosophical ideas of the past centuries with a maximum of objectivity and a minimum of sentimentality, in spite of his "divine impersonality." Ben Jonson's eulogy of the Bard as "Soul of the Age" is a perfect portrayal of that paragon of the English Renaissance.

Chapter One

PHILOSOPHY AND POETRY

THE HISTORICAL SETTING

> "Homer shall have been dishonorably discharged and flogged."
> —Heraclitus, *Fragments*

From the dawn of ancient Greek civilization there has been a long and animated dialogue between the two rival oracles of Western culture, the philosopher and the poet. The champions of "that most noble and sovereign reason" (Ophelia, *Hamlet*) cast their critical eyes on poets and poetry, "the most odoriferous flower of fancy" (Holofernes, *Love's Labour's Lost*) while the poets, shapers of "the forms of things unknown," claimed that they "apprehend more than cool reason ever comprehends" (Theseus, *A Midsummer Night's Dream*) and that they reached for philosophical thoughts but mocked metaphysical ideas as unprofitable speculations: "There was never yet a philosopher that could endure toothache patiently, however they have writ the style of gods" (Leonata, *Much Ado about Nothing*).

The ancient quarrel between philosophy and poetry appeared

in Plato's severe criticism of poetry and dramatic arts and in Aristophanes' mockery of philosophy in his play *The Clouds*. To the Elizabethan age the similar controversy about poetry is nothing but a charming fantasy, and philosophy as the sole vehicle for the discovery of natural, moral, and civil laws, appears in the *Advancement of Learning* by Francis Bacon (1561–1626), in the *Leviathan* of Thomas Hobbes (1588–1679), in the *Defense of Poetry* of Philip Sidney (1552–1584), and in the next century in the *Treatise of Human Nature* of David Hume (1711–1776).

In the nineteenth century Nietzsche speaks of that controversy in terms of two opposing forces symbolized by Apollo as the patron of order and Dionysus as the god of disorderly passion. In his early work, *The Birth of Tragedy,* Nietzsche speculates that "the decline and fall of tragedy is due to the Sophocles-Platonic maxim that virtue is knowledge, and that man sins from ignorance."[1]

Looking retrospectively at philosophy, poetry, and dramatic arts, we must remember that in ancient and Renaissance cultures philosophy was considered to be the queen of knowledge. Gilbert Ryle, the Oxford philosopher, wrote, "the word 'philosophy' up to the middle of the nineteenth century encompassed science and *belles lettres* as well as philosophy in our sense of the term. Our word 'scientist' was not invented until 1840 so there was nothing else to call a Newton or a Harvey other than 'philosophers' or sometimes, 'natural philosophers.'"[2]

Through the centuries, therefore, the protagonists of the debate have radically changed. The seekers of truth through reason have become the scientists and analytic philosophers who use precise language in their arguments against whom are ranged the political and religious advocates who make use of rhetoric and metaphor in their persuasive speeches without much regard for the validity and consistency of their arguments or the verifiability of their theories.

We shall present a summing up of this "ancient quarrel" and the echoes of conflict in the Shakespeare's Folio and in his poems.

SOCRATES ON POETRY

> "There is an ancient quarrel between philosophy and poetry."
>
> —Plato, *Apology*

Socrates in the *Apology* presents poets as unconscious diviners. Aristophanes in *The Clouds* depicts Socrates as a Sophist. Plato banishes Homer from his Utopia in the *Republic* and mocks Aristophanes in the *Symposium*. Aristotle, "the philosopher," as he was called in the Middle Ages, defends poetry as being more philosophical than history, and considered the tragic heroes as the embodiments of the universal—the Platonic form, or the archetype—and looks at tragedy as the artistic display of conflict between the rational and nonrational parts of the soul and as a wondrous medicine for purging repressed emotions.

In the *Apology* Socrates defends himself against his accusers, among them Aristophanes, of being a Sophist, an atheist, a natural philosopher, and a corruptor of youths. He rejects all charges with great eloquence, and goes on telling the court a short history of his intellectual life. He says that his philosophical quest arose out of an oracle's declaration that he is the wisest man in Helas. Knowing that he is not and believing that gods' messages do not lie, he tried to falsify that declaration. "I thought of a method of trying the question. I reflected that if I could only find a man wiser than myself then I might go to the god with refutation in my hand."[3]

Socrates said that first he went to question a politician and found him ignorant, although he was thought wise by many. "So I left him, saying to myself—although I do not suppose that either of us knows anything really beautiful and good, I am better off than he is for he knows nothing but thinks that he knows; I neither know nor think that I know." He said that his "Herculean" labors in search of the wise man made him the enemy of that politician and his followers. "After the politician I went to the poets, tragic, dithyrambic. . . . I took them some of the most elaborate passages in their own writing and asked them what was the meaning of them—Will you believe me? I am almost ashamed to confess the truth but I must say that there is hardly a person present who wouldn't talk better about their poetry than they did themselves. Then I knew that not by wisdom do poets write poetry but by a sort of genius and inspiration; they are like diviners or soothsayers who also say many fine things but do not understand the meaning of them. . . . I observed that on the strength of their poems they believe themselves to be the wisest of men in other things."

Socrates' criticism of poets is understandable if we consider the historical role that poets and playwrights play on the stage, where in the absence of organized religion they were speaking like priests as moral and political advocates. Socrates in his defense referred to that issue when he says that the poets, on the strength of their poems, believe themselves to be the wisest of men in other things. In another dialogue, *Ion*, Socrates again appears as a literary critic. He says, "all good poets, epic as well as lyric, view their beautiful poems not by art but because they are inspired and possessed." He tells Ion, a lover of Homer, "there is a divinity moving you like that contained in the stone that Euripides called a magnet . . . the stone not only attracts iron rings but also imparts to them a similar power of attracting other rings."[4]

Socrates, who himself loved Homer, speaks of the power of poetry and its emotional impact on the actors, while he fears that their passions may transcend reason. He addresses Ion: "I wish you would tell me frankly, Ion, when you produce the greatest effect upon the audience in the recitation of some striking passage such as . . . the description of Achilles rushing at Hector, or the sorrows of Hecuba or Priam, are you in your right mind? Are you carried out of yourself, and does not your soul in ecstasy seem to be among the persons or places of which you are speaking, whether they are in Ithica or in Troy?"

This passage reminds us of Hamlet's instructions to the First Player who is reciting a long passage from the *Aeneid*, where Dido says "Come to Hecuba." After that citation Hamlet provides a description of the sets and speeches of the First Player who, like Ion, identifies himself with the tragic characters. So says Hamlet in his famous soliloquy ("Now I am alone . . ."):

> Is it not monstrous that this player here,
> But in a fiction, in a dream of passion,
> Could force his soul so to his own conceit
> That from his working all his visage wane'd
> Tears in his eyes, distraction in's aspect
> A broken voice, and his whole function suiting
> With forms to his own conceit? and all for nothing!
> For Hecuba!
>   What's Hecuba to him or he to Hecuba
>   That he should weep for her? (HAM, II:2)

The reference is to Virgil's, *Aeneid,* "I saw Hecuba together with her hundred daughters. . . ."[5] It also resembles Ion's recitation of Homer's poems as described by Socrates. The action of the First Player was so moving that even Polonius, the lord chamberlain, that "wretched, rash, intruding fool" could no longer stand it:

"Look! Where he has not turned his colour and has tears in's eyes. Prithee no more." Hamlet is fully aware of the uncanny magic of tragedy when he speaks bitterly about an actor who is performing with mastery his tragic role.

> What would he do
> Had he the motive and the cue for passion
> That I have? He would drown the stage with tears.
> And cleave the general ear with horrid speech,
> Make mad the guilty and appall the free

Blaming himself for his hesitation he goes on,

> Yet I,
> A dull and muddy mettled rascal, peak
> Like John-a-dreams, unpregnant of my cause
> And can say nothing. . . .

He finally resolves to act.

> I have heard
> That guilty creatures sitting at a play
> Have by the very cunning of the scene
> Been struck so to the soul that presently
> They have proclaim'd their malefactions.

If Claudius is guilty can he be tricked into revealing his guilt?

> The play's the thing
> Wherein I'll catch the conscience of the king (HAM II:2)

Thus Hamlet creates "The Mousetrap."

The profound effect of tragedy on the audience and the actor playing the role of tragic hero, praised by Hamlet, offended Socrates' moral sensibility so much that he turned against the performance of Homeric tragedies. In another dialogue, the *Phaedrus*, Socrates again speaks about those possessed diviners who are driven by their imagination. He compares poets, lovers, and madmen as having something in common. "The third kind is the madness of those who are possessed by their Muses which taking hold of a delicate and virgin soul, and there inspiring frenzy, awaken lyrical and all other numbers; with these adoring, the myriad actions of ancient heroes for the instruction of posterity,"[6] a reference to Sophocles' claim that his plays were good for Athens.

Love, too, is a kind of noble madness although there is also a madness of an evil sort. The voice of Socrates speaking of madness of the noble kind, and ranking poets, prophetesses, and lovers on the same level, higher than the ignoble insane, may be heard in *A Midsummer Night's Dream* as Hippolyta and Theseus converse:

> Hip.: 'Tis strange, my Theseus,
>   that these lovers speak of.
> Thes.: More strange than true. I never may believe
>   These antique fables nor these fairy toys,
>   Lovers and madmen have such seething brains,
>   Such shaping fantasies, that apprehend
>   More than cool reason ever comprehends:
>   The lunatic, the lover, and the poet
>   Are of imagination all compact'd,
>   One sees more devils than vast hell can hold,
>   That is the madman; the lover, all as frantic,
>   Sees Helen's beauty in the brow of Egypt:

> The poet's eye, in a fine frenzy rolling,
> Doth glance from heaven to earth from earth to heaven;
> And, as imagination bodies forth
> The forms of things unknown, the poet's pen
> Turns them to shapes, and gives to airy nothing
> A local habitation and a name. (MND, V:1)

This striking resemblance between Socrates' speeches on lovers, poets, and madmen and Shakespeare's exaltation of the poets' creative power also indicates the differences between the philosopher and the poet. Where Socrates boasts that he is a "lover of knowledge" and considers poetry as a kind of madness, Shakespeare lets Theseus speak of poets as godlike creators looking from heaven to earth, while letting their imaginations give form to all that is in the world. The poet's creation, however, is not like God's *ex nihilo*, out of nothing; it is the result of his minute scrutiny of things in heaven and on earth that fires his imagination and enables him to give shape to those "airy nothings." The poet's form, unlike Plato's pure and abstract Forms, is a child of imagination and not of reason.

The ancient charges against poetry and dramatic art that were largely pronounced by Socrates and Plato were evoked in the Elizabethan age by the lovers of natural philosophy upon the emergence of new discoveries in astronomy, physics, physical anatomy, and geography. They were casting a sharp eye, not on Aristotle's philosophy but on the Book of Nature. "There are more things in heaven and earth, Horatio, than are dreamt of in your philosophy"(HAM I:5). Like the Prince of Denmark, the philosophers welcomed the new discoveries "in heaven and earth," although unlike Theseus and Tranio, the lovers of art, they did not vote on behalf of poetry and plays. In their perspective the plays and poems and fiction are nothing but sweet lies, the dormitive opium of the crowd.

Francis Bacon was well acquainted with the poets' circle and the art world in London when Shakespeare, the playwright and actor, was presenting his plays before King James and his lords in the Inns of Court. Thus it is not a surprise that Ben Jonson, who famously eulogized Shakespeare, also wrote an ode, "Lord Bacon's Birthday."[7] Bacon frequently attended performances of plays and was "a friend of the players," and his good report saved the Lord Chamberlain's Company from the charge of helping the rebellious Essex by playing *Richard II* (the king who was forced to abdicate and was deposed by his enemies).[8] What is surprising is the absence of Shakespeare's name and his plays from Bacon's voluminous text that led to the absurd controversy about the authorship of the plays.

Unlike Shakespeare who believed that poetry was a sublime art, Bacon writes, "poetry is nothing else but Feigned History, for God forbid that we shall give our dream of imagination for the pattern of the world."[9] In an essay he warns his fellow theater-lovers against the allure of art.[10] Bacon's cautious appraisal of dramatic art speaks of the uncanny power of drama over the minds of theater-goers, i.e., the common folk and the educated courtiers, lawyers, and university fellows. A noted cultural historian, John Hale, discusses the immense popularity of theatrical performances that were played in the court and public places during the reigns of Queen Elizabeth and King James.[11] In Bacon's warning against art's allure, there is perhaps a hint of envy of Shakespeare's fame and the popularity of the players in the court when "all of Shakespeare's new plays were performed before King James" by the King's Men. The record indicates that Shakespeare was the leading actor in the company.

From Bacon's perspective, art is a child of imagination and represents the flight of imagination versus the cool verdict of reason. Thomas Hobbes, Bacon's friend and one-time secretary, goes further than his master by deprecating imagination as a source of illusion.

In his view, "Imagination is a decayed sense.... Imagination when asleep is dreaming ... and the religion of the gentiles comes of not distinguishing dreams from waking."[12]

In the next century David Hume, a precursor of modern empiricism, expressed ideas similar to those of Bacon and Hobbes though in a milder tone. In his view, what gives life to fiction and poetry is the imagination and experience. "Poets themselves, th'o liars by profession, always endeavor to give an air of truth to their fictions and, where that is totally neglected, their performance, however ingenious, will never be able to afford much pleasure . . . that even where ideas have no manner of influence on the will and passion, *truth* and *reality* are still requisites in order to make them entertaining to the imagination."[13]

The philosophical criticism of poetry and dramatic art by Bacon was sharply rejected by Philip Sidney in his *Apologia for Poetry* when he exalted poets as the prime teachers and makers and declared that the poet affirms nothing and therefore never lies. Sidney rejects those philosophical arguments as an instance of the fallacy of *Ignoratio Elenchi* (irrelevant conclusion). He then provides a view of poetry and dramatic art that anticipates passages in the dialogues of various of Shakespeare's plays.

In Shakespeare's plays the conflicting views of the values represented by reason and imagination can be heard—a sardonic comment opposed by plausive praises of philosophy, mainly some aspects of Platonic, Aristotelian, and Stoic thoughts—sometimes in dialogue between players as Shakespeare uses those differences for the purpose of characterization. When the dialogue is replaced by the monologue the conflict appears as a clash in the speaker's mind between sovereign Reason and rebellious Passion where the Will stands to act like a soldier upon the order of Reason.

Reason is the use of inductive and deductive argument; it is the Promethean fire that is given to humankind to be used for the prediction of events and the reconsideration of the past. So says the philosopher Hamlet.

> He that made us with such a large discourse
> Looking before and after,
> Gave us not
> That capacity and god-like reason
> To fust in us unused. (HAM, IV:4)

Reason is also called silent meditation "In maiden meditation fancy free" along with formal argumentation "large discourse," where it is contrasted with "the dreams of passion—the flight of imagination—and hateful fantasies." In the absence of reason "man . . . is a beast no more."

Since human rationality was identified with thinking, and thinking was seen as a linguistic activity, it was assumed that animals are thoughtless creatures, as Aristotle believed. His common sense idea was taken for granted by Shakespeare, even though it was rejected by Montaigne on empirical grounds based on his observation of elephants, horses, and dogs. It is noticeable that Shakespeare, who quoted some passages from Montaigne's *Essays*, has shown no empathy for that author's defense of animals, for his admiration for American Indian morality, and the simple way of life; Caliban, in *The Tempest* acts like a brute, in contrast to Montaigne's "noble savage." Hamlet's eulogy of man as a paragon of animals draws on the Aristotelian concept of the human species as a rational animal; it resembles certain Renaissance ideas that appear in the writings of Pico della Mirandola (1463–1494), in particular his essay *De hominis dignitato* (*Oration on the Dignity of Man*) in which the author contrasts the mediaeval concept of man with his own Platonic-Christian ideas of humankind. "It is a commonplace to the school," Pico wrote, "that man is a little world, in which we may discern a body mingled of earthly elements and the heavenly spirit . . . and the senses of lower animals, and reason, and the mind of angels and the likeness of God. Animals carry with them from their mothers' bodies all that they are destined to have or be. But God the Father endowed man from birth, with the seeds of every possibility and every life."[14] We may well be reminded of Hamlet's speech in his famous soliloquy about man, and Pico's words are surely not accidental. Consider the segment of his silent meditation:

> What a piece of work is a man,
> How noble in reason;
> How infinite in faculty
> In form, in moving,
> How express and admirable in action!
> How like an angel! In apprehension
> How like a god!
> The beauty of the world!
> The paragon of animals (HAM II:2)

We are reminded, too, of the character in Sophocles' *Antigone* who exclaims, "Many wonders there be, but none so wondrous as man."

Shakespeare in speaking of reason, will, and passion made use of Plato's faculty of psychology, namely, the partition of the soul into three distinct faculties in analogy with the three classes in the ideal state: the philosopher king, together with wise men and women who are highly educated and are rulers of the city-state; the military class, the class of brave and courageous soldiers; and the farmers and workers who are passion's slaves. This was the commonplace mental geography of his age. Consider Hamlet's meticulous and incisive use of Plato's faculty of psychology when he says, "I do not know why yet I live to say, 'This thing to do' sith I have cause and will and strength and means to do it." He has cause (Reason), Will and Strength (the second part of the soul), and Means (like a sword at the service of Passion). While Hamlet says, "I do not know yet why I have to say 'This thing to do,'" the psychoanalysts (Sigmund Freud, Ernest Jones, and others) assign the Oedipus Complex as the reason for Hamlet's long hesitation: his unconscious wish to kill his father cannot be fulfilled since Claudius has already done so.[15] This hypothesis must be rejected, not because as a scientific hypothesis it is nonfalsifiable, and not because of Hamlet's unbounded love for his father or his likening of his father to the Greco-Roman heroes, but because his failure to move is the fource that moves the play forward, which we may see as the playwright playing *with* the audience.

In writing his plays Shakespeare introduced his own ideas about art. This semantic assent in speaking about plays, poems, and the technique of acting by the actors in the course of acting appears in the voices of Hamlet, a prince and the director; Theseus, the Duke; Touchstone, a clown; the Speaker of the sonnet; and in a dialogue between Florizel and Pertita. The questionable inductive inferences from the work of an artist to its maker, is justified here, if ever, for it is quite unreasonable to deny that all those coherent and elegant speeches on art are the reflection of the thought of their maker. The *Sonnets* and *The Tempest*, as it is often mentioned, may tell tales about Shakespeare, but more so does the player's word on the nature of art. Hamlet's detailed and concrete instruction to the players and Florizel's abstract and condensed advice to Pertita in *The Winter's Tale* are reflections of Shakespeare's theory of acting. Forizel's instruction is short:

> Each your doing,
> So singular in each particular,
> Crowns what you are doing in the present deeds,
> That all your acts are queens. (WT, IV:4)

Hamlet's advice to the players, an excellent model for play directing, runs to forty-eight lines. The main points of this speech are the following:

> Speak the speech, I pray you . . . suit the action to the word, and the words to the action; with this special observance, that you o'er-step not the modesty of nature; for anything so overdone is from the purpose of playing, whose end was and is, to hold as it were the mirror up to nature. . . . I have thought some of nature's journeymen had made men and not made them well, they imitate humanity so abominably. (HAM, III:2)

Touchstone in the comedy *As You Like It* defends poetry by pointing to the hypothetical aspects of poetry and fiction. The clown begins by praising Ovid "the most capricious poet, honest Ovid," and alludes to Marlowe the excellent English playwright who was a friend of the Bard and was murdered "in a little room" at an early age. He then starts the following dialogue with his beloved Audrey:

> Tou.: Truly, I would the gods had made thee poetical.
> Aud.: I do not know what poetical is. Is it honest in deed and word?
> Tou.: No, truly, For truest poetry is the most feigning, and lovers are given to poetry and what they swear in poetry may be said as lovers they do feign. (AYL, III:3)

Saying that poetry is the most feigned, Touchstone uses Bacon's words, although for the philosopher to feign is not a virtue, while for the clown it is the highest virtue of true poetry. Likewise Sidney's assertion that the poets "nothing affirm" is the very same as Touchstone's judgment about poetry, where the clown in his conversation with Jacques makes use of a legal disputation. "All these [lies] you may avoid but the lie direct; and you may avoid that too, with an 'if.' I know when seven justices could not take up a quarrel, but when the parties were met themselves, one of them thought 'but of an "If," as If you said so, then I said so,' and they shook hands and swore brothers. 'If Your "If" is the only peace-maker; there is much virtue in If'" (AYL, V:4). In the same play another player, Duke the senior, speaks of art resembling life albeit by asserting that there is much more suffering in life than what is displayed on the stage.

This wide and universal theatre
Presents more woeful pageants than the scene
wherein we play. (AYL, II:7)

For Shakespeare, imagination was the divine spring of poetical inspiration and invention. In the early comedy *Midsummer Night's Dream* Theseus speaks passionately of poets' strong imagination, and claims that poets, like lovers and madmen, "apprehend more than cool reason ever comprehends." In *Love's Labor's Lost*, Holefernes, a school master who speaks of the "elegancy, facility, and golden cadence of poesy, praises 'Ovidius Naso' [noes, in English] for smelling out the odiferous flowers of fancy, the jerks of invention. *Imitare* is nothing, so doth the hound his master, the ape his keeper..." (LLL, IV:3). For Bacon, however, "we have overloaded the beauty and richness of Nature by our Invention." Shakespeare, in his dedication to *Venus and Adonis*, quotes two lines in Latin from Ovid's *Amores* that reveal

Ovid's imaginative inspiration. "Let the vulgar admire vile; to me my golden-haired Apollo shall serve goblets filled from the Castalian spring," the spring from which the muses drink inspiration.

If imagination is the spring of inspiration, for Shakespeare, reason, too, plays an indispensable role in his plays' action. Throughout the plays the foremost role of reason and argumentation in support of action upon facing a problematic situation is often stressed. In Hamlet's view, argument, that is, giving reason and providing justification, is a necessary step for engaging in actions such as taking revenge or going into a war. "Rightly to be great is not to stir without great argument."

In *Troilus and Cressida*, Troilus searches for a better argument in order to fight for Helen:

I cannot fight upon this argument
It is too starved subject for my sword. (TRO, I:1)

and Henry V in his prodding war speech warned his "good yeomen,"

lest they sheathe
their swords for the lack of argument. (H5, III:1)

Shakespeare speaks of philosophy as a subject that includes both natural phenomena and moral issues and uses "philosophers" in the sense of natural philosophers (scientists) and moral and political advocates like the stoics. He uses "metaphysics" once as a philosophical subject but mostly as a synonym for "supernatural event." In *The Taming of the Shrew* references are made to moral and natural philosophy and to metaphysics and mathematics, and to the city of Pisa where Galileo studied Natural Philosophy at its famous university. Lucentio speaks to Tranio, his servant,

> To see fair Padua, nursery of art . . . Lombardy
> I am arriv'd for fruitful Lombardy
> The pleasant garden of great Italy
>
> . . .
>
> Here let us breathe, and haply institute
> A course of learning and ingenious studies.
> Pisa, renowned for grave citizens,
> Gave me my being
>
> . . .
>
> Therefore, Tranio, for the time I study
> Virtue, and that part of philosophy
> Will I apply that treats of happiness
> By virtue especially to be achiev'd.

He asks Tranio "tell me thy mind?" and Tranio answers that he has no objection for his master to study Aristotlean moral philosophy, although he himself prefers Ovid's exuberant poetry over Aristotle's, the schoolmen's idol and the advocate of moderation with regard to moral virtues.

> I am in all affected as yourself,
> Glad that you thus continue your resolve
> To suck the sweets of sweet philosophy
> Only, good master, while we do admire
> This virtue and this moral discipline,
> Let's be no stoics, nor no stocks, I pray;
> Or so devote to Aristotle's check.
> As Ovid be an outcast quite abjur'd
> Balk logic with acquaintance that you have,
> And practice rhetoric in your common talk;
> Music and poetry use to quicken you;

> The mathematics and the metaphysics,
> Fall to them as you find your stomach serves you;
> No profit grows where is no pleasure ta'en;
> In brief, sire, study what you most affect.
>
> (SHR, I:2)

In Tranio's speeches, notwithstanding his preference for Ovid, there is a hint of the importance of Aristotle's check, namely, the golden mean, of "nothing in excess" and the concept of virtue, which lies in doing pleasurable actions.

In addition to many references to Aristotle's moral philosophy and to the Stoics' guide to virtue, there are also allusions in the speeches of various characters to natural philosophy and to Aristotle's idea of causes, the efficient, the material, the formal, and the final (for details, see chapter 4 on Aristotle).

Hamlet's conversation with Rosencrantz about the strange behavior of the courtiers toward his uncle shows his understanding that human actions defy scientific explanation when he says, "there is something in this more than natural, if philosophy could find it out." He is aware that human action is not just a physical motion that is explainable by appeal to the laws of nature but is a purposeful behavior. The same idea is expressed in his conversation with his mother when he resorts to Aristotle's conception that all motion, including human action, is goal directed. "Sense, sure, you have, else could you not have motion." Raising that Aristotelian principle he is pointing to his mother's marrying his uncle as a purposive behavior that makes her responsible for her action. The next sentence clearly indicates that he uses that principle only to strengthen his idea of free choice and not endorsing the schoolmen's teleological idea of universal motion such as the motion of the celestial bodies. "Nor sense to ecstasy was near so thrall'd that,

But it resolved some quantity of choice to serve in such a difference" (HAM, III:4).

Apart from reference to Aristotle's *Ethics*, the Stoics' precept on human conduct appears within the speeches of players in *Much Ado about Nothing*. Leonato, mocking the Stoic philosopher who counsels "Patch grief with proverbs," comments, "For there was never yet philosopher / That could endure the toothache patiently." In *King John* Constance pleads, "Preach some philosophy to make me mad!" (JN, 5:1). In *Romeo and Juliet* Friar Lawrence tries to comfort Romeo who has learned he is to be punished by banishment.

> I'll give thee armour to keep off that word;
> > Adversity's sweet milk, philosophy,
> > To comfort thee, though thou art banished

to which Romeo responds:

> Hang up philosophy!
> Unless philosophy can make a Juliet. (ROM, III:3)

Cassius's speech to Brutus about his neglect of the Stoics' precept that man has power to combat disaster by controlling his mind rather than changing the world when the fighting is lost, states, "Of your philosophy you make no use if you give place to accidental evil." To which Brutus replies, "No man bears sorrow better. Portia is dead" (JC, IV:3).

In *As You Like It* Corin, a shepherd, converses with the clown, Touchstone, when he mocks Aristotle's natural philosophy:

> Cor.: The property of rain is to wet, and fire to burn . . .
> and the great cause of the night is lack of the Sun,

> that he that has learned no wit by nature nor art may complain of good breeding, or comes of a very dull kindred.
>
> Tou.: Such a one is a natural philosopher (AYL, III:2)

The most significant comment on natural philosophy and metaphysics appears in *Hamlet*, where the Prince dismisses the old natural philosophy and welcomes the new spirit of scientific inquiry and Polonius mocks the entire field of philosophy, natural philosophy, moral discourse, and metaphysical speculation. Polonius in his advice to Claudias tells him "to expostulate what majesty should be, what beauty is, why day is day, night, night, and time is time, were nothing but to wait night and day and time" (HAM, II:2). Upon the encounter with the ghost there is a brief dialogue between Horatio, who represents the views of the educated schoolmen against the supernatural, and Hamlet, an open-minded skeptic who, like the modern researcher of ESP and UFO, does not rule out a priori the possibility of such paranormal events. Despite the appearance of the ghost, Horatio is still in doubt about the nature of their experience that may be just an illusion or hallucination.

> Hor.: Oh day and night, but this is wondrous strange!
> Ham.: And therefore as a stranger give it welcome.
> There are more things in heaven and earth, Horatio,
> Than are dreamt of in your philosophy. (HAM I:5)

In Hamlet's comment to Horatio and in his cagey letter to Ophelia (quoted below) there seems to be an awareness of the new discoveries by natural philosophers. That the Copernican revolution became a significant force in undermining the old astronomy and its theological implications is reflected in a poem by John Donne (1572–1631), King James's chaplain and the Dean of St. Paul's.

> The new Philosophy calls all in doubt
> The Element of fire is quite put out
> The Sun is lost and the earth, and no man's will
> Can well direct him where to look for it,
> Tis all in pieces, all coherence gone.[16]

That the sun causes the motions of planets, that comets are no more portents of disaster since they, too, obey the laws of planetary motion, that the nature of heavenly bodies is all earthlike, that there are more things in heaven and earth that are still to be discovered as suggested by the discovery of new stars by Tycho Brahe in 1572 lie beneath Shakespeare's words as he speaks to Horatio about the limits of his philosophy; in Berowne's comment in *Love's Labor Lost* on base authority from others' books, and in Lafeu's dismissal of miracles, "They say miracles are past, and we have our philosophical person to make modern and familiar things supernatural and causeless" (AWW, II:3). Hamlet's skepticism about old natural philosophy is similar to Prince Hector's skepticism about waging war for Helen when he says, "modest doubt is called 'The beacon of the wise, the tent that searches to the bottom of the worst'" (TRO, II:2).

In Hamlet's letter to Ophelia he reveals his understanding that Ptolomaic astronomy is no longer valid.

> Doubt thou the stars are fire;
> Doubt that the sun doth move;
> Doubt truth to be a liar
> But never doubt I love. (HAM, II:2)

The maxim of Protagoras that "Man is the measure of all things" comes to mind in Shakespeare, where villains like Iago or Edmund argue against the objectivity of virtues and vices and for the subjectivity of all moral and political values. They are to them merely expressions of the interest of the stronger.

We have pointed out that Hamlet's speech on the glory of being human is an indirect reference to the Renaissance idea of which Pico de la Mirandola was the outstanding spokesman and yet his own view of humankind is not Pico's but more like the Cynic philosophers and the Epicureans, seeing humankind from the beginning through dark glasses and the end as a particle of dust. Hamlet's famous oration ends with his own cynical view when he exclaims, "But to me what is this quintessence of dust!" Several times Hamlet repeats those two words, "to me"; "how weary, stale, flat, and unprofitable seems to me all the uses of this world." There is a clear indication of Hamlet's cynical view of human beings along with his admiration for those "happy few" who live according to the dictates of reason, such as Horatio, who is "not passion's slave."

The rivalry between philosophers and poet-playwrights as oracles of truth changed in the long centuries since Plato as the urgent questions posed by human needs and desires to know arose amid new challenges, as did also the protagonists: philosophy became allied with poetry as science began to claim the role of most reliable truth-teller while religion rose as challenger to both. The origin of the conflict between philosophy and religion is as old as St. Paul's warning: "beware lest any man spoil you through philosophy," in Tertullian's question, "What has Jerusalem to do with Athens?" and in the account of the angels of the Lord whipping St. Jerome for reading Cicero. The antipathy of the Church fathers to philosophy almost disappeared when Plotinus and Augustine reached for Plato's ideas and when St. Thomas Aquinas used Aristotle's philosophy in support of Christianity but nevertheless the traditional hostility continued as we hear in Luther's bland denunciation "Reason is a Grecian whore," and later in the mockery of rationalism of William Blake (1757–1827):

> Mock on, mock on, Voltaire, Rousseau;
> Mock on, mock on, 'tis all in vain!
> You throw the sand against the wind,
> And the wind blows it back again.
> . . .
> The Atoms of Democritus
> And Newton's Particles of Light
> Are sands upon the Red Sea shore
> Where Israel's tents do shine so bright.[17]

The ancient poet-philosopher dispute that was continued in the Elizabethan age and the following centuries has finally ended in peace when the lovers of poetry and dramatic art came to see, with Aristotle, that poetry is more philosophical than history, and when philosophers came to realize that there are truths in art beside scientific truth. Above all, Shakespeare's works express a happy marriage of Truth and Beauty in this world as reflected in his sonnet.

> But from thine eyes my knowledge I derive,
> And, constant stars, in them I read such art
> As truth and beauty shall together thrive. (SON 14)

Shakespeare himself leaves open the door to hope as he assures us of the constancy of Truth and Beauty.

Chapter Two

FALSTAFF
A PARODY OF SOCRATES

PLATO'S *PHAEDO*;
ARISTOPHANES' *THE CLOUDS*

> "I have a whole school of tongues in this belly of
> mine. . . .And I had but a belly of any indifferency,
> I were simply the most active fellow in Europe."
> Falstaff (2H4, IV:3)

Surely Falstaff must be counted as one of the most beautiful of the philosophical pearls of the Shakespearen deep, inspired as he was by the humanist image of the father of the philosophy of the Western world.

Although the name Socrates appears only in *Taming of the Shrew* and then only in connection with the name of his wife—"[she] is as old as Sibyl and as curst and shrewd as Socrates' Xanthippe"— a caricature of the philosopher himself appears as Falstaff, who acts, fights, mocks the beliefs and values of the heroes and the masses; defends himself in the court against charges of corrupting the youths; and dies like Socrates, though not with hemlock, but because "The King has killed his heart" (H5, II:1). The Folio and the Poems reveal Shakespeare's familiarity with many of Plato's dialogues. In *Henry IV* parts I and II and in the *Merry Wives of Windsor* he presents that great comic artist as an unmistakable parody of the great philosopher.

Harold Bloom in his recent book, *Shakespeare: The Invention of the Human,* speaks in general terms of Falstaff as the "Elizabethan Socrates."[1] Likewise M. M. Phillips, in her work *The Adages of Erasmus,* has observed some resemblances between a clownish Falstaff and a jesting Socrates. She writes, "There are affinities of a general kind between Falstaff and Socrates, especially in the light in which Socrates was sometimes regarded in the sixteenth century."[2] The specific likeness between the death scene of Socrates as reported by Phaedo and Falstaff's death as described by the Hostess in Shakespeare's *Henry V* has been noted by J. R. Moore.[3] However, there are similarities between the Sage of Eastcheap and the gadfly of the Athenians that are more than general, and in the following pages we shall particularize many resemblances between the artist and the philosopher that appear in Shakespeare's plays.

According to Phaedo, the man who gave Socrates the poison looked at his legs now and then, and after while he pressed his foot hard and asked him if he could feel and he said "no," then his leg, and so on upwards and upwards and showed us that he was cold and stiff. He was beginning to grow cold about his groin when he uncovered his face.[4]

In *Henry V,* the scene of Falstaff's death is described by the Hostess: "[F]or after I saw him fumble with his sheets and play with flowers and smile upon his fingers' ends I knew there was but one way; for his nose was as sharp as a pen. 'How now, Sir John,' quoth I, 'What man! Be of good cheer' . . . so bade me lay more clothes on his feet. . . . I put my hand into the bed and felt them, and they were cold as any stone; then I felt to his knees and so upward and upward, and all was as cold as any stone" (H5, II:3).

Socrates, upon taking the poison asked his disciples not to cry. His last words were: "Crito, we ought to offer a cock to Asclepius. See to it and do not forget." Socrates is thanking Asclepius, the god of health, for salvaging his soul from his body.[5] In *Henry V*, part 2, Shakespeare has Falstaff speak as if he believes the prince will recall him to favor while he lets us know that Falstaff feels he had really been dealt a death stroke and, as if about to die, says to Shallow, "I owe you a thousand pounds."

Falstaff's famous soliloquy about honor, in which he mocks the old aristocratic overvaluation of honor as the ultimate value to be paid even by death, is analogous in content though not in form to Socrates' dialogue when he criticizes the simplistic ideas of courage in the *Laches* and piety in the *Euthyphro* as they are held by his naive fellow men as articles of faith. That resemblance, however, ends when we note that Socrates' criticism of those commonly held values was only the first step toward construction of the Idea of true virtue, whereas Falstaff's attacks on honor were purely nihilistic. The famous speech resembles the philosopher's dialectic only qua social critic but not as a moral reformer.

> Well, 'tis no matter if honour pricks me on.
> Yea, but how if honour prick me off when I come on?
> How then? Can honour set a leg? No! Or an arm? No!
>   Or take away the grief of a wound? No.
> Honour hath no skill in surgery, then? No.
> What's honour? A word. What is in that word honour?
>   Air. A trim reckoning; Who hath it? He that dies on
>   Wednesday.
> Doth he feel it? No. Doth he hear it? No. 'Tis insensible,
>   then? Yea, to the deed. But will it not live with
>   the living? No. Why? Detraction will not suffer it.
>   Therefore I'll none of it.
> Honour is mere scutcheon; and so ends my catechism.
>
> (1H4, V:1)

Falstaff's argument, his "catechism," is a serious joke with a certain philosophical point, and some deliberate semantical sophistry in its premises, with a specious conclusion. His questions "Can honour set a leg? Or an arm? Or take away the grief of a wound?" or his comment, "honour hath no skill in surgery" shows that he is aware of all too common mistakes called by moral philosophers the "naturalistic fallacy," that is to identify values or virtues such as "good" or " honour" with natural emotions such as "pleasure" or with supernatural acts such as "divine command." The discovery of that fallacy is due to Socrates' argument wherein he rejects Euthyphro's identification of the essence of the word "piety" with one of its attributes, "what is loved by the gods." Falstaff is saying by implication that "honour" is an expression of value, and when he concludes "Therefore I'll none of it," he is consistent within his own values holding that that sort of honor is not a kind of virtue that he may die for. The same critique of aristocratic virtue is expressed wistfully in the next play of "true valor" and the demise of true virtues in his time (2H4).

However, Falstaff in his speech makes a deliberate semantic blunder when he reduces the meaning of "honour" to its written sign and turns that linguistic symbol to the spoken word, "air." That is the sort of error called by logicians "use-mention confusion" as if "honour" is a name. "What's in a name," cried Juliet, "O! be some other name!" Names, after all, are arbitrary designations and as such may be altered without impunity unless there are sanctions against their alteration.

That intentional blunder that is confusing the meaning or sense of a word with its sign, in the case of honor, or confusing a name with its denotation in the case of Capulet, the family name of Juliet, should be seen in the context of Shakespeare's frequent warnings against the misuse of words or "miscalling," such as "simple truth miscalled simplicity" (SON 66) and incoherent and inconsistent speeches, "O madness of discourse, that cause sets up with and against itself" (TRO, V:2).

Considered from a purely logical point of view, Falstaff's argument that starts with those seemingly factual premises and ends with a statement of his personal values is a specious argument. There is a gap, as David Hume observed, between the "is" and the "ought," and in deriving a prescriptive statement from the factual is to commit a categorical mistake.

Behind Falstaff's diatribe lurks a disguised social criticism, if only we shift our attention from the semantic aspects to the pragmatic dimension of his argument. Let us remember that Falstaff along with the Prince, his loving companion, is obliged to fight in a dynastic war. The heroes of that war were all bloodthirsty warriors. One is Hotspur, "that kills some six or seven dozen of Scots at the breakfast, washes his hand and says to his wife, 'Fie upon this quiet life. I want work.'" In the play he is called "the child of honour." The other is Douglas, a ferocious killer called "the King of honour." So is Prince Hal who has already mocked Hotspur's bloody deeds and yet he is threatening "the child of honour" before he slaughters him saying, "All the budding honours on thy crest I'll crop to make a garland for my head." When Falstaff sees on the battlefield the dead body of another warrior, Sir Walter Blunth, he, like Mark Antony on seeing Caesar's body, points to "that bleeding piece of earth" and says, "there is honour for you." He is so stunned when he sees that noble man soaked in his own blood, for "nothing, for an egg-shell" in Hamlet's words—saying "I like not such grinning honour as Sir Walter hath—Give me life." Hamlet, like Falstaff, speaks in passion of the absurdity of dying:

> when honour's at the stake . . .
> I see the imminent death of twenty thousand men

> That, for a fantasy, and a trick of fame,
> Go to their graves like beds.
> Exposing what is mortal and unsure
> To all that fortune, death and danger dare (HAM, IV:4)

And yet, Hamlet, unlike Falstaff's mockery of the princes of war, envies Fortinbras. who led his soldiers in a war "for a fantasy and a trick of fame."

Honor is not the only subject of Falstaff's derision. In various scenes he makes sardonic remarks about Reason. "Reason, you rough Reason" (MWW) and "If reason were as plentiful as blackberries, I would give no reason upon compulsion" (1H4, II:4).

In contrast to Socrates' praise of reason as a panacea for mental disorder and his injunction that "the unexamined life is not worth living" in his *Apology*, Falstaff puns on reason, and in a more serious vein considers reason to be at best a means to be used in the service of passion. In this Falstaff is with Aristotle who maintained that reason by itself can produce nothing.

Falstaff's assessment of the role that passion played in his life and his attack on the power of pure reason suggests that he would have enjoyed the mediaeval story of "the Buridan's Ass": a passionless person, in Hamlet's words, "thinking too precisely on events," is unable to act, and is thus likened to an ass that is unable to choose between two bundles of hay placed at equal distance to the right and left and thus starves to death for the lack of reason to choose one bundle rather than another. In his identical letter to Mrs. Page and Mrs. Ford, for which on discovery of his deceit they threw him in the Thames, he wrote, "Ask me no reason why I love you, for though love uses reason for his physician, he admits him not for his counselor" (MWW, II:1). The metaphor about reason as a physician to love appears again in a sonnet when the speaker of the sonnet says,

> My reason, the physician to my love,
> Angry that his prescriptions are not kept,
> Hath left me, and I desperate now approve
> Desire is death, which physic did except,
> Past cure I am, now Reason is past care (SON 147)

The speaker of the sonnet explicitly admits the role of reason as a physician to love, albeit ineffective. So does Falstaff in his letters and his amorous conversation with Mrs. Ford: "Why, now is Cupid a child of conscience, he makes restitution." (Folio)

There are many references in the Folio to Cupid, the Roman equivalent of Eros, the Greek god of love. In the apocryphal writing of Homer, quoted by Socrates in Plato's *Phaedo*, there is a reference to Eros as a winged god of love.

> Mortals call him fluttering love
> but the immortals call him the winged one. (*Phaedo*, 252)

In the Folio Cupid is blind, a wise and enlightened god of love, "a child of conscience [who] makes restitution." But in *King Lear* the blind Cupid could not heal Lear's wounds with love and the blinded Gloucester, like the blindfolded Cupid, knows how his world goes sans eyes. On seeing the blinded Earl of Gloucester and hearing his bitter words, "Oh, ruin'd piece of nature! This great world shall so veer out to naught. Dost thou know me?" Lear replies, "I remember thine eyes well enough. Dost thou squiny at me? No, do thy worst, blind Cupid; I'll not love. . . . Read thou this (a letter)."

> Glo.: Were all the letters suns, I could not see one.
> Lear: Your eyes are in a heavy case, yet you see how this world goes.
> Glo.: I see it feelingly.

> Lear: What? Art mad? A man may see how the world
> goes with no eyes." (LR, IV:6)

In *Much Ado about Nothing* Benedick, a Lord of Padua, speaks of that legendary god, "Prove that ever I lose more blood with love than I will get again with drinking, pick out mine eyes with a balladmaker's pen and hang me up at the door of a brothel-house for the sign of the blind Cupid" (ADO, I:1). In Sonnet 153 the sleeping Cupid "got new fire—from my mistress' eyes" and in Sonnet 137 there is an allusion to Cupid without mentioning his name:

Thou, blind fool, Love, what dost thou to mine eyes,
That they behold, and see not what they see?

Rosalind, the witty and learned heroine of *As You Like It*, alludes to blind Cupid and appeals to him as a judge, albeit with her witty remarks:

> The same wicked bastard of Venus that was begot of thought, conceived of spleen and born of madness, that blind rascally boy that abuses everyone's eyes because his own are out, let him be judge how deep I am in love."

In her anger Rosalind would not have agreed with her creator who wrote:

Love's not Time's fool, though rosy lips and cheeks
Within his bending sickle's compass come;
Love alters not with his brief hours and weeks,
But bears it out even to the edge of doom.
    If this be error and upon me prov'd
    I never writ nor no man ever loved. (SON 116)

On the contrary, Rosalind says,

> The poor world is almost six thousand years old, and in all this time there was not any man died in his own person *vide licit*, in a love-cause. Troilius had his brain dashed out with a Grecian club . . . and he is one of the patterns of love. Lender . . . though Hero, hath turned nun, for, good youth, he went but forth to wash him in the Hellespont, and was drowned; and the foolish coroners of that age found it was "Hero of Sestos." But these are all lies: men have died from time to time, and worms haved eaten them, but not for love. (AYL, IV:1)

The kind of love that demands self-sacrifice, if ever it existed, according to Rosalind, "is merely a madness," and in this instance, at least, she was right. Troilus, legendary son of Hecuba, did not die for Cressida but was killed by Achilles in a duel-like struggle between the two men as leaders of the opposing armies of Greeks and Trojans.

The Platonic illusion of love's timelessness does not escape Shakespeare even though it is contrary to his persistent belief that all things, whether in thought or in life, are time's fool, and time itself must have a stop, which vibrates in Hotspsur's dying words:

> But thought's the slave of life and life's time's fool
> And time that takes survey of all the world,
> Must have a stop. (1H4, V:4)

The allusion to blindfolded Cupid is to the god who inspired the earthly and measured love within the mind of the lovers in the plays with some Platonic touch and without the exalted claim for blind love by Florentine Platonists who have spoken of the divine delight in experiencing such a love at which the mystic aims.

The same idea appears also in *A Midsummer Night's Dream*, when Helena says

> Love can transpose to form and dignity,
> Love looks not with the eyes, but with the mind,
> And therefore is winged Cupid painted blind.
>
> (MND, I:1)

Placing love in the mind of the lover, Helena allows for the role of reason in love. In her view, love is not merely a sudden burst of raw feeling of which Philie speaks, "Whoever loved that loved not at the first sight," quoting Marlow, but is a delayed judgment that is called "emotion," and emotion as described by the Stoics is "a judgment," and a judgment stands in need of an objects.

The death scene, the honor soliloquy, the letter to women on the rule of reason and passion, and the references to Cupid are not the end of Falstaff—a parody of Socrates. There are still notable family resemblances between the fictional character and the real philosopher despite their differences. These resemblances include: physical traits, service in war, a sharp tongue and a sharp mind full of a vast inventory of historical knowledge and mythical legends, a sublimated passion for youth, the trial in the court and the unjust death sentence, as well as a death with a broken heart. Falstaff's captious asides in *The Merry Wives of Windsor* on reason go hand in hand with his praise of love by his use of ancient myths that in some respects resemble Socrates' discussion of Eros with the guests in the *Symposium*:

> Now the hot-blooded gods assist me!
> Remember, Jove, thou wast a bull for thy Europa!
> Love sat on thy horns. O powerful love!
> that in some respects makes a beast of man,
>   in some other, a man a beast.

> You were also, Jupiter, a swan for the love of Leda.
> O Omnipotent Love! . . . Think on't, Jove; a fowl's fault.
> When gods had hot backs what should poor men do?
> (MWW, 5:1)

Falstaff's sexual appetite, his dallying with professional madams and his pursuit of married women, his erotic dallying jokes and insatiable desire for sex, sack, and food are attested by his friends and foes. On the Hostess's report, he "cares not what mischief he does if his weapon be out, he will foin like any devil, he will spare neither man, woman, nor child." His companion Point is amazed by Falstaff's sexual desire, saying, "Is it not strange that desire should so many years outlive performance?" and so is Mr. Ford when he became aware of Falstaff's plot for seducing his wife. "What a damned Epicurean rascal is this?" he asks. Responding to Mrs. Ford's sexual challenges,

> Sir John! Art thou there, my dearest, my male deer?

Falstaff exclaims,

> My doe with the black scut
> Let sky rain potatoes
> Let there come a tempest of provocation!
> I will shelter me here [embracing her] (MWW, V:5)

Because of their shape potatoes were considered aphrodisiacal. The white potato was native to South America. It seems likely that Sir Francis Drake brought the first tubers to England in 1586 on his return from the Caribbean, so the potato, newly cultivated, was a luxury vegetable/aphrodisiac that Falstaff would like to see pouring from the skies.

Falstaff's attachment to young, faithless, and fickle Prince Hal is similar to Socrates' love for another handsome traitor, Alcibiades, even though Falstaff's love for the prince was a kind of sensual but fatherly love while Socrates' was a lustless love for the beauty of Alcibiades—an embodiment of the Idea of Beauty: the beloved reported Socrates' rejection of his sexual advances, "I lay during the whole night holding this wonderful monster in my arms, but in the morning when I awoke I rose as from the couch of a father" (*Symposium*).

At his trial Socrates was accused of corrupting youths like Alcibiades who was one of his devoted followers. Falstaff, likewise was accused of being the corrupter of Prince Hal on the ground that both of them at times were "cut purses" (pickpockets). He defended himself against this charge by saying that it was the prince who tried to corrupt him. The prince, the "sweet wag," his treacherous companion in drinking, whoring, robbing, and fighting, was a heartless villain even before he became a king and banished his devoted friend. Prince Hal mocked Falstaff's obesity saying, "Falstaff sweated to death and larded the lean earth as he walked along," and he puts the blame for his own misdeeds on his companion, saying, "Falstaff and the rest of the thieves are at the gate." He looked at him like the trial judge who called Falstaff "that villainous misleader of youth."

The prince, cruelly sarcastic, continues his puns on Falstaff. He calls him "thou globe of sinful continents." He sees his loyal friend as an animal that drinks, eats, and copulates and lives only in the present and is oblivious of time. When Falstaff asks him, "Now Hal, what time of day is it, lad?" the prince replies, "Thou art so fat-witted with drinking of old sack and unbuttoning thee after supper and sleeping.... What a devil hast thou to do with the time of the day?"

Unless hours were cups of sack, and minutes capons . . .
and the blessed sun himself a fair hot wench . . .
I see no Reason why thou
shouldst be so
superfluous to demand
the time of day. (1H4, I:2)

The point of such bitter mockery is that in the prince's opinion, Falstaff lives only in the present. He is afflicted, in Hamlet's words, with this "bestial oblivion" and like a beast "his chief good and the market of his time [is] to sleep and feed,—a beast no more." Socrates was, by his disciple's report, a short, stocky, pot-bellied bearded Athenian, who out-drank all the guests in the Symposium. According to Alcibiades, he could drink any quantity without getting drunk. The parody of Socrates is made more striking by the dissimilarities in character between the two as shown in their war records. Socrates fought for Athens with the utmost show of courage, saved the life of Alcibaides and refused a reward offered to him for his bravery. In contrast, Falstaff behaved like a coward in combat, escaped death by pretending to be dead, and then claimed that he was the man who killed Hotspur, the hero of the opposing army. After that episode, however, he admits he was a coward "by instinct" in that battle. At his trial, his servant defends Falstaff as if he was a Socrates who served the state by fighting in its defense. "He, my lord, but hath since done good service at Shrewsbury."

Falstaff is made of many materials from literature as well from life. He is a sage who, like Archilocus's fox, "knows many things [rather than] a hedgehog, one big one" (Fragments 115).[6] What makes him a sage is his grasp of historical legend and psychological and religious issues that appear within his jocular and pointed conversations with the courtiers and with the common folk. He is known in the town as a jolly scholar. The host of Garter Inn says, "Thou are clerkly, thou are clerkly, Sir John," and so does Mrs. Ford, saying, "I hear you are a scholar." The jester himself speaks as if he could be, like Socrates, the most famous person in Europe, although in contrast to Socrates' disavowal of having true knowledge, Falstaff boasts of the richness of his tongue, his large discourse, and his larger ego. "I have a whole school of tongues in this belly of mine, and not a tongue of them all speaks any other word but my name. And I have a belly of any indifferency, I were simply the most active fellow in Europe" (2H4, IV:1). Like Socrates who described himself as a gadfly on the lazy Athenian horse, Falstaff is a severe critic of the vices and inflated values of the courtiers and war heroes. "Virtue is of so little regard in these costermonger [commercial] times that true valour is turned bear-herd, pregnancy is made a tapster . . . , all the other gifts pertinent to man, as the malice of this age shapes them, are not worth a gooseberry." He makes jokes about his companion, the future heir to the throne, when he says about the beardless Prince Hal, "the prince, your master whose chin is not yet fledged . . . I would sooner have a beard grow in the palm of my hand than he shall get one on his cheek" (2H4, I: 2).

Here Shakespeare lets his Falstaff-Socrates character refer to Plutarch's *Lives*, where the Greek writer recounted,

> Ambassadors of the Parthians [Persians] who were sent to
> Crassus delivered him their message. . . .
> If the Romans try to make war with them then he would
> make war against them.
> Thereto Crassus courageously answered that he would
> make them answer in the city of Seleucia.
> Therewith Vagises, one of the eldest ambassadors,
> fell laughing and showed Crassus the palm of his hand

and told him, "Hair will sooner grow in the palm of my hand, Crassus, than you will come to Seleucia."⁷

Crassus was killed by the Parthians in 53 BCE.

Falstaff is also made to manifest familiarity with the ancient Persian world by referring to the Persian king of the Achaemenid dynasty when he says, "I must speak in passion and I will do it in King Cambyses vein" (521 BCE) (1H4, II:4). He modestly compares himself to Julius Caesar saying, "I can justly say with the hook-nosed fellow of Rome 'I came, saw and overcame.'" And he claims medical knowledge explaining, "This apoplexy is, as I take it, a kind of lethargy . . . a kind of sleeping in the blood, a whoreson tingling. . . . It hath the original from much grief, from study, and perturbation of the brain. I have read the cause of his effects in Galen: it is a kind of deafness" (2H4, I:2). Concerning the role of instinct in human and animal behavior he points to the power of instinct: "[B]eware instinct; the lion will not touch the true prince. Instinct is great matter, I was a coward on instinct" (1H4, II:4). Falstaff justifies his cowardly conduct in the war to his innate disposition for self-preservation. He sees himself as a lion that by instinct does not hurt his cub. His fatherly love for Prince Hal "thou art my son," like his self-love, is an instinctual feeling: "thou know'st I am as valiant as Hercules . . . but beware of instinct, the lion will not touch the true prince . . . what is it for me to kill the heir apparent?" (1H4, II:4). Falstaff's description of the power of instinct in himself and in a lion is in direct opposition to Coriolanus's view of himself as above the instinctual love for his mother. Coriolanus denies he is driven like goslings by instinct "I'll never be such a gosling to obey instinct. I'll but stand as if a man were author of himself and no other kin" (COR, V:3). Although the concept of instinct had emerged in the late middle ages, Shakespeare's reference to this natural phenomenon gives the play a familiar ring to modern ears.

On religious issues Falstaff speaks with sarcasm of the Puritans. He refers to them as weavers and solemn singing: "I would I was a Weaver, and could sing psalms." Prince Hal mocks Falstaff by saying. "Here comes lean Jack, here comes barebones." The Puritans' practice of giving names like barebones, "Damn barebones" or as "ashes" were often mocked in plays.

Falstaff says to Bardolph, "I never see thy face but I think upon hell-fire and Dives that lived in purple; for there he is in his robes, burning, burning. If thou wert any way given to virtue, I would swear by thy face; my oath should be, 'By this fire, that's God's angel,' but thou art altogether given over and wert indeed, but for the light in thy face, the son of utter darkness. . . . O thou art a perpetual triumph, an everlasting bonfire-light!" (1H4, III:3). In Falstaff's words, we recognize an allusion to the parable of the rich man and Lazarus in Luke 16:19-31: "There was a certain rich man which was clothed in purple and fine linen. The rich man died and was buried. And being in hell in torment." Furthermore, in his oath we are reminded of Exodus 2:3: "There the angel of god appeared to him in the shape of a flame of fire." It would seem that the source of Falstaff's diatribe was the Bible, as cited. The word "Dives," however, arouses our curiosity.

According to Harold Bloom, the word "Dive" is Late Latin meaning "rich man" and appears in the Vulgate Bible in the passage quoted above. As Bloom noted, the word "is not to be found in the Geneva Bible," and he comments that "it is not likely that Shakespeare had read Luke in the Vulgate where a certain rich man is a Dive. But Dive in Shakespeare's day was already a name out of Chaucer and common language."[8] Naseeb Shaheen, author of *Biblical References in Shakespeare*, observes that Shakespeare referred to the Geneva Bible more often than any other version and comments that the Geneva Bible was translated by Marian Protestant exiles (from England) in 1557. "The many Biblical references that Falstaff makes were probably suggested by Oldcastle's religious background. Shakespeare makes him a fallen knight who rejects his religious background, factitiously paraphrases the Scripture and frequently mimics Puritans' idiom."[9]

Along with those biblical references there are also references to Zoroastrianism, the ancient Persian religion. After the conquest of Persia by the Arabs, a group of Zoroastrians called Farsi left their homeland for India, where they practiced their rituals of praying to the sun and the sacred fire; hence they were called the sun-worshipers. In the play *All's Well that Ends Well*, Helena speaks of the Indianlike religion and the godlike sun that, like Aristotle's prime mover, moves the world but knows nothing about his worshiper.

> Thus, Indian-like,
> Religious in mine error, I adore
> The sun, that looks up his worshiper
> But knows of him no more.

In the late sixteenth and early seventeenth centuries, there was considerable interest in Persia as a counter to Ottoman power. Reports by travelers, merchants, and adventurers were published, and a play about the Sherley brothers, *Travels of the Three Sherley Brothers*, appeared in 1605.[10] It is not surprising that references to Persia occur in a number of Shakespeare's plays. In *King Lear*, the king, speaking to Edgar, says,

> You, sir, I entertain for one of my hundred;
> > only I do not like the fashion of your garment:
> > you will say they are Persian attire, but let them be
> > > changed. (LR, III:6)

In the *Comedy of Errors,* Angelo's creditor, demanding the repayment of his money, tells Angelo,

I am bound
To Persia and want my guilders for my voyage. (ERR, IV: 1)

In *The Merchant of Venice.* The Prince of Morocco requests of Portia,

Therefore, I pray, lead me to the caskets
To try my fortune. By this scimitar,
That slew the Sophy and the Persian prince,
That won three fields of Sultan Solyman,
I would outstare the sternest eyes that look.
I will not give my part of this sport for a pension if
thousands to be paid from the Sophy. (MV, II:5)[11]

The ancient Persian religion is Zoroastrian in which Ahura-Mazda, the god of light, is symbolized by fire; *Atesh-Kadeh* (the place of fire) is a sacred place where fire is kept burning perpetually. Ahreman is the god of darkness; his followers are Dives, symbols of evil who dwell in *Dozak*, the Persian word for Hell. Reading Falstaff's attack on Bardolph with its light-dark, fiery imagery, his use of the Persian word "Dives" for the rich man who goes to Hell, his reference to an everlasting bonfire-light, we know the imagery was inspired by what Shakespeare with his limitless curiosity had learned about the Persian religion. Perhaps it is not only the

Bible but also echoes from the *Zend-Avesta,* the principal text of Zoroastrianism, and/or even the *Shah-Nameh*, the Book of Kings, the epic poem of Ferdosi in which a "Dive" is mentioned often as an evil mythological character, that underlie Falstaff's outburst.

Given the final judgment of the host of the tavern, Mistress Quickly, one may note a similar judgment about the life of Socrates,

> Well, fare thee well; I have known thee these twenty-
> nine years, come peascod-time; but an honester and
> truer-hearted man,—Well, fare the well. (2H4, II:4)

At the end of *Phaedo* there is a final assessment of Socrates' life where Phaedo says "Such, Echecrales, was the end of our comrade who was, thee may fairly say of all those whom we know in our time, the bravest and also the wisest and most upright man."

Falstaff dies like Socrates and like Sir John Oldcastle he becomes a martyr when his old companion in drinking and carousing, Prince Henry, becomes King Henry and banishes him "on pain of death if he returns." In part 2 of *Henry IV*, in an Epilogue to the audience spoken by a dancer, Shakespeare disclaims Falstaff as Sir John Oldcastle who died a Protestant martyr. The dancer says "Falstaff shall die of a sweat unless already killed with your hard opinions—for Oldcastle died as a martyr and this is not the man." It is known to scholars that the change of the name from Oldcastle to Falstaff was requested by the family of that nobleman and accepted by the playwright. However, the playwright still makes an oblique reference in the play to Oldcastle when Prince Hal calls Falstaff, "my old lad of the castle."

Plato, Aristophanes, and Xenophon each provide different pictures of Socrates. Plato presents an idealized figure of Socrates in his dialogues, the playwright satirizes him in a comic presentation in *The Clouds* and in Xenophon's *Memorabilia* Socrates appears realistically as a prudent man and a practical thinker. That all three writers, the philosopher, the playwright, and the historian, were directly acquainted with the father of Western philosophy and thus had different but authentic perspectives of him is a stroke of fortune for which the intellectual world must be infinitely grateful. Shakespeare thus was able to take advantage of the portraits handed down from antiquity to fashion his own creation in the character of Falstaff.

There are notable resemblances between the Socrates of *The Clouds* and the Falstaff of *Henry IV* and *The Merry Wives of Windsor*. To see Falstaff as a parody of Aristophanes' Socrates, where he also resembles Erasmus's view of Socrates as a jester, we shall present a portion of *The Clouds,* followed by Erasmus's comments in *Adages.*

In *The Clouds,* Socrates appears as a typical Sophist, as a debunker of popular myths and a blasphemer. He is portrayed here by the playwright as a moon-gazer who is not concerned with the lives of ordinary citizens. The playwright sets the stage by presenting Socrates talking to his students in his Phronisterion (think tank) saying that Heaven is a vast fire extinguisher and that we are cinders. He presents Socrates as a teacher of rhetoric and as a Sophist who receives money for teaching sophistry. In a scene with Strepsiades, the father of one of his students, he appears in a basket floating in the clouds.

> Strep.: Hello! Who's that fellow in the basket?
> Stud.: Socrates.
> Strep.: Sweet Socrates.
> Soc.: Mortal! Why call'st thou me?
> Strep.: Please tell me what you are doing.
> Soc.: I walk on air and contemplate the Sun.

Strep.: O, then from a basket you contemplate the gods
and not from earth.

Soc.: Most true
I could not have searched our celestial mother
without suspending judgement. . . .
If from the ground
I were to see those things I could not find . . . ,
So surely doth the earth draw to herself
The essence of our thought.
The same is true in the case of watercress.

Strep.: Come now, do let me learn the unjust logic . . .
Name your own price, by all the gods I'll pay.

Soc.: The gods . . . you must know that gods with us
Don't pass for current coin.

Strep.: Then you must first explain who it is sends the rain.

Soc.: Well, then, let it be known these send it alone.
I can prove it by an argument strong.
Was these ever a shower seen to fall in an hour
When the sky was all cloudless and blue?

The play ends with Strepsiades cursing Socrates and his disciples,

> For with what aim do ye insult the gods and pry around
> the dwellings of the moon?
> Strike, smite them, spare them not for any reason,
> But most because they have blasphemed the gods.[12]

Like Socrates, Falstaff, too, was put in a basket "Have I lived to be carried in a basket, and to be thrown in the Thames like a barrow of butchers offal? . . . [T]hey conveyed me into a buck basket! rammed me in a basket with these smelly clothes . . ." (MWW, III:5).

There are yet other references to *The Clouds* such as the description of Socrates as a wicked old man. Strepsiades taunts him,

> Perhaps you'll urge that childrens' minds be taught by
> blows . . .

> Well, age is second childhood then . . . so when they
> [old men] err they should be punished more severely.

Socrates mutters, "Mortal—mortal man. . . ."

In *Henry IV*, Falstaff echoes the philosopher when answerng the prince's question, "Tell me, Jack, whose fellows are these (the recruits) that come after?" He answers, "Mine."

> Prince: I did never see such pitiful rascals.
> Fal.: Tut . . . tut . . . Good enough to toss;
> food for fodder . . . Tush, man . . . mortal men."
>
> (1H4, IV:2)

Several times Shakespeare attacks the common mockery of old age. He gives to Prince Hal, now exposed as a traitor to friendship, a long speech in which Hal mercilessly insults Falstaff with jibes about being a fat old man, a misleader of youth, an "old white-bearded Satan" (1H4, II:4). Jacques, an unpleasant character, gives a cynical account of human life from infancy to old age, a "second childishness" (AYL, II:7). Falstaff dismisses their comments about his physical infirmities and boasts that he is only old in his wisdom. The Chief Judge in *Henry IV*, part 2 rebukes the aging Falstaff, for continuing to act like a young man, "Have you not moist eyes? A dry hand? A yellow cheek? A white beard? A decreasing leg? And increasing belly? Is your voice not broken? Your wind short? Your chin double? Your wit single? And every part of you blasted with antiquity? And will you yet call yourself young? Fie, fie, fie, Sir John." Falstaff replies, "The truth is I am only old in judgment and understanding" (2H4, I:2).

Falstaff attributes his wisdom to his education by a wise woman. Responding to a question from the Hostess, "Sir John, was there a wise woman with thou?" Falstaff answers, "Ay, that there was . . . one that hath taught me more wit than ever I learned before in my life, but I paid nothing for it neither, but was paid for learning." He is alluding to Socrates' teacher, Diotima: in the *Symposium* Socrates says, "I have told you already Diotima that my ignorance is the reason why I came to you for I am conscious that I want a teacher."[13]

Erasmus in his *Adages* calls Socrates a jester saying that "his eternal jesting gave him the air of a clown. Socrates said that he was sure of one thing and that he knew nothing. And so it was not unjust in a time when philosophers were abundant this jester should have been declared by the Oracles to be wise, and to know more— he who says he knows nothing is wiser than those who pretend to know everything. So that he treated lightly even death—drank the hemlock with as cheerful a face as when he was drinking wine and joking with his friend Phaedo even when he lay dying."[14]

Erasmus's comment on Socrates should be seen in the context of his overall antischolasticism and anti-rationalist theology of the humanists. In his essay *In Praise of Folly,* his spokesman for Folly ridicules the schoolmen's rational theology: "True religion is a form of Folly which comes from the heart rather than the head." He laughs at monkish virtues such as celibacy and fasting: "Without Folly the human race would disappear, for who can marry without Folly." Erasmus's antirationalism is still less severe than that of Montaigne who, in his essay, defends Fideism—declaring that faith without reason is best, since it is not based on some falsifiable judgment in the Folio.

Contrary to Erasmus, Socrates was not a clown or a professional jester. However, on some occasions in Shakespeare's plays fools, jesters, and clowns are called philosophers. King Lear says to the fool, "First let me talk with this philosopher. What is the cause of thunder?" (A similar question was put to Socrates in *The Clouds*, "What is the cause of rain?") Not only fools are called philosophers by Lear but also Edgar, "I will keep still with my philosopher." He calls Edgar "good Athenian" (LR, III:4). It is to be noted that one of the men who speaks in Plato's *Laws* is called "The Athenian Stranger." Lear's fools, Feste and Touchstone, are philosopher-clowns; Touchstone calls Socrates to mind when he says, "I do now remember saying "a fool thinks he is wise but the wise man knows himself to be a fool" (AYL, V:1), and Feste comments in *Twelfth Night*, "better a witty fool than a foolish wit.'"

Shakespeare elsewhere uses the characters of fools and jesters. Kolakowski gives the reason why fools and jesters are called philosophers. "In every era the jester's philosophy exposes as doubtful what seems to be most unshakeable, reveals the contradiction in what appears obvious and incontrovertible, derides common sense, and reads sense in the absurd. They do that because they stand outside good society and observe it from the sidelines."[15]

Shakespeare is not yet through with Socrates as a figure for caricature. In *Timon of Athens* he creates the character of Apemantus, a Cynic philosopher, as another parody of Socrates. The Cynic philosophers followed some features of Socrates' lifestyle such as living simply, self-sufficiently, and honestly. The word "Cynic" referred to canine, and was applied by their opponents to the members of this sect for leading a doglike life. The play is a sardonic representation of Athenian courtly life and takes place in the mansion of a nobleman, Timon, who presides over a dialogue between the artists—a poet, a painter, and a philosopher, Apemantus, described as "a churlish philosopher" in the list of characters. A character given the name Alcibiades also appears as a captain though without much resemblance to the famous lover of Socrates.

The old quarrel between philosophers and poets appears in this play albeit in a simplified and jocular form. Timon resembles Cephalus, a wealthy shield-maker in Plato's *Republic,* who presides over a dialogue between Socrates and other participants. Cephalus speaks of his just and happy life, while Timon expresses himself like a misanthrope who hates everyone, himself above all. Thus it seems that Timon is a parody of Cephalus as Apemantus is a parody of Socrates. (Apemantus is a critic of Homer in Plato's dialogue, the *Lesser Hippias*.)

In the play there is a reference to "real politics" the Machiavellian justification of force for "reason of state" when one of the actors called "The First Stranger" loudly echoes Thrasymachus's idea that "justice is in fact what is good for the stronger," when he says:

I proclaim
Men must learn now with pity to dispense;
For policy sits above conscience. (TIM, III:2)

When Timon asks the philosopher, "Whither art going?" he answers, "to knock out an honest Athenian brain." Timon replies, "That's a deed thou die for." Apemantus says, "Right, if doing nothing be death by the law." Yet unlike Socrates' unbounded love for Athens, Apemantus reveals his love for himself and none for the others. "Apemantus says, great immortal god, I crave no pleft, I pray for no one but myself." In this conversation Apemantus says to Timon, "If thou coudst not please me with speaking to me thou mightst have hit upon it here . . . the commonwealth of Athens is become a forest of beasts." The philosopher accuses the poet of being a liar and the poet defends himself as an artist and hence not a liar. Apemantus, "Then thou liest. Look in thy last work where thou hast feigned him [Timon] a worthy fellow." The poet answers, "That is not feigned. He is so." Apemantus describes a picture of the painter as "a filthy piece of work," and the painter calls the Cynic philosopher a dog. Timon curses the philosopher, "away, thou mangy dog, away thou tedious rogue! I shall lose a stone by thee!" He throws a stone and denounces the poet as a gold digger.

> You have done work for me, there is a payment; hence!
> You are the alchemist, make gold of that
> Out, rascal dogs. (TIM, V:1)

Timon, a misanthrope, presents humankind as if living in Plato's cave. He denounces the Earth and praises the Sun, which in Plato is a symbol for bestowing light on the cave dwellers. "O Blessed Breathing Sun! Draw from the earth the rotten humidity. Blow thy sister's Orb, infect the air." Timon ends his blasting attack with "Come, damned earth. Thou common whore of mankind that put'sts odes among the rout of nations." The furious verbal battle between Apemanthus and Timon ends with name-calling and stone-throwing—another parody of Socrates' dialogues.

Chapter Three

PLATO'S VOICE

"'Fair, kind, and true,' is all my argument, . . .
'Fair, kind, and true,' have often lived alone,
Which three till now, never kept seat in one."

(SON 105)

It is with keen awareness of the spread of the Italian Renaissance into England in the latter part of the sixteenth century, when Shakespeare was born, and its rediscovery of Plato, that we will consider the Bard's plays and poems, and the philosophical ideas reflected in them. Plato's meditations on the Good, the Beautiful, and the True permeate Shakespeare's plays and poems. Plato's reflections on the real Forms and their imitation—the shadows—on self-knowledge and self-deception, on human autonomy, and bondage, on the just city-state and just citizens, on love and lust, on death and intimations of immortality, on time and eternity are dramatically transformed in the actions of Shakespeare's plays mainly following Aristotelian instructions for dramatic art, and into the poems, where he follows the Petrarchan tradition for the sonnets, wherein arguments are condensed and hints and allusions are replaced by demonstration.

Plato's works were translated from Greek into Latin by Marsilio Ficino (1433–1499) and could be found in London in libraries and in book shops.[1] One edition is listed in the catalogue of Frances Bacon's library.[2] Although Ben Jonson famously claimed that Shakespeare had "small Latin and less Greek," modern scholars tend to agree that Jonson was speaking relatively, in view of his own accomplishments; he had been highly educated at Oxford. Shakespeare himself was a schoolteacher and must have known enough Latin to read Ficino's translation. The spread of the Italian Renaissance into England by the late sixteenth century brought with it a taste for *Italianita*—a taste for Italian art and architecture and in living style, which probably accounts for Shakespeare setting twelve of his thirty-seven plays in Italy. There are, furthermore, many references to Italy or Italians: Pico della Mirandola, the ideal man as his Renaissance contemporaries saw him, famous as a Neoplatonist in his own day, was known in England through Sir Thomas More's translation of his biography, which he considered introduced a man "who might be an example for Englishmen as to how to live."[3] His famous *Oration on the Dignity of Man* is doubtless a source for Hamlet's eulogy of humankind, "the paragon of animals" (HAM, II:2). Pico's handsome person and style, for which he was known, comes to mind as we hear Ophelia praising her seemingly mad prince:

Oh, what a noble mind is here o'er thrown:
The courtier's, soldier's, eye, tongue sword.
. . .
The glass of fashion and the mold of form
The observ'd of all observers. . . . (HAM, II:1)

In *Richard II,* the dukes of York and Lancaster lament the present state of England and "the open ear of youth" who listen to

Report of fashions in proud Italy,
Whose manners still our tardy apish nation
Limps after in base imitation. (R2, II:1)

Near the end of *A Midsummer Night's Dream*, Bottom, referring to the beautiful city of Bergamo, widely noted for a particular dance referred to as "the Bergamo dance," asks the company (reversing the verbs seeing and hearing), "Will it please you to see the epilogue or to hear a Bergomask dance . . . ?" (MND, V:1). Shakespeare's knowledge of Italian Renaissance artists seems problematic since in *The Winter's Tale* a player called Third Gentleman speaks of Giulio Romano as "that rare Italian master, Julio Romano" who is copying a statue (WT, V:2). According to Stephen Kegell, "It was indeed *Vasari's Lives* that led Shakespeare's indirect reference to Julio. This is the only allusion in Shakespeare to a modern artist."[4]

THE REAL AND THE SHADOW

> "Now you can understand how much love burns in me for you When I forget our unsubstantiality, to treating shadows as one treats solid things."
> —Dante, *Purgatory XXI,* line 130

Plato in his most poetical Allegory of the Cave speaks of humans as if they are in the cave, shackled in their seats and looking at the wall where they observe only the shadows of the real objects that were placed outside the cave and were projected on the walls. The real objects are illuminated by the sun, the godlike idea of the Good. A cave dweller, a philosopher (Plato himself), unshackles his chain and turns away from the illusory spectacle and moves toward the intelligible realm. On seeing the real world he returns to the cave in order to enlighten the cave dwellers.

In his *Republic* and *Laws* Plato sees himself not only as a traditional author of political constitutions such as Solon, the author of

Athenian laws and the civil code, but also as if he is a Moses, the lawgiver and the idol-breaker, who on seeing the heavenly light and hearing the Lord's voice, descends from the mountain in order to awaken his people from their dogmatic slumber and lead them out of bondage into the Promised Land. The philosopher's godlike idea of the Good, however, is not Jehovah, and Plato is not a messenger but a revolutionary reformer who thinks that possession of knowledge is indispensable for the good life. The distinction between the philosopher and the prophet is even more striking on seeing that Plato at the end of the *Republic*—his thought experiment—is criticizing the viability of his own ideal state. The center of Plato's philosophy is his theory of ideas—*eidas* that are translated as Ideas or Forms although they are not the subjective images in the mind or the objective properties of physical objects. They are common properties of particulars and it is by virtue of this property that they are denoted by their linguistic signs. By assigning the same sign to a number of particular things, that sign is the name of something common to all. The semantic aspect of ideas points to a cardinal distinction between the universal and the particular, to use Aristotle's category or between tokens and types, to use the modern terminology, or between the concept and object in Gottlob Frege's inquiry. Shakespeare reveals his understanding of these categories by providing examples in his plays, and the consequence of ignoring these distinct and separate categories, where proper names are confused with their denotation or titles of kings were replaced by the bearer of that title. (This subject shall be discussed in chapter 4 in a section on Aristotle.)

Socrates in the *Symposium* warns his interlocutor: "But what if man has eyes to see the true beauty, the divine beauty, I mean pure and clear unalloyed, not dogged by the pollution of mutability. He will suddenly perceive the nature of wondrous beauty, beauty absolute, simple and everlasting."[5] His idea of beauty is thus elevated to the metaphysical realm of being and not of becoming, so that if ever we can have knowledge of it we may use it as a paradigm against which a particular beauty is to be measured. The Parthenon, the "Apolo Belvedere" do conform in some degree to the idea of beauty; even though they are all perishable works of art, they participate in the ideal form.

The ideas are also assumed to be the standard for evaluation of particulars; they may be compared to the old standard meter that was once hermetically kept way from changing. Ideas were elevated by Plato to a metaphysical realm, for being atemporal nonspatial entities. "The many are seen but not known, and ideas are known but not seen."[6] They alone are the objects of knowledge, whereas of worldly things, we may have at best "true opinion." Never mind the particulars, those corruptible remains of departed ideas; they are nothing but delusory perceptible objects even though they are the building blocks for the universals.

The core of the theory of ideas is Plato's semantic assumption that conceptual expressions are the abstraction of what all particulars have in common, which is the essence of Aristotle. The theory is modeled after geometry, as pure geometry is the abstraction of the visible geometrical figure, so is the idea of beauty and such abstractions. The clarity and exactness, and the universality of pure mathematics is the model for truth, so much so that Plato imposes that paradigm against all other subjects. The instruction over the entrance of the academy warned the student "No one without geometry may enter." This is the basis of the persistent demand of Socrates for an exact definition of "Knowledge," "Justice," or "Piety." When a disciple in Plato's *Theatatus* provides definitions for "Equality," or for "Mathematical Roots," Socrates demands that he must also define "Knowledge" in the same manner, which the disciple says is beyond his power. It is Aristotle, the distinguished disciple of Plato who reminds the Platonists that, "It is the mark of an educated man to look for precision in each class of things so far as the nature of the subject demands. It is foolish to accept probable reasoning from a mathematician, or to demand from a rhetorician scientific proof."[7]

Plato's famous picture of the two worlds permeates the whole body of Western philosophy, poetry, and theology from Aquinas to Dante and others wherein it is believed that the world of Becoming is a mere illusion and human bodies are nothing but the remains of the departed souls that are permanent inhabitants of the world of Being. The picture closely resembles the idea of duality in Eastern religions, although the latter is more poetical than Plato's reasoned speculation. Certain poetical versions of Plato's worldview appear in Shakespeare where the metaphors in the Cave Allegory such as the illusory world of shadows and the shadows of those shadows that are reflected in the world of art, the darkness of the cave, the world of dreams and waking, and the enlightenment after leaving the cave appear in Sonnet 43:

> When most I wink, then do mine eyes best see,
> For all the day they view things unrespected;
> But when I sleep, in dreams they look on thee,
> And darkly bright, are bright in dark directed.
> Then thou, whose shadow shadows doth make bright,
> How would thy shadow's form form happy show
> To the clear day with thy much clearer light,
> When to unseeing eyes thy shade shines so!

There are yet other allusions to the Platonic vision of the form of beauty and its reflection in bodily frame. In this sonnet the speaker says,

> Mine eye hath play'd the painter and hath stell'd
> Thy beauty's form in tables of my heart;
> My body is the frame wherein 'tis held
> And perspective it is best painter's art.
>
> . . .
>
> Mine eyes have drawn thy shape, and thine for me
> Are windows to my breast, where-through the sun
> Delights to peep, to gaze therein on thee;
>
> > Yet eyes this cunning want to grace their art;
> > They draw but what they see, know not the heart.
>
> (SON 24)

Plato speaks of the trinity of ideas of the Good, Beauty, and Truth, that mirrors with some distortion the trinity of Fair, Kind, and True in Sonnet 105. From Helen Vendler's insightful perspective the sonnet is a reflection of Plato's trinity of ideas of Good, Beauty and Truth, whereas to the other commentators the sonnet alludes to the Christian idea of Trinity. Vendler, however, goes still further by saying that "The speaker of the Sonnet ranks the aesthetic idea of beauty (Fair) in a higher place than the ethical (Kind) and the philosophical (True)."[8] The Good, which is mentioned but once in the *Republic*, is not only an ethical idea, it is the highest form, the idea of all ideas that are participating in that paradigm. Like the sun that is both visible and also is the cause that enlightens objects, the Good is both intelligible and enlightens other ideas. "It is the cause of all that is right and good . . . it is itself sovereign, producing truth and reason unassisted by sight."[9] In the sonnet the speaker speaks of "Fair, kind, and true [that] have often lived alone." However, in the next line he sees unity in the trinity, saying "These three till now never kept seat in one."

> Let not my love be called Idolatry,
> Nor my beloved as an idol show,
> . . .
> Kind is my love today, tomorrow kind,
> Still constant in a wondrous excellence,
> . . .
> "Fair, kind, and true" is all my argument,
> . . .
> "Fair, kind, and true" have often liv'd alone
> Which three till now never kept seat in one. (SON 105)

The beloved is not an idol, he says at the start of the sonnet, but is like the idea of the Good (the *Summun Bonum*); she is a unity of all three separate ideas that once had lived alone. The Beautiful then, stands with the idea of the Good and not above it.

Following the cave allegory is a long discussion about poetry in the *Republic*, book 10, when Socrates speaks to Glaucon saying, "The poet with his words and phrases may be said to lay on the colors of the several arts; himself understands their nature enough to imitate them in meter and harmony. . . . I think you must have observed what a poor appearance that tales of poets make when stripped of color which music puts upon them and recited in simple prose." So it seems to the philosopher that in paraphrasing a poem we may in fact destroy the poem since what remains are only fools' tales and simple thoughts. Plato in his construction of *Poetica* (*Republic*) goes even further than Socrates by banishing Homer from his utopia solely on moral grounds. He considers Achilles, who in Hades laments his fate and prefers to be the meanest slave on earth than a king among the dead and concludes, "We shall expunge all that sort of thing, I say, beginning with Homer—Odyssey."[10] Plato's enchantment with pure reason at the expense of art leads him to a kind of secular puritanism. His proposal about censorship over plays and poems, even over music, by the omniscient philosopher-kings is a consequence of his belief in the Socratic, unwarranted assumption that virtue is knowledge and all wrongdoing is the result of ignorance, that no person does an immoral or illegal act voluntarily.

Plato's view of censorship was effective for centuries. It was promulgated by Augustus, the self-proclaimed reformer of Roman decadence, who banished Ovid, "Honest Ovid," the author of *The Art of Love,* for writing erotic poetry. The practice of state censorship over plays and poems was exercised in Elizabethan times by the office of "Stationery," and extended to Catholic ceremonies such as the prohibition of music in the mass. Catholics suffered far more than censorship, of course: Church property was confiscated, religious symbols destroyed, individuals were subjected to discrimination and abuse, and a number of priests were hung. These and other official abuses were attacked by the Bard in a sonnet where he writes:

> Tired with all these, for restful death I cry,
>> As, to behold desert'd and beggar born
>> And needy nothing trimm'd in jollity,
>> And purest faith unhappily forsworn,
>> And gilded honors shamefully misplaced,
>> And maiden's virtue rudely strumpeted,
>> And right perfection wrongfully disgraced.
>> . . .
>> And art made tongue-tied by authority,
>> And simple truth miscalled simplicity.
>> . . .
>> Tired with all these, from this world I begone,
>> Save that, I die, I live my love alone. (SON 66)

In *Timon of Athens*, there is another reference about the execution of the priests and the confiscation of the wealth of the Catholic Church that occurred during Shakespeare's time.

> Tim.: Nor sight of priests
> In holy vestments bleeding, shall pierce a jot.
> There is gold to pay thy soldiers. (TIM, IV:8)

In the fourth stanza of *The Phoenix and the Turtle* there are again allusions to the anti-Catholic policy of the state such as the repression of the *Requiem* and the "defunctive" church music that resemble Sonnet 66, quoted above:

> Let the priest in surplice white
> That defunctive music can,
> Be the death-devining swan,
> Lest the requiem lack his right.

There are also in the plays and sonnets many Platonic ideas about the sexual desire for unity and about the agony and the ecstasy of love.

In the *Symposium*, the wise philosopher Diotima differs with Socrates on the relation between love and beauty, and provides her own theory of love.

> For love, Socrates, is not as you imagined the love of the beautiful only.
> What then?
> The love of generation out of birth of beauty.
> Yes, I said, indeed. But why generation?
> Because to the mortal creature generation is a sort of eternity and immortality! . . . Love of immortality. . . .

> See you not how all animals, birds as well as beasts,
>> in their desire for procreation are in agony when they
>> take the infection of love whereto is added the care of
>> offspring on whose behalf the weakest are ready to
>> battle against the strongest, even to the utmost,
>> and to die for them. Men may be supposed to act
>> thus from reason but why should animals have these
>> passionate feelings?[11]

In a sonnet, the Speaker encourages his beloved to procreate and so gain a kind of secular immortality by producing offspring.

> From fairest creatures we desire increase,
> That thereby beauty's roses might never die,
> But as the riper should by time decrease,
> His tender heir might bear his memory. (SON 1)

In *Venus and Adonis*, the mythical figure Venus, like the Speaker of the sonnets, tells her chaste lover, Adonis, that the best way of countering mortality is procreation.

> Therefore despite of fruitless chastity,
> Love-lacking vestals and self-loving nuns,
> That on the earth would breed a scarcity
> And barren dearth of daughters and of sons,
> Be prodigal; the lamp that burns by night
> Dries up his oil to lend the world his light. (VEN, 752–756)

In Plato's *Symposium* where the main theme is love, Agathon proclaims, "He whom Love touches not walks in darkness." Pausanius speaks of true love as being superior to vulgar love of the flesh and of true lovers dying for their beloved. A shadowy figure like the winged god of love speaks of vulgar lovers. In his view, "Evil is the vulgar lover who loves the body rather than the soul, inasmuch as he is not even stable because he loves the body which is unstable and therefore when the bloom of youth of what he is desiring is over, he takes wings and flies away."[12]

The contrast between pure, spiritual, and selfless love that makes lovers willing to die for their beloveds and the "vulgar desire" for the body appears in the *Symposium* at the point where Phaedrus is praising Alcestris and Achilles for dying for their lovers, whereas Plato's "wise woman of Maltina," Diotima, questions the legend: "Do you imagine that Alcestris would have died to save Admetis, or Achilles to avenge Patroclus . . . if they had not imagined that the memory of their virtues would be inmortal?" (The legend is attributed to the "foolish error into which Aeschylus has fallen."[13]) Diotima's skepticism about self-sacrificing lovers is echoed by another wise woman, Rosalind, in *As You Like It*, as shown in our previous chapter on Falstaff.

The great themes of life—love, fame, and immortality—pervade Shakespeare's plays and poems. Socrates' wise woman, Diotima, speaks of men seeking fame in order to be remembered for their heroic actions. "Think only of men and you will wonder at the senselessness of their way, unless you can consider how they are spurred for the love of immortality, of fame."[14] And Shakespeare reveals his belief in his own immortality through his art:

> Nor shall Death brag thou wander'st in his shade
> When, in eternal lines to time, thou growest:
> So long as men can breath or eyes can see
> So long lives this, and this gives life to thee. (SON 18)

In Sonnet 107 he promises his beloved,

> . . . thou in this shalt find thy monument
> When tyrants' crests and tombs of brass are spent.

This is a memory from Horace of whom Shakespeare was aware, as we know, from a reference in *Titus Andronicus* (4:2):

> Integer vitae, scelerisque purus,
> Non eget Mauri jaculis, nec arcu.
>
> (The man who is upright in life and free of sin
> has no need of Moorish spears or bow.)

Chiron says, "O! 'Tis a verse in Horace; I know it well: I read it in the grammar long ago."[15] The belief that their works will survive has been recorded in the poetry of the world's great poets: more than one thousand years ago the Persian master Ferdosi proudly proclaimed in his *Ethics: The Book of Kings*,

> Whereas the lofty castles turn to dust by ravages of rain,
>   storm and sunlight,
> This monument will escape the hazards of time.

In the *Symposium* there is a mythical tale about Eros that places love in the yearning of the One for the Other. Aristophanes, who was invited to that banquet, presents his own theory about the origin of humankind. According to his fanciful speculation, Andogynous was a joint female-male creation that was separated by Zeus. Each part thus seeks the other to gain wholeness. Shakespeare takes up this theme in his poem, *The Phoenix and the Turtle,* based on the myth of two birds, the phoenix and the turtle dove, separated but eternally loving each other.

> So they loved, as love in twain
> Had the essence but in one;
> Two distincts, division none:
> Number there in love was slain.
> Hearts remote, yet not asunder;
> . . .
> Single nature's double name
> Neither two nor one was called.

He extends this thought into a nonsexual union in *Twelfth Night* in which Antony speaks of Sebastian's brotherly love:

> Seb.: O Antonio! O my dear Antonio! How have the hours lacked and tormented me since I have lost thee!
> Ant.: How have you made division of yourself?
> An apple, cleft in two, is not more twine than those two creatures.
> Who is Sebastian (TN, V:1)

and in *A Midsummer Night's Dream,* in which Helena speaks of her twin sister, Hermia, from whom she had been separated originally, were seeking each other:

> Double cherries, seeming parted,
> But yet an union in partition;
> Two lovely berries molded on one stem
> So, with two seeming bodies, but one heart; (MND, III:2)

The misery of separation and the longing for union has often lent itself to metaphor in world literature, from the naturalistic reed torn from the reed-bed to the scientific atom seeking atom.

SELF-KNOWLEDGE: THE MIRROR METAPHOR

> "When such a spacious mirror's set before him
> He needs most see himself."
>
> —Antony (ANT, V:1)

The philosophical idea of the privacy of mind, the privileged access to our own mental life, self-knowledge, and the indirect and secondary understanding of others' minds frequently appears in Shakespeare in metaphors and similes, and on some occasions in simple and direct speeches of the players. The main source of these philosophical speeches is in Plato's dialogues and their echoes in Stoic and humanist writings. Consider Plato's early dialogues *Charmides* and *Alcibiades I*. Plato makes Charmides say to Socrates, "For self-knowledge . . . to be the very essence of knowledge, and in this I agree with him who dedicated the inscription 'KNOW THYSELF' at Delphi." Socrates then says, "Self-knowledge to be wisdom . . . in the mirror of the divine he will see his own good."[16]

In the dialogue *Alcibiades I*, Socrates makes use of the eye-mirror metaphor in order to explain our understanding of our own minds as reflected in the other's eyes.

> Soc.: If someone were to say to the eye, "See thyself" as you might say to a man "know thyself" . . . would not his

> meaning be that the eye should be looked at in this in which it would see itself?
>
> Alc.: Clearly, Socrates, in looking at the mirror and the like.
>
> Soc.: Is there not something in the nature of a mirror in our eyes? Did you ever observe that the face of a person looking at the eyes of another is reflected as in a mirror, what is called the pupil, and if the soul is ever to know itself it must look at the soul and not only
> at that part of the soul in which his virtue resides.[17]

The Socratic metaphor of the mirror as the eyes and of knowledge as knowing yourself through the eyes of others though not in the mirror of the divine, appears many times in the Folio and the Sonnets. In *Troilus and Cressida* the Homeric hero Achilles makes use of the mirror metaphor and goes on elaborating on the mirror for self-knowledge through the eyes of others who observe our behavior. In the following passages there is an indirect rejection of the theory called syllopsism by the idealists of modern philosophy who believe that pure introspection is the only viable vehicle for self-knowledge. Achilles is saying, in effect, that without the other, the observer, one would not be aware of oneself as a person. That philosophical idea is restated in our times by the new behaviorists and by a Wittgensteinian who asks, "What is oneness without the otherness?" It is argued by modern philosophers that without language, which we inherit from our culture, pure introspection is as empty of content as the blank mind of the Lockean *tabula rasa*.

In *Troilus and Cressida*, Achilles asks Ulysses "What are you reading?"

> Uly.: A strange fellow here
>   Writes me: "That man, how dearly ever parted, ...

>   How much in having, or without or in,
>   Cannot make boast to have that which he hath,
>   Nor feels not what he owes but by reflection;
>   As when his virtues shining upon others
>   Heat them, and they retort that heats again
>   To the first giver."
>
> Ach.: That is not strange, Ulysses!
>   The beauty, that is borne here in the face
>   The bearer knows not, but commends itself
>   To others' eyes: nor doth the eye itself—
>   That most pure spirit of sense—behold itself,
>
>   . . .
>
>   For speculation turns not to itself
>   Till it hath travell'd and is mirror'd there
>   Where it may see itself. (TRO, III:3)

"The strange fellow" seems to come from *Alcibiades I*. According to Hardin Craig, Churton Collins identified the "strange fellow" as Plato.[18] However, in the *Laws* one of the speakers is called "a stranger" but is not Plato.

The mirror metaphor reappears in *Julius Caesar* in the conversation between Cassius and Brutus:

> Cas.: Tell me, good Brutus, can you see your face?
> Bru.: No, Cassius, for the eye sees not itself
>   But reflection, by some other things.
> Cas.: It is very much lamented, Brutus
>   That you have no such mirror as will trace your hidden
>   worthiness, into your eyes,
>   That you might see your shadow.
>   I have heard where many of the best respected in Rome,

> Except immortal Caesar, speaking of Brutus . . .
> Have wished that noble Brutus had his eyes,
> Since you know you cannot see yourself so well
> as by reflection.
> I am your glass,
> Will modestly discover to yourself
> That of yourself which you yet know not of. (JC, I:2)

In *As You Like It*, Celia questions the possibility of self-knowledge by seeing yourself with your own eyes. "If you saw yourself with your eyes or knew yourself with your judgement, the fear of your adventure would counsel you to a more equal enterprise" (AYL, II:1).

In *Henry VIII,* Cardinal Wolsey echoes the Socratic injunction saying:

> I know myself and I feel
> Within me
> At peace above all earthly dignities. (H8, III:2)

The popular cardinal knows himself through the eyes of his observers.

ON AUTONOMY AND BONDAGE

> "Between the action of a dreadful thing and the first
>   motion, all the interim is
> Like a phantasm or a hideous dream."
>
> —Brutus (JC, II:2)

Shakespeare's characters exhibit a number of persistent mythological, theological, and philosophical beliefs such as predestination, fatalism, and the superstitious belief in "fortune's buffets and rewards" together with rational beliefs in human autonomy and moral responsibility. The main source of the idea of self-knowledge is Plato's dialogues as they were understood by the humanists along with the Stoics' moral doctrine concerning the place of the free man in the cosmos—a microcosm within the macrocosm. We shall provide a brief background on human autonomy and bondage in the ancient world.

The philosophical problem of free will appears first in Socrates when he argues in defense of his own autonomy, against those materialist philosophers who consider that free will is an illusion due to ignorance of cause, where cause for them is only the material cause. Socrates in the *Phaedo* argues against Anaxagoras' mechanistic theory that human action is nothing but bodily motion since that theory does not explain his own moral and political decisions. He offers instead a teleological reason for his actions, which goes beyond the mechanistic operations of his muscles and bones: "I found many philosophers forsaking mind but they have recourse to air and ether and water—and when they endeavored to explain the causes of my several actions . . . they held that I sit here because my body is composed of bone and muscle . . . and they would have a similar explanation of my talking to you which they would attribute to my voice producing sounds. There is surely a strange confusion of causes and conditions in all this . . . it may be said, indeed, that without bone and muscles I cannot execute my purpose. But to say that I do as I do because of them, and not from the choice of the best, is very careless and an idle mode of speaking."[19]

Socrates' philosophical defense of free will had been forcibly expressed by Sophocles (496–406 BCE) who, in *Oedipus*, exalts man as if being a rational animal he is a demigod. We are thus reminded that a great work of dramatic art may eloquently convey abstract philosophical thought and that great poets frequently express metaphorically and allegorically what philosophers express with precision in their intellectual frames.

In the Greek tragedies, the battle between gods and men is ongoing wherein the heroes are guilty of hubris in rebelling against their allotted destiny (nemesis is the ultimate power that rules over all) and they are punished by the gods for their insolence. Homer's *Atlas,* Aeschylus's *Prometheus,* and Sophocles' *Oedipus* all defy the ordeals imposed on them and take their punishment with courage, each in his own style. Oedipus's response to his fate, however, stands above Sysiphus's action in the face of his punishment to roll forever the stone of time and it is even superior to Atlas's passive acceptance of his fate to stand on the edge of earth and bear the sky on his head.

In the first act of *Oedipus Rex* Apollo prophecies that Oedipus is doomed to kill his father and marry his mother. Oedipus on hearing that prophecy at the shrine of Delphi from an oracle feels immortal guilt, even though he has been warned by Jocastra, his mother and his future wife, "don't be afraid that you may marry your mother. Many a man in dreams has shared his mother's bed."[20] Jocastra urges that a dream being just a happening is not an intentional act, hence Oedipus is not responsible for his incestuous dream. Nonetheless the hero believes the warning and vainly tries to escape his fate: in the end he does kill his father and bed his mother without knowing the identities of his parents. When Oedipus realizes that Apollo's prophecies were fulfilled he does something superhuman by plucking his own eyes with his own hand. Thus he shows, to the amazement of the Chorus, that despite the god's decree, a man can act like a god.

> Chor.: You have done a dreadful thing. How could you bring yourself to put out the light of your eyes? What superhuman power urged you on?
>
> Oed.: It was Apollo who brought to fulfillment all my suffering. But the hand that plucked my eyes was mine, and mine alone.

In the next play, *Oedipus at Colonnus*, the hero defends himself against the charge of patricide saying, "I with my father came to blows and slew him Nor knowing what I did, nor unto whom. How couldst thou rightly blame that unconscious sin?" Oedipus's act of self-mutilation, like Socrates' dispassionate act of refusing to escape his prison and accepting his punishment by drinking hemlock, are outstanding examples of free will and disprove the myth of predestination in various forms—astrology, the Pythagorean myth of the transmigration of souls, as well as the pseudoscientific theories of the New Behaviorism. The ancient challenges to predestination and to modern determinism are echoed in Dostoyevsky's insightful observation, quoted by B. F. Skinner, "that even if it could be proved that human behavior is fully determined, a man would still do something out of sheer perversity—he would create destruction and chaos just to prove his point. And if still these could in turn be prevented from occurring then a man would deliberately go mad to prove his point." Skinner, however, responds negatively to that passage and defends behaviorism by saying "We cannot prove, of course, that human behavior as a whole is fully determined but the proposition becomes more plausible as facts accumulate."[21] For the ancient materialists as well as for our contemporary scientific determinists, all events, including human actions, are the effects of antecedent causes; accordingly, human actions are no more free than the motions of the tides. Schopenhauer restates in his *On the Freedom of the Will* the old contention that "a man can surely do what he wills to do, but he cannot determine what he will do."

The philosophical problem of free will is, in part, the unintended result of Plato's faculty of psychology where the Will is assumed to be a faculty along with reason and passion in the human soul. There is a good example of the working of the faculty of psychology in *Julius Caesar* when Caesar first speaks of his own will as the final cause in declining to visit the Senate and provides a reason for that decision; and still another reason for his later decision to attend that assembly.

> Cae.: .... bear my greetings to the senators
> And tell them I will not come today.
> Dec.: Most mighty Caesar, let me know some cause.
> Cae.: The cause is my will. I will not come.
> That's enough to satisfy the Senate.
> But for your private satisfaction
> I will let you know—my wife stays me at home.
> Dec.: The Senate hath concluded
> To give this day a crown to mighty Caesar.
> . . .
> Cae.: How foolish do your fears seem now, Calphurnia?
> I am ashamed I did yield to them.
> Give me my robe, for I will go. (JC, II:2)

Although Caesar speaks of his will as an efficient cause, he also provides a reason for his decision by appeal to a final cause in Aristotelian manner or in a new way of speaking he provides a forward-looking rather than a backward-looking cause for his decision. He gives in effect a reason as final cause just as Socrates did when he declined to escape from his prison.

In our time, philosophers and the cognitive psychologists all dismiss faculty of psychology as folklore-psychology, which was the core of the free will problem. In the new conceptual frame, human action is not just a body reaction or a habitual behavior that can be explained by one-way causal change like any natural phenomena, but is seen as a rational and purposeful motion. New vocabulary such as "the forward-looking behavior," "the intentional negative action," "the pure-chance" or "random event" have replaced the old concept of free will, the "wheel of fortune" and providential design. Such conceptual tools may sharpen our understanding of the speeches and the actions in Shakespeare's plays wherein the causal change, the intentional and positive and negative actions, and in particular the random event all play their allotted roles in the course of human life.

The playwright let some Machiavellian characters like Cassius, Iago, Lysimachus, and Edmund defend man's intentional actions and moral responsibility while they were attacking beliefs in astrology, fortune's buffets and rewards, and miraculous events, as comforting falsehoods. Many times we hear right words and lofty moral concepts coming from a villainous, distorted mouth and twisted tongue. Cassius is all for man's autonomy and for the Republic; Jack Cade, a treacherous rebel, reminds his followers of "Your ancient freedom"; a sly, scheming Polonius teaches honesty to his children; and Hotspur, the bloodthirsty warrior, mocks his cousin for being born with supernatural power. On the opposite side, those characters who resort to the hand of Fortune in shaping human affairs are mostly heroes on the verge of defeat though not at the beginning or the middle scene but at the ending such as Hamlet, Macbeth, Lear, and Coriolanus. In *Julius Caesar,* Brutus and Caesar themselves on some occasions think and act like the stoic Cicero, a Roman sage, who speaks to one of the conspirators who was frightened and seeks Cicero's opinion, saying, "Let not men say 'these are the reasons, they are natural,' for I believe they are portentive things." Cicero replies, "Indeed, it is a strange-disposed time: But men may construe things after their fashion,/ Clear from the purpose of the things themselves" (JC, I:2).

The old Stoic follows Socrates' lifestyle and some aspects of Plato's psychology while inventing his own metaphors for the place of man in the universe. A man is a microcosmic part of the macrocosm and his body, like every physical object, is subject to natural laws. However, the Stoics, like the Epicurean determinists, believed that there is a certain power within the human soul that enables us to experience limited freedom as in forbearing those things that are not in our power. Such mental discipline is a means for attaining ataraxia (contentment), that for the Stoic is the ultimate good. The Stoic Epictetus prescribed his medicine for gaining mental health. "Seek not that thing which happens as you wish but wish the things which happen to be as they are and you will have a tranquil flow of life." The voice of that stoical moral precept is heard in the conversation between Cassius and Brutus:

> Cas.: Of your philosophy you make no use
>   If you give place to accidental evils.
> Bru.: No man bears sorrow better. Portia is dead.
> Cas.: Men at some time are masters of their fates.
>   The fault, dear Brutus, is not in the stars,
>   But in ourselves, ... (JC, I:2)

Hamlet in his famous soliloquy "To be or not to be" faces the dilemma posed by fortune and free will:

> Whether 'tis nobler in the mind to suffer
> The slings and arrows of outrageous fortune,
> Or to take arms against a sea of troubles,
> And by opposing end them. (HAM, III:1)

The stoical concept of forbearance of the inevitable is the first option that Hamlet considers at the outset and then rejects when he makes his decision to fight against a "sea of troubles." He remains, for a long time, however, in an agonizing dilemma before he finally conceives of the "mouse trap" to allay any doubts about Claudius's guilt. It is interesting to note that Hamlet's first option is taken by Edgard, in *King Lear* when he responds to his father's ill thought, when he delivers his lofty stoical maxim: Men most endure,

> Their going hence, even in their coming hither
> Rightness is all. (LR, V:2)

The stoical prescriptions were often offered by friends of suffering souls to help them regain their mental health. In *Romeo and Juliet,* Friar Lawrence offers to Romeo "adversary's sweet milk philosophy," but Romeo responds, "Hang up philosophy! Unless philosophy make a Juliet" (ROM, III:3). In *King John*, Lady Constance, after the loss of her son, wishes for "some philosophy" that would help her endure her grief.

> I am not mad: I would to heaven I were!
> For then 'tis like I should forget myself:
> For being not mad but sensible of grief,
> My visible part produces reason
> How I may deliver'd of these woes,
> O!, if I could, what grief I should forget.
> Preach some philosophy to make me mad. (JN, III:4)

In Brutus's profound reflection about his plan of action we discern the presence of the Socratic contention that human action is not merely a body motion. Similarly we find the Stoic metaphor of the state of man as a little kingdom or microcosm. The metaphor of the missing link between thought and action or in Sartrean language "a Hole in the Being" has been already spoken of in Brutus's brilliant response to Cassius's instigation for murdering his father image.

> Since Cassius first did whet me against Caesar
> I have not slept;
> Between the acting of a dreadful thing
> And the first motion, all the interim is
> Like a phantasma, or hideous dream:
> The genius and the mortal instruments
> Are then in council; and the state of man,
> Like to a little kingdom, suffers then
> The nature of an insurrection. (JC, II:6)

Mark Antony, in Brutus's vein, speaks poetically of a woman's mind on the verge of decision.

> Her tongue will not obey her heart, nor can
> Her heart obey her tongue; the swan's down-feather
> That stands upon the swell as full of tide
> And neither way inclines. (ANT, III:2)

Cassius's remark on man having mastery over his fate "at some times" is expressed by the actor-king in Hamlet's "mousetrap" when he says, "Our thoughts are ours, their ends none of our own" (HAM, III:2). Since thought precedes action and the outcome of action, "their end," is often unpredictable, so is our destiny. The same idea is expressed by the ailing King John saying, "Ay, marry, now my soul hath elbow room" (JN, V:7).

On a deeper level it is Hamlet's conversation with Horatio in the last scene of the play that reminds us again of Cassius's stoical stance about the human power of choice between the limits determined by chance and external impediments. Addressing Horatio, the prince, who has now made up his mind to fight for his life, says,

> Sir, in my heart there was a kind of fighting
> That would not let me sleep
> . . .
> Our indiscretion sometime serves us well
> When our deep plots do pall; and that shall teach us
> There's a divinity that shapes our ends rough-hew them
>   how we will. (HAM, V:2)

In his speech Hamlet uses the word "divinity" as a metaphor for "fortune" or "chance," what we call "random events" without any theological connotation. In the same scene, in response to Horatio's suggestion "If your mind dislike anything, obey it," the prince responds, "Not a whit, we defy augury, there's a special providence in the fall of the sparrow. If it be now, 'tis not to come; if it be not to come, it will be now; if it be not now, yet it will come: the readiness is all. Since no man has aught of what he leaves, what is't to leave betimes? Let be" (HAM, V:2).

The metaphor of the sparrow's fall speaks of the inevitability of death. The sparrow falls at a certain time when gravity and old age do their job. Hamlet defies augury and divination while he speaks of a special providence. He sounds like a Stoic who believes that man should endure what he cannot cure. In Hamlet's last words "the rest is silence," there is a message that he, like the Roman Stoics, welcomes death rather than the prospect of life beyond.

In *King Lear* old musty ideas about fatalism, astrology, and destiny as the wheel of fortune are expressed by the defeated courtiers, namely, the Earl of Kent and the Earl of Gloucester, and are referred to by the king himself. These ideas are brilliantly argued by treacherous Edmund, the bastard son of Gloucester, who mocks such ideas while Edgar, his legitimate son, refers to the stoical remedy as a panacea against the slings and arrows of outrageous fortune. Early in the play, Gloucester, not believing Edmund's words that Edgar is plotting against him, blames the heavenly bodies for all earthly disasters and filial ingratitude. Gloucester says, "These late eclipses in the sun and moon portend no good to us: though the wisdom of nature can reason it thus and thus, yet, nature finds itself scourged by the sequent effects: Love cools . . . in cities, mutinies . . . in palaces, treason; and the bond cracked between son and father" (LR, I:2). He is resorting to astrology in order to explain the total breakdown of loyalty and family affection. He says in effect that scientific astronomy does not explain these disasters but that astrology does, "Though the wisdom of nature can reason it thus and thus, yet." The blinded Gloucester put the blame on the gods for his misfortune,

> As flies to wanton boys, are we to the gods.
> They kill us for their sport. (LR, IV:1)

Another defeated courtier, the Earl of Kent, blames the stars.

> It is the stars,
> The stars above us, govern our conditions;
> Else one-self mate and make could not beget
> Such different issues. (LR, IV:3)

Edmund, the bastard and treacherous son, and Elgar, the legitimate and loving one, are different issues; so are the loving Cordelia, "A soul in bless," and her sister Regan who regrets not killing Gloucester. "It was great ignorance, Gloucester's eyes being out, to let him live, where he arrives and moves the heart against us" (LR, IV: 4). Filial ingratitude is the conspicuous theme in the play. King Lear addresses the same subject when he speaks in passion: "Filial ingratitude. Is it not as the mouth shall tear this hand for lifting food to it?" The idea of making the supernatural agent the main cause for man's disasters is as old as the biblical story in which Eve blames the Serpent for her fall. "Yahweh God asked the woman 'what is this you have done?' The woman replied, 'The serpent tempted me and I ate.'"[22] In the Homeric mythological tales it is Helen who blames Cypris for running off with a stranger to a strange land, and Agamemnon blames Zeus for his madness. Such supernatural beliefs are mocked with great eloquence by Edmund in his famous soliloquy.

> This is the excellent foppery of the world, that, when we are sick in fortune—often the surfeit of our own behavior—we make guilty of our disasters the sun, the moon, and the stars, as if we were villains by necessity, fools by heavenly compulsion, knaves, thieves and treacherous by spherical predominance, drunkards, liars, and adulterers by an enforced obedience of planetary influence; and all that we are evil in by a divine thrusting on: our admirable evasion of whoremaster man, to lay his goatish disposition to the charge of a star! My father compounded with my mother under the dragon's tail and my nativity as under ursus major; so that it follows that I am rough and lecherous. (LR, I:2)

Edmund goes on mocking also Elgar's astrological beliefs:

> "Do you busy yourself with that? . . .
> How long have you been a secretary astronomical?"

Cultural historian John Hale questions the intention of the playwright here without considering Shakespeare's mockery of astrology through his plays and poems. He writes, "Whether the intention was to put the audience on the side of Edmund in *King Lear* or, more probably, condemn his disbelief, is unclear."[23]

A similar voice is heard in *All's Well that Ends Well* when Helen says,

> Our remedies oft in ourselves do lie
> Which we ascribe to heaven: the fated sky
> Gives us free scope; only doth backward pull
> Our slow designs when we ourselves are dull. (AWW, II:1)

And in *The Winter's Tale*, Camillo protests,

> Swear his thought over
> By each particular star in heaven and
> By all their influences, you may as well
> Forbid the sea for to obeying the moon. (WT, I:2)

Dante in *Purgatory* echoes Socrates' philosophical argument for free will. His defense of free will and his rejection of astrological explanations for human actions repeat the argument of Socrates in the *Apology* regarding his vision of human destiny.

> The world indeed has been stripped utterly
>   of every virtue;

> ...
> Some place the cause in heaven, some, below;
> but I beseech you to define the cause
> ...
> You living ones continue to assign
> to heaven every cause, as if it were
> the necessary source of every motion.
> If this were so, then your free will would be
> destroyed and there would be no equity
> in joy for doing good, and in grief for evil
> ...
> Misrule, you see, has caused the world to be
> malevolent, the cause is clearly not
> celestial forces—they do not corrupt.[24]

King Lear argues against predestination and astrology and for moral responsibility in this life although not in the hereafter as is the main theme of Dante's *Divine Comedy*.[25]

The ethical idea of good and evil that is attached only to actions of a person and not to heredity or to title or social standing is a favorite theme of Shakespeare. In *All's Well that Ends Well,* it is pointedly the king who defends that idea while Bertram, the courtier, was unwilling to marry a virtuous maid because she lacked the courtly title.

> Good alone
> Is good without a name; vileness is so:
> The property by what it is should go
> Not by the title. She is young, wise, fair;
> In these to nature she's immediate heir
> And these breed honour:

. . .
honours thrive,
When rather from our acts we them derive
Than our foregoers: (AWW, II:3)

Along with astrology the Pythagorean speculation about the transmigration of the soul became a laughing stock in various scenes. Pythagoras (ca. 570–500 BCE), philosopher-mathematician credited as having been the first to use the term "philosophy," believed in the transmigration of souls and preached certain rituals for the purification of the soul; he prohibited meat eating as a form of practicing cannibalism. There is a satirical story about Pythagoras having called upon a man to stop beating a dog because he recognized in the yelps the voice of a departed friend. In *As You Like It*, Rosalind says, "I was never so be-rimed since Pythagoras' time, that I was an Irish rat which I can hardly remember" (AYL, III:2). In *Twelfth Night* there is a clear reference to that story.

> Clo.: What is the opinion of Pythagoras concerning wild foul?
> Mal.: That the soul of our grandam might haply inhabit a bird.
> Clo.: What thinkest thou of his opinion?
> Mal.: I think nobly of the soul, and no way approve his opinion.
> Clo.: Fare thee well. Remain thou still in darkness . . . I . . . fear to kill a woodcock lest thou dispossess the soul of thy grandam. (TN, IV:2).

All through the plays, astrology, witchcraft, and miracles, which were the popular folklore of the medieval and Renaissance periods, are satirized. (Queen Elizabeth was present at the trial of witches and King James wrote a book on demonology.) In *Henry IV*, part 1, Glendower claimed that he was in love with a supernatural power that he called "Spirit," and the devil like a prophet and that he is not an ordinary man because at his birth certain miraculous events happened. Hotspur, his cousin, ridicules his argument, which for him is a simple case of an old fallacy, *Post hoc ergo proptee hoc* (after this, because of this). He then tries to provide a naturalistic explanation for disastrous events like earthquakes and volcanic eruptions.

> Glen.: At my nativity the front of heaven was full of
> fiery shapes, . . . and at my birth
> The frame and huge foundation of earth
> Sha'k like a coward.
>
> Hot.: Why, so it would have done at the same season,
> if your mother's cat had but kittened,
> though yourself had never been born.
>
> . . .
>
> Glen.: The heavens were all on fire, the earth did remble.
>
> Hot.: O! Then the earth shook to see the heavens on fire,
> And not in fear of your nativity.
> Diseased nature oftentimes breaks forth
> In strange eruptions; oft the teeming earth
> Is with a kind of colic pinch'd and vexed
> By imprisoning of unruly wind
> Within her womb; which, for enlargement striving
> Shakes the old bedlam earth and topples down
> Steeples and moss grown towers.
>
> . . .
>
> Glen.: I am not in the role of common men,

>   . . .
>   I can call a spirit from the vasty deep.
> Hot.:   Why, so can I, or can any man;
>   But will they come when you do call them?
> Glen.: Why I can teach thee cousin to command The devil.
> Hot.:   And I can teach thee, coz, to shame the devil
>   By telling truth; tell truth and shame the devil.
>
>   (1H2, III:1)

ON DEATH AND INTIMATIONS OF IMMORTALITY

> "For in that sleep of death
> What dreams may come When we have shuffled off this mortal coil."
>
>   —Hamlet (III:1)

Socrates in the *Apology* addresses the assembly of judges by saying that he has no fear of death, rather he welcomes its prospect when he delivers his elegant argument that, on close reading resembles Hamlet's soliloquy, "To be or not to be" in its form—the excluded middle and its subject matter—life and death, and in the imagery of death as a dreamless sleep.

We shall first listen to the voice of Socrates in the Athenian court that was recorded by Plato, then to Hamlet's meditation by pointing to a certain resemblance and some distinct differences between the speakers of that historical figure and the fictional prince. I quote a portion of Socrates' argument in the *Apology*.

Either death is a state of nothingness and utter unconsciousness or, as men say, there is a change and migration of the soul from this world to another. Now if you suppose that there is no consciousness, and a sleep like him who is untroubled even by dreams, that will be an unspeakable gain. For if a person were to select the night in which his sleep was undisturbed even by dreams, and were to compare with the other days and nights of his life, and then were to tell us how many days and nights he had passed in the course of his life better and more pleasant than this one, I think that any man, even the great king, will find many such days or nights, when compared with others. Now if this be of such a nature, I say that to die is a gain, for eternity is then only a single night. But if death is the journey to another place, what good, oh, my friends and judges, can be greater than this? . . . He is detained from the pleasure of justice in this world and from the true judges. But what would not a man give if he might converse with Orpheus, Homer, and Perseus?[26]

I quote *in extensio* Hamlet's profound soliloquy for its philosophical ideas and its historical allusions to the ancient literature.

> To be, or not to be: that is the question:
> Whether 'tis nobler in the mind to suffer
> The slings and arrows of outrageous fortune,
> Or to take arms against a sea of troubles,
> And by opposing end them? To die: to sleep:
> No more; and by a sleep to say we end
> The heartache and the thousand natural shocks
> That flesh is heir to, 'tis a consummation

> Devoutly to be wish'd. To die, to sleep:
> To sleep: perchance to dream: ay, there's the rub;
> For in that sleep of death who knows what dreams may
>   come
> When we have shuffled off this mortal coil,
> Must give us pause: there's the respect
> That makes calamity of so long life;
> For who would bear the scorns and whips of time,
> The oppressor's wrong, the proud man's contumely,
> The pangs of despised love, the law's delay,
> The insolence of office, and the spurns
> That patient of the unworthy takes,
> When he himself might take his quietus make
> With a bare bodkin? Who would fardels bear,
> To grunt and sweat under a weary life,
> But that the dread of something after life,
> The undiscover'd country from whose bourne
> No traveler returns, puzzles the will
> and makes us rather bear the ills we have
> Than fly to others that we know not of?
> Thus conscience doth make cowards of us all;
> And thus the native hue of resolution
> Is sicklied o'er with the pale cast of thought,
> And enterprises of great pitch and moment
> With this regard their currents turn awry,
> And lose the name of action. (HAM, III:1)

We have noted that Socrates, on being presented by the court the choice between choosing life by paying a monetary penalty or suffering the ultimate penalty by drinking the hemlock, chooses to die which for him on any account is a blessing in disguise, since for him death is a release of his soul to heaven or a dreamless sleep. Hamlet in like manner considers the very same option either to live or to die though not by a court's order but by the verdict of his own conscience, with his own hand, using a "bare bodkin." Early in his speech he, too, like Socrates thinks of death as a blessing. "Devoutly to be wished," but in contrast to Socrates' image of death as either a window into immortality or a dreamless sleep, Hamlet speaks of "a sleep of death" and then of the possibility of dreams, "perchance to dream," and still of "the dread of something after death."

Of all Hamlet's eleven soliloquies, "to be or not to be" is the most thought-provoking artistic creation where Hamlet pronounces his philosophical contemplation in Shakespeare's unmatched poetical language. In that pregnant monolog there are three occasions when Hamlet seems to echo the voices of Socrates in the *Apology*, Aristotle's metaphor in *Nicomachean Ethics*, and Virgil's simile in the *Aeneid*, as well as the words of Montaigne in his *Essays*, wherein there is an allusion to Socrates' image of dreamless sleep.[27] Among the many comments about this soliloquy by literary critics and even by philosophers I quote a page from a book on the philosophy of science by a logical empiricist Hans Reichenbach for its perspicuous logical analysis of this soliloquy.[28]

> To be or not to be—that is not the question but a tautology. I am not interested in empty statements. I want to know the truth of a synthetic sentence; I want to know whether I shall be. Which means whether I shall have the courage to avenge my father. I have good evidence. The ghost was very convincing in his argument. But he is only a ghost. Does he exist? I could not very well ask him. Maybe I dreamt him. But there is other evidence. The man had a motive to kill my father. My father had always been a healthy man. It is a good piece of inductive evidence. But that is it; nothing but indirect evidence. Am I allowed to

believe what is only probable? The logician tells me that probability has no meaning for an individual case. How then could I act in this case? That is what happens when you ask a logician. The native hue of resolution is sicklied over with the pale cast of thought. Is the logician so bad? He tells me that if something is probable I am allowed to make a posit and act as though it was true. In doing so I shall rewrite in the greater number of cases. But shall I rewrite in *this* case? No answer. The logicians say you act, you will be right in the greater number of cases. I see a way out. I shall make the evidence more conclusive. It is really a good idea (that I shall put on). It will be a *Crucial Experiment*. If they murdered him they will be unable to hide their emotions. That is a good psychologist. If the test is positive I shall know the whole story for certain. See what I mean? There are more things in heaven and earth than are dreamed of in your philosophy, my dear logician.

The reference to making the evidence more conclusive, i.e., "the mousetrap" is to the crucial experiment that was devised by Hamlet. The test was indeed positive, although not perfect, as Hamlet proudly claimed. Saying to Horatio, "would not that still get me a fellowship?" Horatio: "have a share." To which Hamlet says, "a whole one." The "mouse trap" idea brings to mind Francis Bacon's *Esperimentum Crucible*.

In the play there are some allusions to the ghost resident for a certain time in Purgatory when the ghost proclaims:

I am thy father's spirit
Doom'd for a certain term to walk the night,
And for the day confined to fast in fire
Till the foul crimes done in my days of nature
Are burned and purged away. (HAM, I:5)

Stephen Greenblatt, in his book *Hamlet in Purgatory*, writes about the Church of England's rejection in 1562 of the idea of Purgatory on the grounds that there is no warrant for it in Scripture. Hamlet's farewell to the Ghost, "Rest, rest perturbed spirit," and his reference to St. Patrick, the patron of Purgatory, "Yes, by St. Patrick it is an honest ghost," all in all points to Hamlet's awareness of that concept despite the absence of the word "Purgatory" in the folio except on a single occasion where Romeo complains, "There is no world without Verona/But Purgatory, torture, hell itself" (ROM, III:3).

Greenblatt writes about Hamlet's forgetfulness, "His father's ghost has told him quite explicitly how his audit stands but once again, Hamlet has forgotten, as he earlier forgot, that a traveler has in fact returned from the bourne of the dead, undiscovered country." It seems however, that Greenblatt, following other commentators, has forgotten the temporal sequence in Hamlet's speeches. Hamlet speaks "of the undiscovered country" in act three, scene one, that is prior to the subsequent events such as the performance of the "mouse trap" and on hearing his uncle's voice praying for his sins, "Oh! My offense is rank" in act three, scene two. It is only after the occurrence that Hamlet suspends his earlier doubt and believes in the ghost and his charges, saying, "I'll take the ghost's word fire a thousand pound" (HAM, III:2).[29]

Hamlet's overall perspective on death and on the prospect of a hereafter is naturalistic and secular, without a hint on how to prolong life by appealing to religion wherein death is denied. What is missing in Hamlet's last reflection on life and death is the Christian belief in an afterlife and eternity and the denial of the idea of immortality, which is eloquently spoken of by Shakespeare's contemporary John Donne, King James's chaplain and the Dean of St. Paul's cathedral.

According to a recent Shakespeare biographer, Peter Ackroyd, "There is no reason why he [Shakespeare] should not have heard or read Donne's poetry in manuscript. . . . Donne had been a member of Lincoln's Inn and had also served with the Earl of Essex, he can be said to have moved in the same London circles as Shakespeare himself. There was also the milieu in which Donne's poems were circulating in manuscript, and there seems to be echoes of his work both in *King Lear* and in *The Two Noble Kinsmen*."[30]

In the series of poems called "Divine Poems" the following poem appears,

> Death be not proud, though some have called thee
> Mighty and dreadful, for thou are not so,
> For those whom thou think'st thou dost overthrow
> Die not poor death, not yet canst thou kill me.
> . . .
> Thou art slave to fate, chance, king and desperate men
> . . .
> One short sleep passed, we wait eternally
> And death shall be no more, death, shall die.[31]

Shakespeare in Sonnet 146 makes use of the very same metaphor of dying death. The body will die, but the soul will conquer death.

> Poor soul, the center of my sinful earth
> [Thrall to] these rebel powers that thee array,
> Why dost thou pine within and suffer dearth,
> Painting thy outward walls so costly gay?
> Why so large a coat, having so short a lease,
>
> Dost thou upon thy fading mansion spend?
> Shall worms, inheritors of this excess,

> Eat up they charge? Is this thy body's end?
> Then, soul, live thou upon thy servant's loss,
> And let that pine to aggravate thy store;
> Buy terms divine in selling hours of dross;
> Within be fed, without be rich no more:
> So shalt thou feed on Death, that feeds on men,
> And Death once dead, there's no more dying then.
>
> (SON 146)

Shakespeare in this powerful sonnet makes use of the same idea of dying-death and thus the survival of the soul that appears in Donne's poem. The body, "my sinful earth" shall die, but "the pour soul," the center of the body should outlive its servant, by the speaker of the sonnet's command: "Thou, soul, live thou upon thy servant's loss," which follows with another command, "Buy terms divine in the selling hours of dross." While Donne firmly declares his belief in immortality, "one short sleep past, we wake eternally" there is only an intimation of immortality in this sonnet. The speaker of the sonnet wishes that the soul on selling his body should purchase divine salvation. The idea of bargaining between the dying body and the soul may allude to the practice of paying priests in order that the prayers may shorten their stay in Purgatory.

The fantasy in this sonnet, with its similarities to Donne's contention about immortality and his denial of death, runs against the focal point in other sonnets and in some plays that, in the main, the intimation of immortality, if any, is in the belief that the poet's sonnets and plays will be everlasting as exemplified in Sonnet 81:

> Your name from hence immortal life shall have,
> Though I, once gone, to all the world must die
>
> . . .

> You still shall live—such virtue hath my pen
> Where breath most breathes, even in the mouths of men.

and in Sonnets 55, 56, and 107 and in the hope of the survival of the race by procreation in Sonnet 1 that resembles Diotima's idea in her conversation with Socrates, as we have already noted.

On the same subject, Shakespeare scholar Helen Vendler writes, "The speaker of Shakespeare's sonnets scorns the consolations of Christianity and afterlife in heaven for himself and a Christian resurrection of his body after death."[32]

Let us look more closely at Hamlet's encounter with the Ghost, his philosophical comment about miraculous events, and his method of testing the veracity of the Ghost's claim, which is an ingenious device. From a modern scientific perspective any hypothesis, be it empirical, mathematical, historical, or religious, should be testable (either verifiable or falsifiable), that is, it should have a possible truth-value, or at least probability value where truth or probability is regarded as a property of a statement. However, no hypothesis, even those well confirmed, is regarded as an eternal verity but true only upon further notice, and no theoretical canvas is considered to cover every event, since surprises may force theory to tear it all up and consider a new one. Such methodological approaches may be taken toward any hypothesis, as simple as the Ghost's claim in *Hamlet*, the witches' prophetic messages in *Macbeth,* or the acclaimed miraculous recovery of a born-blind in *Henry IV,* part two. The Ghost once more appeals to Hamlet while he is speaking to his mother but not seen by her.

> Ghost: Do not forget: this visitation
> Is but to whet thy almost blunted purpose.

Hamlet then talks to the Ghost but the queen thinks he is hallucinating.

> Que.: This is the very coinage of your brain:
>   This bodiless creation ecstasy is very cunning in.
> Ham.: It is not madness
>   That I have utter'd, bring me to the test,
>   And I the matter will re-word, which madness-
>   Would gambol from. (HAM, III:4)

He says then,

> I am essentially not in madness, but in craft.

Hamlet is not only not mad, as he himself says, and Polonius concurs: "There is a method in his madness"; on the contrary, he is a paragon of reasonableness. His initial open-mindedness, welcoming the strange event, his subsequent skepticism that is finally removed by sufficient evidence, his method of testing the hypothesis, and his readiness to be tested by his mother resemble the Baconian method of inquiry in the search for truth; all point to his intelligent mind. Had Bacon himself undergone the same ordeal he would have believed the Ghost as Coleridge already said about a would-be reaction of David Hume, the famous skeptic. "Hume himself could not but have faith in *this* ghost dramatically, let his anti-Gnosticism be as strong as Samson against ghosts less powerfully raised."[33]

> What a wounded name. Things standing thus unknown
>   shall leave behind me!
> Absent thee from felicity a while,

> And in this harsh world draw thy last breath in pain
>> to tell my story.

Hamlet dies with equanimity like the Roman stoics, Brutus, Mark Antony, and Caesar. He is pleased with himself, "Cheering himself up," (Eliot) with no trace of Christian humility or hope for redemption. His conception of the human body as the quintessence of dust and his images of "Imperial Caesar died, and turn'd to clay" is contrary to the scholastic belief that there is no such thing as a dead body; there are only the remains of a living one.[34]

Thus the foremost question, "To be or not to be," is finally answered in the last scene when Hamlet utters his ominous words, "Let it be" which paradoxically means "not to be." "But let it be. Horatio, I am dead."

In the play *Measure for Measure,* there is an exchange of ideas between the duke, who speaks of death as an Epicurean materialist, and Claudio, who expresses Hamlet's dark perspective of death in the first scene, and of Achilles' preference for "the most loathed worldly-like to that hellish existence beyond" as mentioned in Plato's *Republic*.

> Clau.: Death is a fearful thing.
> Isab.: And shameful life a hateful
> Clau.: Ay, but to die and go we know not where;
>> To lie in cold obstruction and to rot;
>> This sensible warm motion to become
>> A kneaded clod; and the delighted spirit
>> To bathe in fiery floods, or to reside
>> In thrilling region of thick-ribbed ice;
>> 'tis too horrible!
>
>> . . .

> The weariest and most loathed worldly life
> That age, ache, penury and imprisonment
> Can lie on nature is a paradise
> To what we fear of death. (MM, III:1)

When Claudio, condemned to die, expresses his fear of death, the duke responds

> Merely thou art death's fool;
> . . .
> For thou dost fear the soft and tender fork
> Of a poor worm Thy best of rest is sleep,
> And that thou oft provok'st; yet grossly fear'st
> Thy death, which is no more. Thou art not thyself;
> For thou exist'st on many a thousand grains
> That issue out of dust. (MM, III:1)

He goes on speaking of the universal fear of death,

> What's yet in this
> That bears the name of life? Yet in this
> Lie hid more thousand deaths: yet death we fear. (MM, III:1)

The duke's conception of death is an echo of the Epicurean maxim, "When we are, death is not yet, and when death comes, then we are not."

The Roman philosopher poet Lucretius, a disciple of Epicurus, argues that Materialism may free humankind from the irrational fear of death and the dread of Hell as if philosophy is a kind of therapy for restoring mental health. That philosophical reflection has been restated in our time by Wittgenstein and his followers. Wittgenstein in his early work, the *Tractatus Logico-Philosophicus*, writes, "Death being an annihilation is not an event of life. Death is not lived through. As in death, the world does not change but ceases." Claudio's images of death as if the corpse goes through experiencing those dreadful events and resembles Epicurean Lucretius's picture of death in *The Folly of Fear and Death* in the mind of a simpleton who is projecting sentiments of his live body onto his corpse.

> He pictures his state, dividing not himself
> Therefrom
> Removing not the self enough
> From the body fleeing away, imagining
> Himself that body, and projecting there
> His own sense, as if he stands beside it, hence
> He grieves that he is mortal born, not marked
> That in true death
> There is no second self
> Alive and able to sorrow for self destroyed
> Or stand lamenting that the first lies there mangled or burning.[35]

It is the fear of death that gives birth to myth, religion, and mystical ideas, and, according to Schopenhauer, "Philosophy. " If there were no fear of death, says the philosopher, there would have been no philosophy. He should have said the same about religion as was said by Lucretius.

In the Folio there are certain skeptical remarks about the survival after death, about ghosts and the supernatural. Horatio at one point calls the Ghost "illusion." Macbeth early in the play claims that he has no fear of what may happen to him in the afterlife.

> But here, upon this bank and shoal of time
> We'd jump the life to come.
> But in these cases we shall have judgement here.
>
> (MAC, I:7)

Lady Macbeth mocks her husband's fear of death:

> O, Proper stuff!
> This is the very painting of your fear,
> . . .
> A woman's story at a winter's fire
> Authoriz'd by her grandam. Shame itself. (MAC, III:4)

Macbeth himself at that stage is incapable of distinguishing reality from illusion.

> And nothing is but what is not.

Yet after his encounter with Banquo's ghost he tries to subdue his fear by resorting to a naturalistic explanation of death.

> The time has been,
> That when the brains were out, the man would die
> And there's an end, but now they rise again. (MAC, III:4)

In contrast to Macbeth's skepticism about the afterlife, Shakespeare presents also the Christian perspective in *Henry VIII* when Katherine, a good Christian queen, sees a heavenly vision on her death bed. Here is her exchange with her usher, Griffith:

Kath.: Spirits of peace where art Ye? . . .
Griff.: Madam. We are here.
Kath.: It is not you I called for:
Saw ye none enter since I slept?
Griff.: None, Madam.
Kath.: No! Saw you not, even now, a blessed troop
Invite me to a banquet, whose bright faces
Cast thousand beams upon, me like the sun?
They promised me eternal happiness.
Griff.: I am most joyful, Madam, such good dreams
Possess your fancy. (H8, IV:2)

We shall end this section by observing that there are specific clues that reveal Shakespeare's knowledge of Dante's *Inferno*. In *Richard III*, the Duke of Clarence speaks of his nightmare in which he saw horrible wrecks of men and war and treasure destroyed and himself being ferried into Hell. His vision recalls Dante's *Inferno*, canto three, where the poet writes of Charon who ferries souls to Hades, "the kingdom of perpetual night." The Duke of Clarence, who was imprisoned in the Tower by order of Richard III and was soon murdered by the kings' hired murderers, recounts with fear and trembling his terrifying long dream.

O, I have pass'd a miserable night
So full of ugly sights, of ghostly dreams,
That, as I am a Christian faithful man,
I would not spend another such night,
. . .
my dream was lengthen'd after life;
O, then began the tempest to my soul,
I pass'd, methought, the *melancholy flood*

> With that grim ferryman which *poets* write of
> Upon the kingdom of *perpetual night*. (R3, I:4)

In Canto three Dante writes,

> When we have stopped along the melancholy shore . . .
> All these matters will be plain to you
> . . .
> Now silence fell upon the wooly cheeks
> of Charon, pilot of livid marsh
> Whose eyes were ringed about with wheels of flames.[36]

Dante's "melancholy shore" becomes Shakespeare's "melancholy flood" and his "Charon, pilot of livid marsh" becomes our poet's "grim ferryman."

Notwithstanding occasional religious statements by some players, there is an absence of religion in Shakespeare in contrast to Dante and Chaucer, as has been noted by Santayana.[37] More significantly, there is a total absence of the dramatic presentation of conflict between faith and reason that is eloquently expressed by Søren Kierkegaard, a Danish Protestant preacher and philosopher, a lover of Shakespeare who complained of the Bard's negligence in presenting on the stage the agonizing drama of the choice between faith and reason. Kierkegaard was upset with Abraham's absolute faith in God, in his adamant refusal to raise a Hamlet-like doubt, "that the spirits I have seen may be the devil," that he never even questioned that it was God that commanded him to commit murder by killing his innocent son. Kierkegaard is not concerned with the allegorical aspect of the story and its happy ending when God replaced a lamb for Isaac. He is focused on Abraham's fear and trembling. "He knew, had faith by virtue of the absurd, for human calculation was out of question, a paradox that makes murder into a holy act—because faith begins precisely when thought stops."[38]

We hear a lover's complaint when in his "Eulogy of Shakespeare" he says, "Thanks to you, great Shakespeare, you who can say everything, everything, everything just as it is *and yet why did you never articulate this* [Abraham's] torment?" A strange comment, as if he expected that the poet-playwright, one who tells us all about Hamlet's torturous search for truth, shared the intense emotions invested in Abraham's passion for faith. The biblical Abraham and the fictional Hamlet are two contrasting paragons, and so are the Renaissance poet and thinker and Kierkegaard, a new Augustinian philosopher mystic for whom the truth of religion has nothing to do with the question of rational proof and ethical maxims.

Immanuel Kant's judgment about Abraham's actions reminds us of Hamlet's skeptical remark that the spirit may be the devil. Kant observes that "Abraham ought to have replied to the pretendedly divine voice that I must kill my innocent son is quite certain, but that you who appears to me as God, of that I can never become certain. How can man know that it is God who speaks? In some cases one can be sure that it is not God whose voice a man may believe to hear."[39]

Chapter Four

ARISTOTLE
POETRY AND HISTORY

THE UNIVERSAL AND THE PARTICULAR

> "The poet's function
> is to describe
> not the thing that has happened,
> but the *kind* of thing that might happen."
> —Aristotle (*Poetics*)

> "Will you see the players well
> bestowed . . . for they are
> the abstract and brief chronicles of the times."
> —Hamlet (II:2)

The presence of philosophical ideas in the speeches of the players and the speaker of the sonnets reflect certain Aristotelian philosophical points and their counterpoints that were the intellectual background of the late Renaissance; even though they were gradually losing their voices in the Elizabethan Age due partly to the return to Plato and to Platonism in Italy, but mostly because of the new discoveries in science and technology. The anti-Aristotelian stance of philosophers, poets, and the essayists, like

Bacon, Dryden, and Erasmus against making the philosopher an idol is a clear indication of the power and authority that Aristotle's ideas had on the intellectual life of Europeans, not only on subjects such as cosmology, physics, logic, and ethics but also on the dramatic arts that were adopted by playwrights without serious objections.

Long before Shakespeare's time, during the reign of Henry VIII and after, England had been gradually Italianized as the Italian Renaissance changed the cultural life of that country. The Parliament had ended the political, cultural, and Catholic authority in England, where Aristotle's philosophy had been regarded as the essential curriculum in the schools and universities. Given such cultural surroundings it is not surprising that certain ideas of "the Philosopher" in the *Poetics* and the *Nicomachean Ethics* appear in the Folio and in the sonnets, some with a kind of mitigated skepticism such as Hamlet's retort to Horatio's "philosophy" or Polonius's antimetaphysical expostulation or in Tranoi's mocking comment about "Aristotle's checks." However, there are also positive remarks about Aristotle's ideas, in particular about the crucial distinction between a particular historical or fictional figure, in contrast to the tragic heroes and comic players who on the stage are embodiments of universals.

The most notable similarity between the philosopher and the poet is in their concern with the concrete specificity of objects and events, of tokens and types, or of the individual, even though one is the lover of knowledge who writes in the clear and cold style of a logician and the other writes as a maker "Vates" who speaks the Ovidian language. Aristotle's concern with particulars is in contrast to Plato's sedulous search for universals. When the ethical idea of the good life is an issue, Plato in the *Republic* speaks of the supernatural Form of the Good, which is the highest object of knowledge and thus beyond the reach of all but the philosopher-kings, whereas Aristotle enumerates many kinds of virtues that are achievable by action. He offers, for example, descriptions of various kinds of courage rather than an exclusive definition of courage in the manner of the Euclidean definition of "triangle." Aristotle's famous statement that poetry is more philosophical than history and his psychological comments regarding the habits of conduct and the idea of the great-souled man, about thinking and imagination and the place of metaphor in poetry, on the psychology of the spectator, and on virtues are poetically displayed within Shakespeare's plays and poems.

Plato, as we have shown, would have banished from his Utopia the theater that was the crown jewel of Greek civilization, strictly censored poetry and dramatic art, and did in fact denounce oratory as a technique that pandered to the crowd's emotions. It was Aristotle, his most renowned fellow of the Academy and his severest critic, who wrote the *Poetics*, the first and the best work of literary criticism. In contrast to Socrates' and Plato's dismissal of poetry as a Siren Song, Aristotle exalts poets and playwrights as conveyors of universal truth in the medium of art: "The poet's function is to describe not the thing that has happened but a kind of thing that *might* happen." The distinction between historian and poet is not in the one writing in prose and the other in verse. You might put the works of Herodotus into verse and they will still be a species of history. Hence, poetry is something more philosophic and of graver import than history since its statements are of the nature of universals, which is the aim of poetry, whereas those of history are singular. "By universal statement I mean one as to what such a kind of man will probably or necessarily say or do . . . though it applies proper names to those acts or character."[1]

In Aristotle's view the origin of poetry has two causes, "Imitation is natural to man from childhood, one of his advantages over the lower animals being this that he learns at first by imitation; also it is natural for one to delight in the works of *imitatio*; although the objects themselves may be painful to see, we delight to view the most realistic representations of them in art. To be learning something is the greatest of pleasures, not only to the philosopher but also to the rest of mankind."[2] Then comes his answer to Plato's criticism of poets and playwrights. "If the poet's description be criticized as not true to fact one my urge perhaps that the object ought to be described—an answer like that of Sophocles who said that he drew men as they ought to be while Euripides drew them as they were. If the description, however, is neither true nor of things as they ought to be, the answer must be then, that it is in accordance with opinion. The tales about gods, for instance, may be as wrong as Xenophanes thinks, but they are certainly in accordance with opinion."[3] Aristotle in this passage refers to Xenophanes' famous mockery of anthropomorphism—that man makes gods in his own image. "The Ethiopians . . . black and snub-nosed, Thracian as blue-eyed and red-hair. . . . If oxen and horses and lions had hands or could draw . . . horses would draw their god's shape like horses and the lions like lions . . ." (fragment from Xenophanes).

The Aristotelian distinction between the particular and the universal and its applications to the historical persona, and the actor as the universal figure, reappears in modern semantics without its metaphysical baggage. Gottlob Frege in his famous essay "On Sense and Reference" retained the old Stoics' logical distinction between Signs and Sense and Reference or Denotation. In his logical investigations he considers as an afterthought the language of dramatic art and the role of the actors in their speeches. He writes, "On hearing an epic poem, for instance, apart from the euphony of the language we are interested only in the sense of the sentences and the images and the feeling thereby, aroused." The question of truth would cause him to abandon aesthetic delight for attitudes of scientific investigation, hence, it is a matter of no concern to us whether the name Odysseus, for instance, has reference as long as we accept the poem as a work of art. It is striving for truth that drives art always to advance from the sense to the reference. In the footnote he writes, "it would be desirable to have a special term for signs making only sense. If we name them, say, representations, the word of the actor on the stage would be a representation, indeed, the actor himself would be a representation."[4] We may make use of Frege's idea about actors and their speeches as "representations" in Shakespeare's plays. Hamlet, for example, considers the players on the stage as "representations." He in his conversation with Polonius about players makes a significant philosophical remark, for they are the abstract and brief chronicles of the time (HAM, II:2). Hamlet's view of players, "they are" alludes to the universal features of the players, namely, their words and their actions, and not to their personal aspects.

There is another interpretation of this passage wherein the word "abstract" appears. Jonathan Bate provides a historical account for the occurrence of that word. "According to contemporary dictionaries, an abstract was 'a little book or volume gathered out of a greater' ... an abridged epitome, summary. In the age of long sermons, interminable homilies, and closely printed treatises on ethics and politics the players provided a crash course in the way of the world, an instant summary ... of manners and light."[5] Bates's historical reference, however, is about "a little book" that was used by a player but not about the abstract role that a player, of many other players, may act upon. The words "they are" surely denote the roles that are designed for the players. As we have noted, Cassius speaking about the play *Julius Caesar* that it would be played in many ages in many states, and Brutus in similar words saying, "How many times Caesar would bleed in sport," surely point to the universal aspect of the plays.

In Francis Bacon's *On the Advancement of Learning* there is an important remark on the issue of abstract knowledge that was noted by scholar Ann Barton, "It is the duty and virtue of all knowledge to abridge the infinity of individual experiments as the conception of truth will permit, and remedy the complaint of *'vita bravis, ars lunga'* [life is short, art endures]." Barton's insightful passage ends with the caveat, "He [Bacon] was not thinking of poetry or dramatic art but the statement has always seemed to me peculiarly applicable to that special brand of knowledge which imaginative literature can provide."[6] Bacon in fact was thinking about the abstract features of natural law; however, in Barton's words, that saying also speaks of the abstract features of the players who are "abstract and brief chronicles of the time." Actors' words and acts on the stage are as abstract as concepts in pure mathematics and hence should not be confused with their references just as numbers are not to be identified with the numerals and their denominated objects. One may affix any sign or any proper name to the actor, as Aristotle observed, unless the connotation of the name conveys information about its bearer, such as the puns, "Justice Shadow" or "Mistress Overdone." Names in the plays behave like common nouns rather proper names: Richard II, Richard III, Falstaff, Hamlet, Macbeth, Lear, Rosalyn, Cleopatra, Desdemona, and Ophelia, to mention some, are each particular characters; they are at the same time universal paradigms like the Standard Meter or pure geometrical forms. Although various players may perform the same roles, none of them should be identified with either the fictional or historical character in the plays.

Such meticulous interest in the categories is an indication of Shakespeare's Aristotelian perspective. It is as if the poet knows Aristotle's "Categories." The primary substance is the first item in the list of the categories. The substance, he writes, in the truest and the most definite sense of the word is the individual thing... "the this," such as a man, Socrates, the horse, Bucophlus.[7] That is, things that are definable by what is called, in semantics, the ostensive definition rather than "the such" as the genus animal and the species man. The secondary substances, the universals, are the stuff of natural philosophy, pure mathematics, and of the abstract figures in the dramatic arts. To put it in the new vocabulary, we may take a species, man, as a class, whose members are each individual, a primary substance, and the genus animal is the class of all classes of animals. Now consider the issue of universals as common names, when Macbeth, the regicide and unabashed murderer hires a murderer who says about himself and his comrades that "We are men, my liege." Macbeth mocks them for claiming to be human. He points out that, "the valued file" conveys a true description of its particular figure that is enclosed in the universal. There is a semantic regularity or correct sense of the word "man" as there is "dog" that designates the particular property or the essence of each species, unlike proper names that are just arbitrary designations. According to Macbeth:

> Ay, in the catalogue, you go for men,
> As hounds, and grey hounds, mongerers, espaniels, curs,
> Shaughs, water-rugs, and demi-wolves are clept
> All by the name of dog: The valu'd file
> Distinguishes the swift, the slow, the subtle,
> The housekeeper, the hunter, every one according to the
>   gift which this bounteous nature Hath in him clos'd,
>   whereby he does receive
> Particular addition, from the bills
> That write them all alike: and so of men (MAC, III:1)

Shakespeare's text is an ocean of the minute particulars that are denominated within their specific catalogue. The particulars are the real stuff of this universal discourse. There are as many kinds of men and women with their unique characters as different as Hamlet from Falstaff, and Cleopatra from Ophelia. Polonius enumerates eight kinds of plays from tragedy and comedy to comedy-historical. Touchstone, in response to Jacque's question: "Can you nominate in order now the degree of the lie?" He lists seven kinds of lies from "the lie direct" to "the retort courteous," and Macbeth, as we have mentioned, counts eight kinds of dogs. In the Folio and the Poems, there are the names of one 108 variety of plants, many kinds of birds, insects, the names of many cities, and the names of instances of time: seconds, minutes, hours, weeks, months, years, and ages. Aristotle's remark about the token representation of historical events in dramatic art is alluded to in *Henry V* when the chorus sings, before the beginning of act I.

> O! For a muse of fire, that would ascend
> The brightest heaven of invention;
> A kingdom for a stage, princes to act
> And monarchs to behold the swelling scene. (Prologue)

At the beginning of act V the chorus reminds the audience that the play is of necessity a microscopic picture of history.

> Vouchsafe to those that have not read the story,
> That I may prompt them: and of such as have,
> I humbly pray them to admit the excuse
> Of time, of numbers, and due course of things,
> Which cannot in their huge and proper life
> Be here presented.

Some historical plays such as *Henry VI* are more closely related to actual historical events than others, and yet there are great artistic inventions. Compare the plays with the historical sources, for example, the richness of *Richard III*, where historical events are presented along with those exuberant philosophical speeches, with the cold poverty of the history of the kind in *Holingshed's Chronicles* (1577) or the play *Julius Caesar* with Plutarch's account of Julius Caesar's life.

Finally, let us consider Aristotle's theory of tragedy and its relation to Shakespeare's tragedies. "A tragedy, then, is the imitation of an action that is serious, and also as having magnitude, complete in itself, in language with the pleasurable occasions in accessories, in dramatic, not in narrative form, with incidents arousing pity and fear wherewith to accomplish the catharsis of such emotions. . . . We have laid it down that a tragedy is an imitation of an action that is complete in itself, as a whole of some magnitude. Now a whole is that which has beginning, middle, and end."[8] The "Praxis" denotes action done for achieving an end and tragedy is concerned with the actions of demigods, great men and women, and noble heroes having certain flaws of character that cause their fall. Comedy, on the other hand, is about ordinary people, the traveling sophists, soldiers, beggars, and whores. The character in tragedy, in Aristotles's view, should be better than the average man and those of comedy should be worse.

Aristotle's description of tragedy is a philosophical redescription of Greek tragedies that was familiar to the philosopher when they were performed on the stage and appear in the manuscripts. In later ages that description became the standard model for tragedy with the emphasis on the unities of time and the continuity of place and even of the consistency of character. Some aspects of Aristotle's theory, in particular the idea of imitation, of mirroring nature, and the effect of tragedy on the audience are presented in Shakespeare's tragedies, evident in Hamlet's instructions to the players, although not the idea of space-time-character that was unsuitable for the vast stage and discontinuity of time and complexity of human behavior. On Aristotle's model, tragedy and comedy are worlds apart. Shakespeare did not accept that worn-out model. In many of his tragedies, comic fools and jesters, drunken porters, and singing grave diggers appear within the tragic scene, and many of his comedies have their unhappy maidens and melancholy youths. His tragic heroes are not humorless, dark, rigid figures of the old plays but are quick-witted, self-conscious, many-sided persona. "Hamlet and Lear" says Yeats, "are gay. Gaiety transfigures all the dread." The Shakespeare scholar Jonathan Bate in his charming essay overstates the issue when he writes, "we might even say that all Shakespeare's plays are tragico comedies and that is one of the principal reasons why his drama is, as Dr. Johnston also recognized, 'the mirror of life' and why it remains so brilliantly alive on page, stage, and screen some four centuries after his death."[9]

THE PRESENCE OF ARISTOTLE'S ETHICS

Aristotle's idea that cultivation of moral and intellectual virtues is the means to happiness, the principle of the Golden Means, the psychology of habit and conduct, and the idea of the ideal Great-Souled Man are all displayed in the Sonnets. There are six notable direct and indirect references to Aristotle although the name of the philosopher is mentioned in only a few places. Aristotle begins his *Nicomachean Ethics* with the commonly accepted belief that good is happiness and virtues are only means to that ultimate goal.[10] He then considers what he calls moral virtues, which are achieved by learning good habits and the intellectual virtues that pertain to the rational part of the soul and are the virtues of the Great-Souled Man—the magnanimous—the shades of Plato's philosopher-kings.

The guardians of moral virtues are the legislators who make young citizens moral by teaching them to acquire good habits which in turn make their actions pleasurable even while performing difficult tasks. In *Hamlet* the prince, in his speech to his mother, makes use of Aristotle's idea that acquiring good habits, such as rejecting the sexual demands of her husband, makes her virtuous even by pretending virtue and may restrain her own sexual temptation.

> Good night; but go not to mine uncle's bed;
> Assume a virtue, if you have it not:
> That monster, custom, who all sense doth eat,
> Of habit's devil, is an angel yet, in this,
> That to the use of actions fair and good
> He likewise gives a frock or livery
> That aptly is put on.
>   Refrain tonight
> And that shall lend a kind of easiness
> To the next abstinence; the next more easy;
> For use almost can change the stamp of nature,
> And master e'en devil or throw him out
> With wondrous potency. (HAM, III:4)

In the churchyard scene it is Horatio who, in his response to Hamlet's outrage in hearing a clown singing while digging a grave, explains his behavior by the same theory of habit.

> Ham.: Has this fellow no feeling of his business while he sings at grave-making!
> Hor.: Custom hath made it in him a property of easiness.

In both cases, acquiring a habit (that monster, customs) such as the sexual desire of Gertrude and the natural repulsion of playing with human remains that was suppressed in the clown. Hamlet, while clasping York's skull, shows that revulsion when he says, "my gorge rises at it," and yet he recalls the fond memory of the king's jester. "Here hung those lips that I have kissed I know not how oft."

In another play, *Coriolanus*, the hero of the same name speaks of the irresistible force of custom and tradition,

> Custom calls me to it,
> What custom wills, in all things should we do,
> The dust of on antique time.

However, he is torn between obeying the customary advice of the citizens who are defending the military tradition or the voice of his mother,

> I never be such a goosling to obey instinct, but
> Stand as if a man were author of himself and
> No other kin. (COR, V:3)

He at first proudly claims proclaims that he, unlike gooslings, is not the slave of his instinct—that biological instinct, innate disposition, toward their mother and his children (as if he knew the biological data on gooslings' instinct that were recently researched by Konrad Lorenz). That biological instinct at the end overcomes the forces of social custom and ends his life. Despite seeing the danger in disobeying his army and risking his own life he follows his mother's advice.

> O my mother, mother! O!
> You have won a happy victory to Rome;
> But, for your son, believe it! O! believe it,
> Most dangerously you have with him prevail'd (COR, V:3)

On the other side, his mother's maternal instinct gave way to her political decision that led to her son's death. Custom and habit are often at war with instinct, and habits are pictured in a dark frame, "that monster, custom" (Hamlet) "this slave-like habit" (Apemantus), the repeated metaphor "the plague of custom" in spite of its occasional benefit, as noted by Aristotle, appears in many plays.

An outstanding example of the plague of custom appears in *King Lear* with Edmund's reaction to his bastardly birth and to his brother's legitimacy.

> Thou, Nature, art my goddess; to thy law
> My services are bound. Wherefore should I
> Stand in the plague of custom, and permit
> The curiosity of nations to deprive me,
> For that I am some twelve or fourteen moonshines
> Lag of a brother? Why bastard? wherefore base?
> When my dimensions are as well compact,
> My mind as generous, and my shape as true,
> As honest madam's issue? Why brand they us
> With base? With baseness? bastardly? base, base?
> Who, in the lusty stealth of nature, take
> More composition and fierce quality
> Than doth, within a dull, stale, tired bed,
> Go to the creating of a whole tribe of fops,
> Got 'tween asleep and wake? Well, then,
> Egitimate Edgar, I must have your land (LR, I:2)

Against the plague of custom stands the human and animal love for their offspring such as wrens defending their offspring to the death against owls. Lady Macduff on hearing of her husband's flight observes,

> He loves us not.
> He wants the natural touch;
> The poor wren
> (That most diminutive of birds) will fight,
> Her young ones in her nest, against the owl (MAC, IV:2)

However, instinct in humans is not the sole cause of action when there are other overriding values, as Ross points out to Lady Macduff in defending Macduff's flight to save his life.

Consider another idea of Aristotle, namely, the standard of balancing the extremes of too much against too little: for example, excessive fearfulness in the face of danger is cowardice while the unreflective response to danger is rashness: the Golden Mean between cowardice and rashness would be courage. The so-called Golden Mean expresses the ancient Grecian maxim, "Nothing in excess." That, Aristotle says, is to be applied only to moral virtues, not to intellectual excellence. Aristotle's idea also appears in in *The Taming of the Shrew* when Tranio refers to "Aristotle's checks" even though he shows his preference for an Epicurean lifestyle rather than that of the Stoics.

> Glad that you continue your resolve
> To suck the sweets of sweet philosophy
> This virtue and this moral discipline,
> Let's be no Stoic, I pray
> Or so devote to Aristotle's checks. (SHR, I:1)

Tranio continues his moral discourse by referring to Aristotle's logic in the *Rhetoric* and to the philosopher's idea of pleasurable intellectual pursuits. "Balk logic with acquaintance that you have and practice rhetoric in your common talk. . . . No profit grows where no pleasure takes." In the same play another player, Lincentio, speaks of Aristotle's conception of happiness without mentioning the philosopher's name.

> And therefore, Tranio, for the time I study
> Virtue and that part of philosophy will I apply that
>   treats of happiness
> By virtue especially to be achieved. (SHR, I:1)

Aristotle's standard appears again when Hamlet wonders whether "To take arms against a sea of troubles and by opposing end them."

An example of Aristotelian criticism of rashness is his comment regarding the behavior of the Celtic warriors when, fighting a losing war, they drew their swords to attack waves rather than show fear by flight. The Celts in attacking the waves were displacing their rage like herring gulls that when under attack pull grass. Aristotle states that "A man is not brave if knowing the magnitude of danger he faces [he acts] through passion, as Celts up their arms to meet the waves." Rashness is an automatic and a fast response to a problematic situation. Courage is a delayed action which is a result of knowing what to fear and what not to fear. In *Macbeth*, Ross expresses that idea.

> But cruel are the times when we are traitors
> And do not know ourselves, when
> We hold rumor
> From what we fear, yet know not what we fear
> But float upon a wild and violent sea
> Each way and move. (MAC, IV:2)

In this passage there is a reminiscence of "take arms against a sea of troubles" in Hamlet's soliloquy when Ross, after repeating Aristotle's definition of courage "to know what to fear and what not to fear" speaks like Hamlet, "but to float upon a wild and violent sea each way and move."

There is yet another reference to Aristotle in the play *Troilus and Cressida* when Hector, soldier-philosopher, rebukes Paris and Troilus, saying, "Not much unlike young men who Aristotle thought unfit to hear moral philosophy."[11] The old criticism against Shakespeare's ignorance, about the chronology when he let Hector mention Aristotle, is off the mark since it is based on the unwarranted assumption that the poet must follow the chronology of events or the exact description of geographical locations, or the true characterization of the historical figure (for example, that Richard III was not a hunchback).

In *As You Like It*, Touchstone (a clown) makes reference to Socrates' admission of ignorance and then to Aristotle's idea of the purposive function of the eye and the lips in the presence of food. Touchstone, joking, points to Aristotle's practical syllogism, for example, a deduction from the premises: "Dry fruit is good to eat," and "There is a dry fruit," to the conclusion "One eats dry fruit." Touchstone says, "I do now remember a saying, 'The fool thinks he is wise, but the wise man knows himself to be a fool.' The heathen philosopher, when he has a desire to eat grapes, would open his lips when he put them into his mouth, meaning, thereby, that the grapes were meant to eat and the lips to open" (AYL,V:1).

Finally, in addition to all these references to Aristotle in the plays there is yet another significant allusion to the philosopher's idea of the ideal man, and to the Stoics' moral prescription.

> They that have power to hate and will do not
> That do not do things they must do show

> Who, moving of others, are themselves as stone
> Unmoved, cold, and to temptation slow,
> They rightly do inherit heaven's graces
> And husband nature's riches from expense,
> They are the lords and owners of their faces
> Others but stewards of their excellence. (SON 94)

The sonnet doubtlessly alludes to Aristotle's god, the Unmoved Mover, who moves the world as the "First Cause." He is not the creator of the world *ex nihilio* but he is like the magnet that not only causes the motion of iron rings but also endows them with its power. As Plato mentions in the dialogue *Ion*, the speaker of the sonnet anticipates Aristotle's Great-Souled persons who are proud, rational, self-controlled, and are able to impose their magnetic power on others who are but the "stewards of their excellence."

That moral stance is contrary to the experience of Christian humility since those who inherit heaven are the Great-Souled persons, not the meek or poor in spirit. The Sermon on the Mount declares, "Blessed are the meek for they shall inherit the earth." Commenting on Sonnet 94, Stephen Booth points out that, "the plural graces have only secular meaning."[12] However, he does not seem to see Aristotle's stance on this sonnet. In his view "this love . . . inappropriately echoes the Scripture." In this sonnet the allusion to Scripture as we have pointed out is contrary to the Christian moral stance. In Sonnet 121 the speaker goes further in mocking the Trinity, as one critic (G. G. Lone) writes: "[It] is decidedly blasphemous—it parodies the Trinity." According to another critic (Irvin Leigh), "in saying 'I am that I am' Shakespeare adapts God's name (Ex.3) as though he were God himself."

> For why should others' false adulterate eyes
> Give salutation to my sportive blood?
> . . .
> No, I am that I am; and they that level
> At my abuses reckon up their own.

Such interpretations are suggestive of Santayana's judgment in his essay "The Absence of Religion in Shakespeare," where he writes, "the only kind of religion we get in Shakespeare is that of an occasional Oath."[13]

The same idea about "the blessed magnanimous" is echoed in Hamlet's unbounded admiration for his "blest" school fellow, Horatio.

> For thou hath been
> As one, in suffering all that suffers nothing,
> A man that fortune buffets and rewards
> Hath ta'en with equal thanks; and blest are those
> Whose blood and judgement are so well commingled
> That they are not a pipe for fortune's finger.
>
>   Give me that man
> That is not passion's slave and I will wear him
> In my heart's core,
> Aye, in my heart of hearts
> As I do thee. (HAM, III:2)

Hamlet's search for the man who is not passion's slave is Aristotle's idea of the magnanimous men who are the masters of their passions; where the rational parts of their souls dominate through the agency of the will over the lower parts. In Hamlet's estimate, Horatio is near kin to Aristotle's ideal man, yet Hamlet himself is a paragon of reasonableness.

Aristotle's magnanimous man, however excellent in thought and action, is still a rational animal, not an omnipotent god. Aristotle in observing that no one, not even a god, can undo what has been done, is pointing to future deliberations. He writes, "For no one deliberates about the past, but about what is future and capable of being otherwise, hence Agathon is right in saying, 'for this almost is lacking even to god to make undone things have since be done.'" In *Macbeth* there is an echo of Aristotle when Lady Macbeth pleads, "Come, come, come, come, give me your hand. What is done cannot be undone." Macbeth murdered his guest, Duncan, knowing that what he is doing is an outrageous crime; even though his queen saw his deed cannot be undone, he did not learn from the past when he continued to murder others.

Against the Socratic contention that all wrongdoing is due to ignorance, Aristotle argues that one may choose to do evil deeds in the full knowledge that what he is doing is wrong. Shakespeare seems to be aware of that Socratic contention when he lets Polonius "that wretched, rash, intruding fool" say to his son, "'Tis above all to thine own self be true, and it must follow as the night the day, thou canst not then be false to any man."

In *The Merchant of Venice,* it is Portia who questions the Socratic equation of knowledge and virtues—that whoever is endowed with knowledge becomes *ipso facto* a benevolent godlike human—when she responds to Nerissa's comment,

> Ner.: It is no mean happiness therefore . . . to be seated in the mean: superfluity comes sooner by white hairs, but competency lives longer.
> Por.: Good sentences and well-pronounced.
> Ner.: They would be better if well-followed.
> Por.: If to do were as easy as to know what were good

> to do, chapels had been churches, and poor men's cottages princes' palaces. It is a good divine that follows his own instructions. . . . The brain may devise laws for the blood, but a hot temper leaps o'er a cold decree. . . . O, the word "choose"! I may neither choose whom I would nor refuse whom I dislike. . . .

Portia then goes on rejecting various candidates to be her mate, among them, "The Count Palatine. I fear he would be the weeping philosopher when he grows old" (MV, I:2).

Portia echoes Aristotelian moral philosophy when she speaks about the gulf between action and reason, and about passion and reason, and "good divine[s]" who, unlike others, are able to follow the dictates of their own reason. Her idea of her limited options in choosing her mate, and her reference to the "weeping philosopher" (the epithet given to Heraclitus by his enemies) recalls Aristotle's moral philosophy.

Chapter Five

ON THINKING AND SPEAKING

> "What's in the brain, that ink may character,
> Which hath not figur'd to thee my true spirit?
> What's new to speak, what new to register,
> That may express my love, or thy dear merit?"
> —SON 108

The discovery of certain intimate links between the cognitive act of thinking and the speech act of talking to others or silently to ourselves is ages old. Plato has spoken of the identity of thought and verbal speech while allowing for unuttered conversation of the soul with itself. "Are not thought and speech the same, with this exception, that what is called thought is the unuttered (silent) conversation of the soul with itself."[1]

Shakespeare speaks of the togetherness of thought and ideas in the brain and the items of language, words, phrases, and verses that, "ink may character," or tongue may utter. The word "character" as used refers to Hamlet's manner of forming the letters as in, "'Tis Hamlet's character" and in speaking about the letter of Aptigous that "they knowest his character." The use of the word "brain" here also needs explanation. Shakespeare often speaks of the brain as the organ that produces mental phenomena, rather than the indestructible ghostly substance of the idealist philosophers and poets. For

Shakespeare, mind is more like a moving stage where players act for a time and then are seen no more, rather than the unknowable substance lurking behind the scenes. His idea of mind anticipates that of David Hume who famously argues that when he introspects to find his mind he only stumbles on some ideas and impressions. When, in Sonnet 30, the speaker evokes his silent thought: "When to the sessions of sweet silent thought / I summon up remembrance of things past," his mind wanders to a variety of friends, events, and places. Concerning silent thought there is yet another reference where in *Troilus and Cressida* Agamemnon speaks of

> That unbodied figure of thought
> That gave't surmise shape. (TRO, I:3)

The relation of thought to language and action is expressed in an ingenious metaphor, "the engine of thought." The word "engine" is derived from Latin as used in "ingenium nature." In a usage now obsolete, it could be associated with a source of power such as mental power or a clever invention, such as a metaphor, or by extension any markedly agreeable manner of speaking. Shakespeare saw it as the power that "drives" speech, the human tongue used for the spoken language and appears in the play *Titus Andronicus*, where Martius speaks of Lavinia whose tongue has been torn from her:

> O! That delightful engine of her thoughts,
> That blabb'd them with such pleasing eloquence,
> Is torn from forth that pretty hollow cage. (TIT, III:1)

In the poem "Venus and Adonis," the metaphor of the engine of thought is used about the words of the feminine goddess Venus. "Once more the engine of her thoughts" began to speak of her sexual drive for Adonis, "Nothing but my body's bane would cure thee" (VEN, 367).

Shakespeare on many occasions speaks of Nature as the mainspring of Nurture in the sense of the birth of contemplation and imagination and of the priority of thoughts over their expression by words. His poetic epistemological insights were reflected in the writing of the later British empiricists such as David Hume who writes of the impression or sense-data as the cause of ideas or thoughts, and of words that convey genuine ideas or sometimes meaningless symbols that signify nothing. In our time these philosophical issues became the subject of scientific inquiry by psycho-linguists about the nonverbal thought of animals and infants, and the poets' wordless images prior to their appearance in their speeches or in the written word. In Sonnet 85 there is an allusion to the priority of the speaker's thoughts to their expression and then the speaker mockingly compares his rival "good words" with his "dumb thoughts."

> I think good thoughts whilst others write good words,
> And, like unletter'd clerk, still cry "Amen"
> To every hymn that able spirit affords,
> In polish'd form of well-refined pen
> Hearing you prais'd, I say, "'Tis so, 'tis true,"
> And to the most of praise add something more;
> But that is in my thought, whose love to you,
> Though words come hindmost, holds his rank before,
> When others for the breath of words respect
> Me for my dumb thoughts, speaking in effect. (SON 85)

Shakespeare, who sees a close link between thought and experience, sees also the privacy over our thoughts, "our thoughts are ours," (HAM, III:2); in *The Tempest*, Stephano, the butler, sings,

"Flout 'em and scout 'em. . . . Thought is free" (TMP, III:2). Thought is free and yet it is bounded within the frame of discourse, namely, the semantic definitions of words and the rules of grammar and logic that distinguishes thought from daydreams and free association of words and images. Caliban, prior to his education by Prospero, was a thoughtless savage, said his master-teacher,

> When thou did'st not know, savage
> Know thine own meaning but would'st gabble like
> A thing most brutish. (TMP, I:3)

In the same play Stefano rebukes his brother's manner of speaking,

> It is a sleepy language, and thou
> Speak'st out of your sleep. (TMP, II:1)

Hamlet speaks intentionally off the mark to Guildenstern who says to him, "Good, my lord, put your discourse into some frame and start not so widely from my affairs" (HAM, III:2). In *Henry VI* Lady Margaret speaks of a courtier that, "He talks at random; sure, the man is mad" (1H6, V:3).

The speaker of the sonnet speaks also of the power of thought: "For nimble thought can jump both sea and land" (SON 44). Thus it seems that the poet in effect is cognizant of the philosophical idea that there is no one-way causation between our thoughts and our words, that thoughts are not a mere mechanical by-product of experience since, besides biological determinism, there are other factors such as cultural input that enable us to choose our words from the multitude of words available. On the power of thought that enables the rational animal to communicate Frege writes that thoughts are directly communicable and thus they are objective since we can share our thoughts and know of Plato's and Shakespeare's meditations. The objectivity of thought of which Frege writes may be contrasted with the subjectivity of private experience. Hamlet, while he speaks of human rationality and nobility, speaks also of the beast hidden in the human heart and of the beast that lacks the discourse of reason. Hamlet speaks of "a beast like oblivion," of a man "whose chief good and the market of his time be to eat and sleep—a beast no more." For Troilus even infants are devoid of thought. "Give as soft attachment to thy senses/ as infant empathy of all thought" (TRO, IV:2).

Caliban without language is the beast in the jungle; even when he learns to speak to Prospero he is still a savage "a devil, a born devil, on whose nature nurture can never speak" (TMP, IV:1). It has been pointed out that this the first occasion in the English language when the word "nature" is opposed to "nurture." This "beast" paradoxically speaks the most exuberant poem in *The Tempest*.

> Be not afeard: the isle is full of noises,
> Sounds and sweet airs, that give delight and hurt not.
> Sometimes a thousand twangling instruments
> Will hum about mine ears, and sometime voices
> That, if I then had waked after long sleep,
> Will make me sleep again: and then, in dreaming
> The clouds methought would open and show riches
> Ready to drop upon me; that, when I waked,
> I cried to dream again. (TMP, III:2)

Shakespeare's references to Montaigne's ideas about cannibals and on the primitive simple lifestyle of the American Indians should not be taken as an endorsement of Montaigne's counter-civilization fantasies and about the beauty and simplicity of noble savages.

Montaigne maintains in comparing man and animals that men have no wonderful faculties that animals lack. In support of his theory he provides examples from Sextus Empiricus about the ability of dogs when in chasing a cat make use of a disjunctive syllogism: either the cat goes this way or the other way (P or Q); since there is no sign of the cat going this way (not P), therefore he has gone that way (Q).[2]

Montaigne who held that religion should be based on faith alone and not on any shaky rational argument, says that even religious faith is not exclusive to humans but seems to exist among elephants that appear to pray. Shakespeare, in contrast to Montaigne's delight in primitivism, expresses his deep love for civilization and for orderly political and social life; nonetheless there are occasions when he lets the old King Henry VI express his longing for a shepherd's simple lifestyle:

> For what is in this world but grief and woe?
> O God! methinks it were a happy life,
> To be no better than a homely swain;
> To sit upon a hill, as I do now,
> . . .
> how sweet! How lovely!
> Gives not the Hawthorne bush a sweeter shade
> To shepherds looking on their silly sheep,
> Than doth a rich embroider'd canopy
> To kings that fear their subjects' treachery? (3H6, II:5)

On the relationship of thought to life, Hotspur, the wounded hero of *Henry IV* part 1, speaks:

> O, Harry! Thou robb'st me of my youth.
> I better brook the loss of brittle life,

>   Than those proud titles that thou won of me.
>   They wound my thoughts worse that thy sword my flesh:
>   But thought's the slave of life, and life time's fool. (1H4, IV:4)

Richard II speaks of his little world, a microcosm, and of the birth of thought in his brain and in his soul.

>   My brain I'll prove the female to my soul,
>   My soul the father; and these two beget
>   A generation of still-breeding thoughts
>   And these same thoughts people this little world,
>   In humours like the people of this world,
>   For no thought is contented. (R2, V:3)

Macbeth, too, speaks of the brain and thought when he orders a doctor to make use of medicine and erase the written thought in his wife's brain: "Raze out the written trouble of the brain" (MAC, V:3).

THE SEMANTIC ASCENT

> "My language! heavens!
> I am the best of them that speak this speech,
> Were I but where 'tis
> spoken."
>
> —Ferdinand (TMP, I:2)

Shakespeare, the master-mistress, of the English language, is a self-conscious critic and a severe judge of the uses and abuses of the spoken word by warlords, demagogues, priests, dishonest lawyers, and lovers; but language can also heal wounds and give comfort. He rises above the spoken words of the players by making a semantic ascent when he turns his sharp eyes upon his own sonnets and plays. When Hamlet gives instruction to the players about their speech-acts or when Cassius and Brutus make predictions about performances of the plays in the future "in states unborn and accents yet unknown" or when the speaker of the sonnets speaks of his art outlasting all gilded monuments, they speak about what they are saying while performing their roles.

Shakespeare's mastery of language is largely acknowledged by his contemporaries and by modern scholars who are still shifting through his worlds of words. By some estimates, he used about 884,647 words including 29,066 different words. He created 3,000 new words from Latin and Greek words. There are 31,459 speeches in the plays. He was acquainted with the Greek, Latin, French, Italian, and Welsh languages. Shakespeare himself knows that he is the best speaker of the language when he lets Ferdinand, the Italian prince, and Troilus, the Greek prince, speak for him.

> Ferd.: My language! Heavens! I am the best of them
> that speak this speech.
> Were I but where 'tis spoken.

And when Troilus speaks of "My love with words" while reading Cressida's letter saying, "Words, words, mere words, no matter from the heart" (TRO, V:3).

We may hear the voice of the poet in Thomas Mowbray's speeches about the English language. Here is a bit of Mowbray's eloquent speech about his language after he was sentenced to exile by King Richard II.

> The language I have learned to speak this forty years
> My native English, now I must forego

> And now my tongue's use is to me no more
> No more than an unstringed viol or a harp
> What is thy sentence than but a speechless *death*
> Which robes my tongue from breathing native breath?
>
> (R3, I:V)

In order to investigate the Shakespearean language and clarify certain misrepresentations of his works by critics we shall make use of semiotics, the general study of linguistic signs and its division into pragmatics, semantics, and syntatics (a la Rudolf Carnap) along with the earlier work of Gottlob Frege in the semantics of sign, sense, and denotation of signs; and the more recent inquiries into the performative use of language in contrast to its descriptive functions (J. L. Austin).

"Pragmatic" refers to the study of language and its relation to the speaker, the author, the audience, and the reader of the text. In this domain the subjects of the study are the social and political background of the author, his beliefs and motifs, and the impact of his message upon the audience and the reader of the text. While such pragmatic information may very well enhance the understanding of the plays, it is not, however, a substitute for the text, since the playwright's background was not intended to be a part of the play but was taken for granted by him that the audience, in particular, the educated "fellows" are aware of the historical and social surroundings of his plays. In "the language-game" of dramatic art, to use Ludwig Wittgenstein's metaphor, it is assumed that the audience does understand not only the "brute facts" of birth, copulation, and death, but also "the institutional facts" of baptism, marriage, funerals, and the courtly ceremonial language of coronations, abdications, and entitlements in rank and position. Given a poet's background, it is also necessary that the audience look at the play as if the actors are expressing their true emotions, as if the ghost, the witches, and all those fantastic scenes are real. The "willful suspension of disbelief" is an indispensable requirement for the aesthetic experience in observing plays. Let us be reminded that Shakespeare is fully aware of the importance of make-believe in listening to his fictions—for example, when a player says "much virtue in 'If'" he is alluding to the hypothetical aspect of plays.

We shall speak of the Semantic Dimension of language when we eliminate the speaker and the hearer of the text and focus on the linguistic symbols, words that denote objects and events, and those descriptive sentences that in a certain sense picture the world albeit various segments of the same world. When the issue of truth or untruth of descriptive sentences arises we shall hold unto the old Aristotelian concept of truth or falsity: "To say of what is that it is not, or of what it is not that it is, is false, whereas to say of what is that it is, or what is not that it is not, is true" (*Metaphysics*). In the semantic dimension of language "the play's the thing," we let the authors alone.

Last, we shall abstract from the semantic domain all references to objects and events and focus on the grammatical and poetic aspects, the rhyme and rhythm, and the logical structure of the argument, which is called the "Syntactics." The syntactic aspects of the Folio does not fall within the scope of this inquiry except for a bare reference to syllogistic logic and the use of tautology by some "unlettered small-knowing souls."

Shakespeare's semantic ascent into language appears when the players speak about signs, tokens, the meanings of words, sense and nonsense, the magic of proper names and their connotations, and on the abuse of rhetoric by political and religious leaders.

Consider the following passages on word, thought, and action. In *Othello*, Brabantio says to the duke,

> But words are words, I never yet did hear
> That the bruised heart was pierced
> Through the ear. (OTH, I:3)

Troilus says to Cressida, "Why you have berefet me of all words, lady." To that, Paudarus comments: "Words pay no debts / Give her deeds" (TRO, III:2). On occasion tears may replace words, so says Henry VIII: "He has strangled his language in his tears" (H8, V:1).

Shakespeare is cognizant of what in modern semantics is called "The Speech Act." J. L. Austin calls the "Speech Act" uttering words such as making a promise or reciting "The Pledge of Allegiance." In such cases, one does not describe the content of the mind, rather one is performing an act. In *Henry VIII* there is a passage where words are used as a compliment. "This is a kind of good deed to say well, and yet words are not deeds." The first phrase shows that the king recognizes that the utterance of certain words such as "well" amount to an act of paying a compliment. The second phrase, however, indicates that not any use of a word amounts to performing an act. Words may be used as swords and on occasion may heal the afflicted heart.

Shakespeare's contemporary, Francis Bacon, a philosopher and a statesman, in his voluminous work has written much against the scholastics' "word-play." The idols of "the market-place" stand for the tyranny of words over the cloudy minds of scholastic philosophers. He considered that words are the counter of the wise, but the money of the fools. He used the metaphor of counter in order to point out that the counter as a piece of paper is valuable merely by convention; otherwise it is worthless paper. For the fool, however, all words including metaphysical expressions such as "Essence," "Substance," "Prime Mover," are gold. We shall consider many variations of these Baconian semantic ideas, which were familiar to the scholars of the late Renaissance and that occur in Shakespeare's plays. For example, when Polonius asks Hamlet, "What do you read, my lord?" Hamlet replies, "Words, words, words."

> Pol.: What is the matter my lord?
> Ham.: Between who? (pretending to misunderstand the question).
> Pol.: I mean the matter that you read, my lord.
> Ham.: Slander, sir. (HAM, II:2)

The word "matter" that is used in this exchange means both the subject matter of the book and also the sense of the word. Shakespeare often makes use of the word "matter" that stands for sense and in a certain context for "denotation," in contrast to its symbolic representation. The distinction that is made between a linguistic symbol and its purported denotation goes back to Aristotle's metaphysical idea about "matter and form," and to the Stoics' theory of sign, sense, and denotation. A barbarian, says the Stoic, may hear a spoken Greek word though not understand its meaning unless he learned the Greek language. In *Hamlet,* the king, while praying on his knees, speaks of his thoughtless words, "words without thought," which is the same as nonsense, or form without matter. So does the Fool in *King Lear* when he complains of priests' empty words, saying, "When priests are more in word than matter."

In *Love's Labours Lost* a player mocks the word-play of the schoolmen when the king reads a letter written by that "unlettered, small-knowng soul—that hollow vessel" (LLL, I:1). By using such words he in effect reversing Aristotle's idea of the "great-knowng soul" much praised by the philosopher. In *Twelfth Night*, Feste, the clown, in the manner of Francis Bacon, slights the use of Aristotelian syllogism as useless argument, which says nothing new in the conclusion that has not already been said in the premise.

If that this simple syllogism will serve, so,
It will not, what remedy? (TN, I:1)

In the same play the clown points out that what the illiterate person says is an empty tautology. "As the old hermit of Prague, that never saw pen and ink very wittily said so a nieve of kings, Gorbeduc, 'that, that is, is that that is; and being master parson am master parson; for, what is 'that' but 'that' and 'is' but 'is'" (TN, IV:1). It is interesting that on the grave of Lucretius there is reference to empty words: "Out, idle words; servant to shallow fools—this helpless smoke of words does me no right." Words are also used for deception like the use of politically dangerous words such as "equivocation," where a Jesuit priest in the trial known as "The Gunpowder Plot" used misleading and ambiguous answers, under oath without lying. A book called *A Treatise of Equivoation* was written by Henry Garnet who was condemned to death for treason. In *Macbeth,* a porter says, "Faith, here is equivocation, that could swear in both the scales against either scale, who committed treason enough for God's sake, yet could not equivocate to heaven. O! Come in equivocator, O!"

Macbeth also speaks of an equivocator in the last scene of the play when he says to a messenger

I pull in resolution and begin
To doubt the equivocation of the fiend
That lies like truth. (MAC, V:3)

Consider the host of critical remarks about the pedantic use of language and the misuse of words and the use of rhetoric for deception. Viola speaks of the misuse of words and sentences in *Twelfth Night*, and Hamlet points to the broken pledge in the marriage ceremony of his mother: "Sweet religion makes a rhapsody of words." And Polonius expresses his loathing for religious hypocrisy:

> 'Tis too much proved
> That with devotion's visage
> Any pious action
> We do sugar'd o'er
> The devil himself. (HAM, III:1)

The most satirical lines against the use of rhetoric appears in *The Merchant of Venice* when Bassanio declares

> The world is still deceived with ornament
> In law, what plea so tainted and corrupt
> But, being reason'd with gracious voice,
> In religion,
> What damned errors but some sober'd brow
> Will bless it and approve it with a text,
> Hiding the grossness with fair ornaments. (MV, III:3)

In *King John,* a player called Bastard speaks of words and sentences. "Zounds! I was never so bethup't with words—Since I called my brother's father dad!" The same semantic point about the "boundless" uses of words is also spoken by Bastard when he mentions words such as "maid" and "commodity" "this old-changing world."

> He that wins of all
> Of kings, of beggars, old men, young men, maids
> Who having no external thing to use
> But the word "maid" cheats the poor maid of that;

> This commodity,
> This baud, this broken, this all-changing world
> Clapped on the outward eye of sickle France (JN, II:1)

The semantic aspect of language looms large in *The Tempest* where Ferdinand boasts of his mastery of language and when Sebastian admonishes Antonio's sloppy manner of speaking.

> It is a sleepy language
> Thou speak'st out of thy sleep. What is it thou dids't say?
> This is a strange repose, to be asleep
> With eyes wide open, standing, speaking, movin
> And yet so fast asleep. (TMP, II:1)

Prospero, like colonial officers who were trying to civilize the Indians, teaches Caliban language, though he regrets that all his efforts did not turn the savage into a civilized person.

> I pitied thee,
> Took pains to make thee speak, taught thee each hour
> One thing or other: when thou dids't not, savage,
> Know thine own meaning, but wouldst gabble like
> A thing most brutish, I endow'd thy purposes
> With words that made them known: But thy vile race
> Though thou didst learn, had that in't which good natures
> Could not abide to be with; therefore wast thou
> Deservedly confined into this rock,
> Who hadst deserved more than a prison. (TMP, I:2)

Thus again the idea that language is an engine of thought and without it man is a beast in a jungle is spoken by the master of language.

Miranda speaks to her father of his power over language: "Your tale, sir, would cure deafness" (TMP, I:2). Shakespeare emphasizes the special uses of language not only when he speaks of the brute facts of nature such as birth, copulation, and death, but also when he speaks of the institutional facts of birth, marriage, funerals, and of acts as diverse as the performative speech act of changing the behavior of lovers, soldiers, parishioners, courtiers, or for flattery such as Hamlet saying to Horatio, "Let candid tongue lick absurd pomp." Or for cursing, when Caliban, in response to Prospero's admonition, says,

> You taught me language; and my profit on't
> Is, I know how to curse. The red plague rid you
> For learning me you language! (TMP, 1:2)

Malcolm, like a psychologist, advises Macduff to make use of words for healing wounds:

> Give sorrow words: the grief that does not speak
> Whispers the o'er fraught heart and bids it break. (MAC, IV:3)

The eloquent oration of King Henry V, which begins,

> Once more into the breach, dear friend, once more.
> Or close the wall up with English dead! (H5, III:1)

Mark Antony's speech:

> O! pardon me thou bleeding piece of earth
> That I am meek and gentle with these butchers! (JC, III:1)

These words used for the purpose of inciting soldiers or citizens to take arms, or revenge against their enemies, are examples of the performative utterances where sword-like words were used by leaders. However, Aristotle observed in the *Poetics*: "the greatest thing by far is to be a master of metaphor. It is the one thing that cannot be learnt from others, and it is also a sign of genius, since a good metaphor implies an intuitive perception of the similarity in the dissimilarities."

Shakespeare is the master-builder of a vast number of new and enlightening metaphors. In Aristotle's opinion this is a sign of genius. The poet is fully conscious of the richness and novelty of his own creations when he speaks of the poverty and dryness of metaphorical expressions that were invented by unlettered pretentious fools. In his comedy *All's Well that Ends Well*, one player, Parolles, says to the Clown:

Paro.: You need not to stop your nose, sir
I speak but by metaphor.
Clo.: Indeed, sir, if your metaphor stinks,
I will stop my nose, or against any man's metaphor.
(AWW, V:3)

In another comedy, *Twelfth Night,* Maria says to Sir Andrew Aguecheek that since "thought is free" she can create her own metaphor. It turns out to be a dull and "dry metaphor."

Mar.: Now, sir, "thought is free": I pray you
bring your hand to the buttery-bar and let it drink.
Sir And.: Wherefore sweetheart? What's your metaphor?
Mar.: It's dry, sir. (TN, I:3)

In discussing metaphor we shall look back to the best literary critic of the ancient world, Aristotle, who meticulously described the nature of metaphor and its cognitive and emotive power in some detail. Aristotle's views are meticulously mirrored in the pages of the Folio and the Poems.

Aristotle in the *Poetics* says, "Metaphor consists in giving the thing a name that belongs to something else," in "transference being either from genus to species or from species to genus" is examplified in, "Here stands my ship," for lying at anchor is "the standing of a particular kind of thing." He says, "There is also another form of qualified metaphor. Having given the thing the alien name, one may by a negative addition deny it one of the attributes naturally associated with its new name. An instance of this would be to call the shield a "cup that holds no wine, the simile is also a metaphor—the difference is but slight."[3] To convey Aristotle's idea in modern terms we may say that metaphor is the transference of meaning of one set of expressions to another, where there is some correspondence between members of the two sets (though not one-to-one of the identical sets) and where meaning covers sense and denotation.

Metaphorical expressions are distinct from the literal meaning of an expression, which conveys semantic regularities that are recorded in dictionaries. We may replace in a poem a metaphorical use of an expression with its ordinary use, and in so doing rob its cognitive, novel, and emotive power, turning it into a dull, recondite expression, in particular where metaphors breed metaphors. Thus, in place of "Macbeth does murder sleep," we may say "Macbeth suffers insomnia." However, doing so, we miss the point that it is Macbeth who has murdered his innocent guest, Duncan, in his sleep, and sleep is described metaphorically by Macbeth: "Methought I heard a voice cry 'sleep no more.'" Macbeth does murder sleep, innocent sleep, "Sleep that knits up the ravell'd sleave of care; the death of each day's life; great nature's second course. Chief nourisher in life's feast" (MAC, II:1). The overwhelming force of these metaphors would be lost by any literal alternative expression.

Shakespeare's metaphors show him to be a discoverer-artist. Wallace Stevens's dictum that "Metaphor creates a new reality from which the original appears to be unreal," speaks in particular of Shakespeare's metaphors in which the poet selects many novel, illuminating, emotionally charged and unscanned similarities between sets of events while inventing a conceptual apparatus to capture those phenomena, which often slip through the sieve of our perceptions.

Such metaphors are antidotes to our habitual ways of perceiving the world. They are artistic discoveries on a par with discoveries in science such as meteorological discoveries that start with Luke Howard's classification of cloud forms under the names, "cumulus," "cirro," and "stratus," hailed by Goethe as "giving form to the indeterminate." Hamlet's perception of a cloud in the shape of a camel, a weasel, or a whale is more poetic than scientific. "The poet's pen," says Theseus, in *A Midsummer Night's Dream*,

> Doth glance from heaven to earth, from earth to heaven;
> And, as imagination bodies forth
> The forms of things unknown, the poet's pen
> Turns them to shapes, and gives to airy nothing
> A local habitation and a name. (MND, IV:2)

The poets' discoveries expressed in metaphors are not just literary devices used for ornamentation; both models and metaphors are indispensable parts of scientific theory. Consider the use of metaphors in science such as "natural selection" in biology, "big bang" the birth of the universe, or the "big crunch" when the universe ultimately will collapse of its own weight, in cosmology. The art historian E. H. Gombrich writes that "Goethe, the great morphologist, haled Howard's effort as a further conquest of the mind 'giving form to the indeterminate.'"[4]

Shakespeare gives us poetic metaphors about cloud shapes. In *Antony and Cleopatra*, Mark Antony observes,

> Sometimes we see a cloud that's dragonish;
> A vapour sometimes like a bear or lion,
> A tower'd citadel, a pendant rock
> A forked mountain, or blue promontory
> With trees upon't, that nod unto the world
> And mock our eyes with air. (JC, IV:12)

The use of metaphor is not limited to poetry and other arts. There are numerous metaphors that are used in the theoretical sciences such as "the arrows of time" or "string theory" in atomic physics. There is, however, a difference between the use of metaphor in the sciences and in poetry. In poetry, the cognitive and emotive aspects of metaphors are commingled; they are taken to be both true and beautiful, whereas their use in the sciences is only as tools for providing information about the world. They are not used to evoke emotion.

From the vast number of Shakespeare's metaphors that shine through the pages of the plays and poems we shall select for discussion certain philosophical metaphors such as those on Time-Eternity, World-Stage, Ladder-Ambition, and put aside others such as the erotic metaphors on deflowering, and on homosexual and heterosexual love—for example, in *A Midsummer Night's Dream*—since they do not fall within the scope of this philosophical inquiry. Moreover, we shall omit some overused metaphors in our language, which, in Harold Bloom's metaphor, is "a cemetery of dead metaphors."[5]

ON METAPHOR

> "A moving image of eternity
> . . . this image we call Time."
> —Plato, *Timaeus*

> "Thou by thy dial's shady stealth mayst know
> Time's thievish progress to eternity."
> —Shakespeare (SON 77)

Natural Time/ Eternity

Aristotle sees the world in ten categories. From the ontological perspective, categories are the catalogues of what there is in the world, and from the epistemological view they are the objects of thought. The basic category, as we mentioned before, is the primary substance—the particular thing; the rest, such as the universal, place, time, action, and the others owe their being to the existence of the primary substance so that there is no such thing as the universal, time, place, number without being an aspect of the primary substance. Aristotle, unlike Plato, does not resort to myth and metaphor in speaking of time. He considers that time, like extension, or weight, is an aspect of a moving entity and not something that exists by itself. He writes that time is the "number of movements in respect to the before and after, and continuous since it is an attribute of what is continuous."[6]

In Shakespeare's plays the categories of Time and Place are the scaffolding for the category of Action, and Actions, the intentional bodily motions and speech-acts, are the main concerns of the players. The players, while acting in the Time-Place framework, often speak philosophically of objective, or natural time; subjective, or personal time; the divisions of time into present, past, and future; and of the union of time and motion. Time is seen in the Aristotelian perspective as a measure of change, and change is the ordeal of life, and life is "time's fool." In the Shakespeare *Concordance* there are about two thousand entries under Time, and many under Time/Species.

There are close resemblances, however, between Plato's and Shakespeare's Time metaphors, where time is seen as a "moving image of eternity" and by Shakespeare as a "ceaseless lackey of eternity," a "progress to eternity," and as "the devouring- time [that] makes us heirs to all eternity." Shakespeare even presents time as the omnipotent God in *A Winter's Tale* and as a king in *Pericles*. "I see that Time's the king of men. He is both their parents and he is their grave and gives them what he will not what they crave" (PER, II:5).

Except for Frederick Turner, commentators have not noticed the philosophical aspect of time in the texts, and even Turner does not recognize its roots in Plato's *Timaeus*. He writes, "Although it is *highly unlikely that Shakespeare had read any of the Greek philosophers,* nonetheless what they had to say about time was inevitably part of the intellectual syntax of his period."[7] To the contrary, I argue that Shakespeare was more than "highly likely" aware of Plato's *Timaeus*, which was translated into Latin by Cicero and was the only one of Plato's dialogues known in the West before Marsilio Ficino's translation of the complete works of Plato into Latin in 1484.

The *Cicero's Timaeus* begins with a summary of the first of the five divisions of the *Republic*; thereafter Timaeus, who was a Pythagorean cosmologist, recounts a myth from an Egyptian source. It has been said that its speculative cosmology about the creation of the universe from Chaos and the place of Time and Eternity in the Cosmos, "the order," had a significant impact upon Scholastic theology. According to the myth, at the beginning all was chaos, which resembles Hesiod's idea in the *Theogony*, "First of all chaos came into being." The Bible describes the creation of the universe from a "formless void," not from "chaos"; the word "chaos" does not appear in *Genesis*. However, the biblical idea of the world created out of nothing is not a Greek view either of Plato or Aristotle. For them, the Divine is an architect or prime mover; Time and Eternity are two different concepts and Time coexists with the Cosmos. Only by annihilation of the cosmos is it the case that "Time must have stop." Plato explains, "When the creator saw the creature which he made moving and living, the created image of the eternal gods, he rejoiced . . . wherefore he resolved to have a *moving image of eternity* . . . he made this image Eternal but moving . . . eternity itself rests in unity for there are no days and nights . . . before heaven was created . . . the past and future are created species of time, which we unconsciously but wrongly transfer to the *eternal* essence, for we say that he 'was,' he 'will be,' but the truth is that 'is' alone is properly attributed to him, and that 'was' and 'will be' are only to be spoken of becoming in time . . . but that which is immovably the same cannot be older or younger by time. . . ."[8] There are other indications of the Bard's familiarity with this book and with the translation of Plato's complete dialogues into Latin by Ficino.

Apart from the Platonic metaphors of Time and Eternity, there are some references to the *First Book of the Republic*. Simonides, who was a lyric and elegiac poet and author of many epigrams, was mentioned in *The First book of the Republic* when Cephalus quotes the poet's idea of justice, or righteousness as "to tell the truth and pay one's debt." Cephalus's casual remark is the first movement that starts the whole dialogue about the nature of justice in the commonwealth. In Shakespeare's play, *Pericles: Prince of Tyre*, there is a dialogue between the prince and three fisherman near the seaside that resembles certain passages in the *Republic*.

> Third Fish: Master, I marvel how the fishes live in the sea.
> First Fish: Why, as men do a-land; the great ones eat up the little ones; I can compare our rich misers to nothing so fitly as to a whale; a' plays and tumbles, driving the poor fry before him, and at last devours them all at a mouthful. Such whales have I heard on o'the land, who never leave gaping til they've swallowed the whole parish, church, steeple, bells, and all.
> Per: [aside] A pretty moral.
> Third fish: But, Master, if I had been the sexton, I would have been that day in the belfry.
> Second Fish: Why, man?
> Third Fish: Because he should have swallowed me too, master. . . . But if the good King Simonides were of my mind,—
> Per: [aside] Simonides!
> Third Fish: He would purge the land of these drones that rob the bee of her honey.
> Per: [aside] How from the finney subject of the sea These fishers tell the infirmities of men.
>
> (PER, II:1)

What the fishermen say is similar to Thrasymachus's theory of justice, which states that justice is nothing but what is the interest of the stronger party. Although the name Cephalus does not appear in this play a variation of the name does appear in the form of "Shafalus" in *A Midsummer Night's Dream.*

> Pyr.: Not Shafalus to Procrus was so true
> Thi.: As Shafalus to Procrus, I to you. (MND,V:1)

In *Troilus and Cressida* and in *The Tempest* there are allusions to Plato's idea of the just state in which Plato describes in detail the structure of his utopia. That state is free from "drones" and all other kinds of parasites. "They exist in a cell, an affliction to the hive." Plato writes. The same expression that was used in the *Republic* appears in the saying of the Third Fisherman, "We would purge the land of these drones, that rob the bee of her honey," as above.

Shakespeare's numerous uses of Time fall between three categories: the Natural or Objective Time, the Subjective, and the Private. Let us now consider the category of Objective Time and the idea of the End of Time. In *Henry IV,* part 1, we hear the voice of the dying Hotspur.

> O, Harry! Thou hast robb'd me of my youth
> I better brook the loss of brittle life
> Than those proud titles thou has won of me;
> They wound my thoughts worse than thy sword my flesh;
> But thought's the slave of life, and life *time's* fool.
> And *time, that takes survey of all the world,*
> *Must have a stop.* O, I could prophesy,
> But that the earthly and cold hand of death
> Lies on my tongue. No, Percy, thou art dust
> And food for—[he dies]
>
> Prince: For worms, brave Percy. Fare thee well, great heart!
> Ill-weaved ambition, . . . how much art thou shrunk!
> When that this body did contain a spirit,
> A kingdom for it was too small a bound
> But now . . . (1H4, V:4)

"Time that takes survey of all the world" is natural or objective time. It is that "thievish Progress to eternity," that "ceaseless lackey to eternity" of *Poems*. It will have a stop only by doomsday, speaking theologically, only upon the death of the entire universe. Time cannot be stopped by his death. So it seems that Hotspur speaks of two kinds of time: one is natural that eventually ends with doomsday and the other "private or personal time" (using Heidegger's metaphor), the time that life is it's fool and thus in this case, the end of his own life. Just before the battle of Shrewsbury Hotspur anticipated the death of all, saying "Doomsday is near, die all, die manly" (1H4, IV:1). Hotspur's view of time— that life is its fool and must have a stop with his death— perfectly fits Heidegger's concept of "Private" or "Personal" time. In *Being and Time*, in contrast to "world time," which is public, being measured by a clock, there is also a "Private-Time." Heidegger writes: "When one is concerned with making an appointment one designates the time publicly by saying 'when the shadow is so many feet long, then we shall meet yonder.' . . . [I]t is tacitly supposed that the 'locations' at which the shadow gets paced off are at the same latitude. This clock is one which Dasein does not have to carry around with it; in a certain manner Dasein itself is the clock."[9]

Heidegger thought that for a human to exist is to be a being whose future is closed off by death: *Sein-Zum-Tode*. As soon as an individual comes up against the finite limits of his own existence, he is obliged to make a time of his own. Heidegger brings together the idea of *Dasein*, "being there" of a human as a conscious being and the idea of death. *Dasein* determines its own character in terms of all possibilities, and death is "the possibility of impossibility of any existence" celebrated by him as an *Ausgezeichnete Moglichkeit* (splendid possibility).

But what of Eternity? We have noticed that time is said to be a moving image of eternity; it moves toward and is a servant of eternity. Thus there is a distinction between what is in constant motion and what is outside the temporal order—the unmoved mover of Aristotle's cosmology. Since the expression "eternity" like "time," or "number" is a nondenotated expression, the poet had to use metaphorical language in order to convey its sense. One sense of "eternity" is the idea of endless time, just like a continual series of prime numbers getting larger all along without ever becoming "the greatest prime." The other sense of it is simply the absence of time such as Leibniz's conception of "the eternal truth" of the laws of logic and mathematical axioms.

Knowing that the category of time, as well as space, does not cover logical and mathematical truths, "when and where" may as well be called "eternal truths," or in Leibniz's metaphor, "true in all possible worlds." It is that sense of "Eternity" that is often displayed in Shakespeare's poems.

Metaphors apart, consider a reason for each invention. Bertrand Russell writes, "Philosophically inclined mystics unable to deny that whatever there is in time is transitory have invented a conception of eternity as not persistence through endless time, but existence outside the whole temporal process." In another passage he writes, "mystical doctrines as to the relation of time to eternity are also reinforced by pure mathematics, for mathematical objects such as numbers if real at all are eternal and not in time."[10]

We have already noted that the poet many times says that whatever is in time is in fact transitory, with the exception of his Platonic vision of Beauty and Love and his own sonnets as if they were as time-independent as those of Leibniz's eternal truths. Yet it is assumed that the poet commits "a conventional literary conceit that while time sweeps everything, his own verses are indestructible" as Russell suggests of him, quoting two lines from Sonnet 60,

And yet to times in hope my verses shall stand,
Praising thy worth despite his cruel hand.

The fanciful views of "to time in hope" is not to be taken as literal truth. The poet himself says in Touchstone's words, "for the truest poetry is the most feigning; and lovers are given to poetry, and what they swear in poetry may be said as lovers they do feign" (AYL, III:2).

The category of objective time (and its species the present-yesterday-tomorrow) is the running theme that vibrates through the whole tragedy of *Macbeth*. It appears in act 1, scene 1 when Banquo addresses the witches saying, "If you can look at the seeds of time and say which grain will grow and which will not/ Speak to me." Soon after, Lady Macbeth, in conversation with her husband, predicts that Duncan shall never see another day.

> Mac.: Duncan comes here to-night
> Lady M.: And when goes hence?
> Mac.: Tomorrow, as he proposes
> Lady M.: O! never
> Shall sun that morrow see!
> . . .
> To beguile the time,
> Look like the time; bear welcome in your eye,
> Your hand, your tongue: look like the innocent flower
> But be the serpent under't. (MAC, I:5)

In the next scene Macbeth looks at the river of time and its banks and decides to jump over it so that he may shorten the course of events and replace the king without waiting for his term. However, he considers the consequence of murdering the king.

> But, here, upon this bank and shoal of time
> We'd jump the life to come. But in these cases
> We still have judgement here. (MAC, I:7)

He is saying in effect that he is not concerned with what may happen in an afterlife but with the judgment of his peers here on earth.

It is time, indeed, that strikes the spark for Macbeth's most philosophical, sophisticated, and terrifying soliloquy.

> Mac.: Wherefore was that cry?
> Sey.: The queen, my lord, is dead.
> Mac.: She should have died hereafter;
> There would have been a time for such a word.
> To-morrow, and to-morrow, and to-morrow
> Creeps in this petty pace from day to day,
> To the last syllable of recorded time;
> And all our yesterdays have lighted fools
> The way to dusty death. Out, out, brief candle!
> Life's but a walking shadow, a poor player
> That struts and frets his hour upon the stage
> And then is heard no more; it is a tale
> Told by an idiot, full of sound and fury,
> Signifying nothing. (MAC, V:5)

Macbeth's relentless obsession with "tomorrow" in this play is in stark opposition to the biblical injunction: "Take therefore no thought for the morrow for the morrow shall take thoughts for the things of itself...."[11] Here it seems that the playwright presents a naturalistic view of time in contrast to that biblical command to ignore the future. Another skeptical remark about the afterlife, in addition to his saying "we'd jump the life to come," appears when

Macbeth shows his disbelief about the ghost of his departed victim. "The time has been that, when the brains were out the man would die. And there's an end, but now they rise again."

In the last scene, Macduff enters with Macbeth's head on his arm.

> Behold where stands the usurper's cursed head;
> The time is free. (MAC, V:7)

"Time with its sprouting seeds, the flowing river, the double-faced august tyrant with his lion's paw" at last is free—cleaned from the bloody acts of men. The image of seeds, the river, the traveler, the out-of-joint gates (Hamlet), suggest a picture of a moving object in space. Since Time, like Eternity falls under the category of pure concepts, the playwright has to use a spatial metaphor in order to speak of "Time."

But what about that "nothing" in the contents of a tale told by an idiot "signifying nothing"! *Nothing* has been as puzzling a concept for philosophers as for literary critics. Consider Heidegger's playing with "nothing" in his essay, *Was ist Metaphysik? (What Is Metaphysics?)*. He writes that "science is concerned with the exploration of the real, and aside from that with nothing." He then immediately asks the question, "How about this nothing?" "Since science has preempted the realm of the real there is nothing left for metaphysics but the exploration of the nothing." Rudolf Carnap comments on Heidegger's elevation of a simple negation sign to something called *Nichthight,* "Nothingness," pointing out that "nothing" is not a name, even if it appears as a name, as in "life signifies nothing."[12] To say that is to say that it is false that life signifies anything, that there is any transcendental value to life, beyond the value we bestow on life.

Northrup Frye comments on Richard II's soliloquy in which the word "nothing" is used in a metaphor.

> Think that I am unking'd by Bolingbroke
> And straight am nothing, but what e'er I be,
> Nay I nor any man that but man is
> With nothing shall be pleas'd, till be eas'd
> With being nothing. (R2, V:5)

"Ever since the beginning of language probably 'nothing' has meant two things, not 'not anything' and 'something called nothing.' Richard is saying here (not very dramatically) that every human being including himself is discontent, not pleased with anything, until he becomes something we call nothing, i.e. in this context, dead."[13] Frye writes again elsewhere, "The word 'nothing' has two meanings; it is a grammatical negative meaning 'not anything' and it is a positive noun meaning 'something called nothing.' In Shakespeare the word nothing, when it means something called nothing, usually refers to the loss of essence, not the end of existence." These comments are good examples of where a metaphor may create hypostasized entities in which the use of mere negation signs are taken as if they stand for something concrete. The use of "meaning" as a positive noun, though grammatically correct, is semantically misleading, for it may force us to fabricate a denotation for it where there is none. As Wittgenstein observed, where language suggests a body that is not there we invent something like a soul to take its place.

In *King Lear* the Fool says, "Then 'tis like the breath of unfee'd lawyer, you give me nothing for't. Can you make no use of nothing, nuncle?" meaning that he was not paid for what he said, although one could make use of his words. To which Lear evokes the ancient philosophical maxim, *Ex Nihilo Nihio Fit,* that nothing comes of nothing; there is a cause for every event. Lear states, "Why, no, boy, nothing can be made out of nothing." The Fool then continues with his philosophically loaded puns.

> I marvel what kin thou and thy daughters are; they'll have me whipped for speaking true, thou'lt have me whipped for lying. . . . I had rather be any kind o' thing than a fool; and yet I would not be thee, nuncle; thou hast pared thy wit o' both sides, and left *nothing* i' the middle. . . . Now thou art an O without a figure. I am better than thou at now; I am a fool, thou art nothing. (LR, I:4)

Here, "nothing" is compared to a null-set class, a zero, without an adjoining number, and that metaphorically compares to a naked king, sans power and love, "sans everything." Again, in the same play "nothing" is used as the absence of significance when Gloucester asks his son, Edmund,

> Glo.: What paper were you reading?
> Edm.: Nothing, my lord.
> Glo.: No? What needed then that terrible dispatch of it into your pocket? The *quality of nothing* hath no such need to hide itself. (LR, I:2)

The expression "quality of nothing" is poetic language standing for "the absence of significance" and not a metaphysical idea of the quality of "Nothngness" as alleged by a critic.

In *A Winter's Tale* "nothing" is used as the absence of significance as in the title *Much Ado about Nothing*.

> Is whispring nothing?
> Is leaning cheek? Is meeting noses?
> Kissing with inside lip?
> . . .
> Is this nothing?

> Why, then the world and all that's in' t is nothing;
> The covering sky is nothing; Bohemia;
> my wife is nothing; nor nothing have these nothings,
> If this be nothing. (WT, I:2)

Finally, there is Hamlet's Time, after his encounter with the ghost and his cutting remarks with Horatio in the first act:

> The time is out of joint; O cursed spite,
> That ever I was born to set it right! (HAM, I:5)

followed with another metaphor in the third act, "For who would bear the whips and scorn of time?" (HAM, III:1). The first metaphor conveys a visual picture of an unhinged gate waiting to be set right. The ghost's report of Claudius's treachery is so outrageous that someone (Hamlet) is needed to avenge it. Hamlet curses his lot when he feels the burden of revenge. As reluctant as he is to shoulder that unholy task he nevertheless feels it is up to him to do so.

Certain unwarranted inferences have been drawn from the first metaphor by critics such as Gille Deleuze, a noted philosopher, who begins his book *Kant's Critical Philosophy* by seeing similarities between Kant's concept of time and Hamlet's metaphor on time "out of joint." He writes, "On four poetic formulas which might summarize *Kantian Philosophy*, the first is Hamlet's great formula 'The Time is out of joint.' Time is out of joint, time is unhinged. The hinges are axes around which the door turns. *Cardo,* in Latin, designates the subordination of time to the cardinal points through which the periodical movements that it measures pass. As long as time remains on its hinges, it is subordinate to movement.... This was the view of ancient philosophy. But time out of joint signifies the reversal of the movement. Time is no longer related to the movement which it measures, but movement is related to the time . . . this is the first great Kantian reversal. Everything which moves and changes is in time, but time itself does not change, does not move, say then it is eternal."[14]

Deleuze's interpretation of Kant's concept of time is questionable. It does not explain how Hamlet's metaphor is Kantian. Kant views Time and Space as a pure form of sensibility, *Anschung*, which our mind imposes on nature, in order that the raw material of experience becomes intelligible Such views make both Time and Space subjective—"subjective" in the sense that one cannot speak of Space and Time in the absence of some perceiver (but not psychological subjectivity such as one's feeling of the passage of Time). They are, after all, lenses of our spectacles through which we look at the world. Such a Kantian perspective is incongruent with Hamlet's objective view of Time.

Subjective, Objective, and Private Time

Let us first introduce briefly the subjective view of Time that was expressed eloquently by Augustine in his *Confessions*. He asked, "What is Time? . . . [I]f no one asks of me, I know, if I wish to explain to him who asked I know not."[15] He seems to concur with Plato's idea that Time and the world were created together. God, however, like Aristotle's unmoved mover, stands outside of the stream of time. Not satisfied with that mythical version, Plato resorts to a kind of speculative psychology and speaks of the three subjective species of time. The presence of things past is memory, the presence of thinks present is sight, and the presence of things future is expectation. "Some such different times do exist in the mind but nowhere else that I can see."

The objective and subjective contrast appears in dramatic form in Shakespeare's text. In one of his early plays, *A Midsummer Night's Dream*, Theseus, the Duke of Athens, speaks to Hippolyta, the queen of the Amazons:

> The.: Now, fair Hippolyta, our nuptial hour
> Draws on apace; four happy days bring in
> Another moon; but O! methinks, how slow
> This old moon wanes; she lingers my desires
> Like to a step-dame or a dowager
> Long withering out a young man's revenue.
> Hip.: Four days will quickly steep themselves in night;
> Four nights will quickly dream away the time;
>
> (MND, I:1)

Here the queen speaks of the subjective in comparison with objective time.

Objective time is depicted as an omnipotent tyrant, an all-destroyer with his "whips" in his hand and "scorn" on his lips such as Gloucester's gods, "As flies to wanton bay are we to gods. They kill us for their sport" (LR, IV:1).

In contrast, subjective time's existence is contingent upon our personal perspective of the world. It is that "that goes slow in sorrow, and swift and short in folly and sport and travels in diverse paces with diverse person" (AYL, III:2). It is a lover's time, a lover waiting for her lover, as Juliet laments, . . . my lord, my love, my friend!

> I must hear from thee every day in the hour,
> For in a minute there are many days:
> O! By this count I shall be much in years
> Ere I again behold my Romeo. (ROM, III:5)

In other plays there are allusions to what is called "Private Time," such as "my true time" in *Richard II,* "time must have a stop" with Hotspur's death; "life" as a "a poor player that struts and frets his hour upon the stage and then is heard no more," in *Macbeth*, and "my dear time's waste," spoken by the speaker of Sonnet 30.

We find in the texts an important philosophical understanding that the very existence of subjective and private times presupposes objective time, which is knowable by appeal to external criteria such as a sand clock, as mentioned by Aristotle, or a dial or by measuring shadows. The famous observation of Wittgenstein that "an inner process stands in need of outer criteria" applies also to the idea of subjective time—subjective only in contrast to objective time, since a concept of time without a legitimate contract is an empty concept.[16]

We have already spoken of objective time, as in the Sonnets:

> Thou by dial's stealth mayest know
> Time's thievish progress to eternity (SON 77)

and

> Thou ceaseless lackey to eternity. (LUC verse 139)

In *Richard II* the king responds to hearing music with thoughts about three kinds of time. At first time is objective.

> Music do I hear?
> Ha! ha! Keep time. How sour sweet music is
> When time is broke and no proportion kept!
> So is it in the music of men's lives.
> And here have I the daintiness of ear
> To check time broke in a disorder'd string

Time becomes private in the following lines,

> But for the concord of my state and time
> Had not an ear to hear my true time broke.

He returns to objective time then remembering,

> I wasted time, and now doth time waste me
> For now hath time made me his numbering clock

Time becomes momentarily subjective with

> My thoughts are minutes, and with signs they jar

But immediately objective time returns,

> Their watches on unto mine eyes, the outward watch
> Whereto my finger, like a dial's point
> Is pointing still, in cleansing them from tears.
> Now sir, the sound that tells what hour it is
> Are clamorous groans, that strike upon my heart
> Which is the bell: so sighs and tears and groans
> Show minutes, times and hours

Private time returns as he bids the music stop.

> but my time
> Runs posting on in Bolingbroke's proud joy
> While I stand fooling here, his Jack o'the clock.
> This music mads me: let it sound no more. . . . (R2, V:5)

In *Henry IV*, part 2, King Henry speaks of objective time in his prayer,

> O God! that one might read the book of fate
> And see the revolution of the times
> Make mountains level, and the continent,—
> Weary of solid firmness,—melt itself
> Into the sea! and, other times, to see
> The beachy girdle of the ocean
> Too wide for Neptune's hips; how chances mock,
> And changes fill the cup of alteration
> With divers liquors! (2H4, III:1)

In *Love's Labour's Lost*, a philosophical play, there is a dialogue between the king and Berowne wherein the king hopes that by fighting "the huge army of the world's desires," he would blunt the scythe of devouring time:

> Let fame, that all hunt after in their lives
> Live register'd upon our brazen tombs
> And then grace us in the disgrace of death;
> When, spite of cormorant devouring Time
> The endeavour of this present breath may buy
> That honour which shall bate the scythe's keen edge,
> And make us heir of all eternity. (LLL, I:1)

In *All's Well that Ends Well*, the King of France speaks metaphorically of time as a thief, reminding Bertram of his father's gloomy outlook on life.

> Not one word more of the consumed time.
> Let's take the instant by the forward top.
> For we are old, and on our quick'st decrees
> The inaudible and noiseless foot of time
> Steals ere we can effect them. (AWW, V:3)

and

> Methinks I hear him now, his plausive words . . .
> "Let me not live,"
> Thus his good melancholy oft began
> On the *catastrophe and heel of pastime.* (AWW, I:2)

It is the clock, the dial, and the shadow that tell time, but without an objective clue we speak sometimes of our subjective estimate of time, "There is no clock in the forest," says Orlando (in *As You Like It* [III:2]); sometimes time is personified: Time may "turn back an hour in a day," as Dromio of Syracuse says in *The Comedy of Errors* (IV:2). In Sonnet 57 time is both subjective and objective:

> What shall I do but tend
> Upon the hours and times of your desire?
> . . .
> Nor dare I chide the world-without-end hour
> Whilst I, my sovereign, watch the clock for you,

There are many visual metaphors all through the poems and plays where we may see many faces of objective and subjective time. ("Subjective" not in the Kantian but almost in the Augustinian sense.)

> Let him have time to mark how slow time goes
> In time of sorrow, and how sweet and short
> His time of folly and his time of sport.
>
> (LUC, verse 142)

In *Cymbeline* the character Imogen says,

> Why, one that rode to 's execution, man,
> Could never go slow: I have heard of riding wagers,
> Where horses have been nimbler than the sands
> That run i' the clock's behalf. (CYM, III:3)

In *As you Like It*, Orlando says to Duke senior,

> Under the shade of melancholy boughs,
> Lose and neglect the creeping hours of time. (AYL, II:3)

In Orlando's view consciousness of objective time is detrimental to love, but by closing one's eyes and ignoring the flow of time, one may gain a kind of secular bliss. Neither remembering past happiness nor anticipating future happiness can engender the experience of present happiness. Orlando's advice reminds us of Matthew 6:34, "Take therefore no thought for the morrow: for the morrow shall take thought for the things of itself. Sufficient unto the day is the evil thereof." In act IV time becomes personified in the dialogue between Rosalind and Orlando:

> Ros.: I pray you, what is t'o clock?
> Orl.: You should ask me what time o' day; there is no clock in the forest.
> Ros.: Then there is no true lover in the forest; else sighing

every minute and groaning every hour should detect
the lazy foot of Time as well as a clock.

Orl.: And why not the swift foot of Time? had not that
been as proper?

Ros.: By no means, sir. Time travels in diverse
paces with diverse persons. I'll tell you who Time
ambles withal, who Time trots withal, who Time
gallops withal, and who he stands still withal.

Orl.: I prithee, who doth he trot withal?

Ros.: Marry, he trots hard with a young maid between
the contract of her marriage and the day it is
solemnized . . .

. . . ambles with a priest that lacks Latin . . .

. . . [he gallops] With a thief to the gallows;

. . . he thinks himself too soon there

. . . [he stays it still] With lawyers in vacation,
for they sleep between term and term and then they
perceive not how Time moves. (AYL, III:2)

When Orlando arrives to keep their tryst, Rosalind chides him for being late, and calls on Time as a measure of love.

Orl.: My fair Rosalind, I came within an hour
of my promise.

Ros.: Break an hour's promise in love! He that
will divide a minute into a thousand parts, and
break but a part of the thousandth part
of a minute in the affairs of love, it may be
said of him that Cupid hath clapped him o' the
shoulder.
But I'll warrant him heart-whole. (AYL, IV:1)

In *The Comedy of Errors*, in this exchange between Dromio and Adriana, Time turns into a bankrupt merchant.

> Dro.: It was two ere I left him, and now the clock strikes one.
> Adr.: The hours come back! That did I never hear
> Dro.: If any hour meets a sergeant
> a' turns back for very fear.
> Adr.: As if Time were in debt! How fondly Dost thou reason!
> Dro.: Time is very bankrupt and weds more than he's worth to season
> Nay, he's thief too . . .
> If Time be in debt and theft and a sergeant be in the way,
> Hath he not reason to turn back an hour in a day?
> (IV:2)

In *Othello,* Time is a pregnant woman who will gave birth to many ominous events. According to Iago, "There are many events in the womb of time which will be delivered." While in *A Winter's Tale*, Time is personalized as an omnipotent god.

> I, that please some, try all, both joy and terror
> Of good and bad, that make and unfold error,
> Now take upon me, in the name of Time
> To use my wings. Impute it not a crime
> To me or my swift passage, that I slide
> O'er sixteen years and leave the growth untried
> Of that wide gap, since it is my power
> To o'erthrow law, and in one self-born hour
> To plant and o'erwhelm custom. (WT, IV:1)

Time is also an august tyrant with his "lion's paws" who occasionally may do some good by cooling the roaring king's blood, and by revealing hidden truth as is granted in the metaphor "Truth is Time's daughter." Time is perhaps most powerful as she appears as Truth's greatest ally in *The Rape of Lucrece*:

> Time's glory is to calm contending things,
> To unmask falsehood and bring truth to light.
>
> (LUC, verse 135)

The Ladder Metaphor

In *Julius Caesar* there appears the Pyrrhonian ladder metaphor, and in *Love's Labour's Lost* there is a reference to the skeptic reasoning against reason. The ancient skeptical claim that knowledge is impossible is rebutted by a clever argument that skepticism refutes itself inasmuch as the skeptic in claiming to know nothing is declaring to know something. The skeptic's answer was even cleverer: our reasoning is a ladder of premises, go and climb it step by step and when you reach the roof, the conclusion, then throw it down.

Wittgenstein in his *Tractatus* used this Pyrrhonian answer, the ladder metaphor, by saying that "He who understands me recognizes it's senseless (he must so to speak throw away the ladder after he has climbed up on it)." The skeptic rebuttal is indeed a strong argument if taken as a metalanguage about the object-language. "That we know nothing" is not a self-referential assertion since it is about the totality of sentences claiming truth and not about itself. Thus the ladder may stand if taken as a metalanguage about the object-language. The ladder metaphor in *Julius Caesar* as voiced by Brutus is a true description of politicians who appeal to the masses for climbing to the top and upon achieving their goal ignore their campaign promises and scorn those who helped them.

> But 'tis a common proof,
> That lowliness is young ambition's ladder,
> Whereto the climber-upward turns his face;
> But when he once attains the upmost round,
> He then unto the ladder turns his back,
> Looks in the clouds, scorning the base degrees
> By which he did ascend. So Caesar may. (JC, II:1)

In *Love's Labour's Lost*, Berowne argues against learning from books written by the ancients such as the Aristotelian and astrological treatises. The king points out the paradoxical feature of reasoning against reason—the skeptics trying to overthrow arguments by argument.

> Ber.: And give him light that it was blinded by
> Study is like the heaven's glorious sun,
> That will not be deep-search'd with saucy looks;
> Shall have continual plodders ever won
> Save *base authority from others' books*.
> These earthly godfathers of heaven's lights
> That give a name to every fixed star,
> Have no more profit of their shining nights
> Than those that walk and wot not what they are.
> Too much to know is to know nought but fame;
> And every grandfather can give a name.
> King.: How well he's read, to reason against reading!
>
> (LLL,1:1)

THE MAGIC OF NAMES

On Names and Titles: Denotation and Connotation

> "Oh tell me friar, tell me
> In what vile part of this anatomy
> Doth my name lodge?"
>
> —Romeo (ROM, III:3)

> "Good name in man or woman, dear my lord Is the
> immediate jewel of their souls:
> Who steals my purse steals trash; 'tis something, nothing
> 'Twas mine, 'tis his and has been slave to thousands;
> But he that filches from me my good name
> Robs me of that which not enriches him,
> And makes me poor indeed."
>
> —Iago (OTH, III:3)

Poets, novelists, logicians, and magicians have been fascinated by the protean functions of names. They were often charmed with the connotation that the phonemes and morphemes of personal or place-names carry with themselves and may awaken the memory of sundry bits of information about bearers of names. Even a bare mentioning—a mere echo of the name of some significant persons or place—may occasion the floating of forgotten images, as if the given name that supposes to be just an identification mark tries to tell tales about its bearer. Marcel Proust was enchanted by the multifarious functions of place-names—"I thought of some names," he writes, "not as the inaccessible ideal but as a real and enveloping substance into which I was about to plunge, the life not yet lived, the life intact and pure which I enclosed in them. The name of Parma, one of the towns that I most longed to visit, after reading the Chartreuse . . . seeming to me compact and glossy, violet-tinted, soft ... if anyone were to speak of such or such a house in Parma ... he would give me the pleasure of thinking that I was to inhabit a dwelling that was compact and glossy as I could imagine it only by the aid of that heavy syllable of the name Parma, in which no breath of air stirred and all that I had made it assume of Stendhalian sweetness. . . . And when I thought of Florence, it was of a town miraculously embalmed; as for Balbec, it was one of those names in which one depicted still the representation of some abolished custom."[17]

From ancient times philosophers such as Plato (in *Philebus*) and the Stoic logicians have spoken about the meanings of signs and the function of proper names. Modern philosophers' interest in proper names and the denotation and sense of signs is subsidiary to their concern with language. The technical vocabulary of logicians such as the use of terms such as "constant" and "variable" in place of proper names and common nouns and the semantic distinction between the use and mention of signs is meant to provide a perspacious language free from obscurity by translating an ordinary language into precise symbolic language.

Magicians' concerns with names, signs, and numerals stem from an ancient belief that names are bounded by mysterious ties to persons or places so that by invoking or abusing names one may cause beneficial or harmful changes to their bearers. The injunction that "Thou shall not take the lord's name in vain," and the warning that blasphemy, disrespectful mentioning of God's name, is a sin, and the belief that bestowing saints' names on infants is salutary are all consequences of that belief. The old Puritans gave such names as "Tribulation," "The Lord is near" and "If Christ-had-not-died-for-you you had been damned Bare-bones" (shortened to Damned Bareborns) to their children. Falstaff is called "bare-bones" in jest, by the prince.

The Puritans' practice of bestowing foreboding names continued in their new home, New England. Hawthorne in *The Scarlet Letter* mocks the practice by letting Hester plead, "Do anything, save to lie down and die? Give up this name Arthur Dimmesdale, and make thyself another, and a high one such as thou canst wear without fear or shame."[18]

Shakespeare mocks the widespread superstitious beliefs of kings and queens, soldiers and maids in the magic of names. He shows that the use of a name as if it identified the character, or characteristics, or prophesied the destiny of an individual of that name may damage the reputation of the bearer of the name and have tragic consequences. A proper name is just a sign for a person's identification; it is like a model of a house, and not a house. "A model of a house that one draws beyond the power to build," said a player in *Henry IV*, part 1. We may compare Shakespeare's realistic account of proper names and titles while exorcising their magic with Goethe's romantic fascination with names. In *Romeo and Juliet*, Juliet of Capulet laments that her lover, Romeo, is of the Montague clan, long feuding with her own family.

'Tis but they name that is my enemy;
Thou art thyself, though, not a Montague.
What is Montague? It is nor hand, nor foot,
Nor arm. Nor face, nor any other part
Belonging to a man. O! Be some other name;
What's in a name? That which we call a rose
By any other name would smell as sweet;
So Romeo would, were he not Romeo call'd
Retain that dear perfection which he owes
Without the title. Romeo, doff thy name;
And for that name, which is no part of thee,
Take all myself. (ROM, II:2)

but Goethe writes,

> A man's name is not like a cloak that merely
> Hangs around him, that may be loosened and
> Tightened at will. It is a perfectly fitting
> Garment. It grows over him like his very skin.
> One cannot scrape and scratch at it without
> Injuring the man himself.[19]

Romeo of Montague seeks to relinquish his clan name:

> Call me but love, and I'll be new baptiz'd
>   By a name
> I know not how to tell thee who I am;
> My name, dear saint, is hateful to myself
> Because it is enemy to thee;
> Had I it written, would tear the word. (ROM, II:2)

The denotation cannot be freed from the sign, and the lovers are doomed. Romeo is aware of this tragic magic. He laments that his name "grows over him like his very skin," as Goethe writes, he "cannot scrape and scratch at it without injuring himself." Romeo continues:

> As if that name,
> Shot from the deadly level of a gun,
> Did murder her, as that name's cursed hand
> Murder'd her kinsman. O, tell me, friar, tell me
> In what vile part of this anatomy
> Doth my name lodge? Tell me, that I may sack
> That hateful mansion. (ROM, II:3)

To be sure, "Capulet," "Montague," clan names, as well as "Romeo, "Juliet," are proper names; are all linguistic signs and hence are arbitrary designations. However, clan names and proper names are more artificial than the common noun. We would not violate any semantic regularity by changing the proper names as we would by replacing "rose" with other common nouns. Since it is a Sense of a Sign that does determine Denotation of a sign and "rose" has its own determinant sense, it designates a particular kind of flower according to the English dictionary. It would be a deviant usage if we replaced it with any other name. Although a proper name may be changed without much ado, not so the sense of a common noun that exhibits a certain semantic regularity.

Juliet abjured the magic of names when she announces that she is in love with Romeo, never mind his name, and when she speaks of words in general as mere artifacts she in effect is expressing the Aristotelian naturalistic idea of the primacy of things such as a person or a flower over and above the particulars and the universal. However, when she makes Romeo a personal name, an analogue of rose, she is making a category mistake that should be dismissed as a lover's poetic license.

In the same play once more the magic of names is displayed when Juliet's nurse asks Romeo,

>Nur.: Doth not *rosemary* and Romeo begin both with a letter?
>Rom.: Ay, nurse, what of that? Both with an R.
>Nur.: Ah! Mocker; that's the dog's name.
>R is for the _____ No,
>I know it begins with some other letter;
>and she had the prettiest sententious of it,
>Of you and rosemary, that it would do you good to hear.

It is to be noted that while both Juliet and Romeo tried to free themselves from the spell of their clan names, Juliet's nurse, in contrast, is a captive of that magic. Such superstitious belief in the magic of names is also expressed by the Queen Lady Grey with a catastrophic outcome in *Richard III*. Here Gloucester (later, King Richard III) asks his brother the cause of his arrest.

> Glo.: Upon what cause?
> Clar.: Because my name is George.
> Glo.: Alack! My lord, the fault is none of yours,
> He should, for that, commit your godfathers.
> . . .
> Clar.: He harkens after prophecies and dreams;
> And from the cross-row plucks the letter G,
> And says that by the letter G
> His issue disinherited be,
> And, for my name George begins with G
> It follows in his thought that I am he.
> Glo.: Why, this it is, when men are ruled by women.
>
> (R3, I:1)

At any rate, if there is a fault in the name George, it is a fault of the bestower of the name, his godfather, not of the bearer of the name; it is Gloucester who disinherited the king. The wizard, after all, was right about a name beginning with G.

In *As You Like It*, a similar point is made when Jacques asks Orlando,

> Jacq.: Rosalind is your love's name?
> Orl.: Yes, just.
> Jacq.: I do not like her name.

Orl.: There was no thought of pleasing you when
she was christened. (AYL, III:2)

In *Hamlet*, Fortinbras's army is going to fight for the name of a worthless piece of land. Here the captain states:

We go to gain a little patch of ground
That hath in it no profit but the name.
To pay five ducats, five, I would not farm it. (HAM, IV:4)

Hamlet, as he is dying, speaks metaphorically of the wounded name but not his wounded body. Here his name is a token for his life. This happens when the name of a person is replaced with its bearer as in two sonnets in which Shakespeare identifies his own name with the person who carries the name.

Make but my name thy love and love that still
And then thou lov'st me, for my name is *Will*. (SON 136)

And in another sonnet

Whoever hath her wish, thou hast thy *Will*
And *Will* to boot, and *Will* in overplus;
. . .
Let no unkind, "No" fair beseechers kill;
Think all but one, and me in that one *Will*. (SON 135)

It has been noticed that there is an oblique pun that refers to the name Ann Hathaway in the sonnet where he writes,

"I hate" from hate away she threw,
And saved my life, saying, "not you." (SON 145)

In *Julius Caesar*, Cassius tries to persuade Brutus that there is nothing in the name "Caesar" in order to demythologize the magic of the name, the name that was associated with all the honor bestowed on Caesar.

> Brutus and Caesar: What should be in that "Caesar"?
> Why should that name be sounded more than yours?
> Write them together, yours is as fair a name;
> Sound them, it doth become the mouth as well;
> Weigh them, it is as heavy; conjure with 'em,
> "Brutus" will start a spirit as soon as "Caesar."
> Now, in the names of all the gods at once,
> Upon what meat doth this our Caesar feed
> That he is grown so great? (JC, I:2)

However, in *Antony and Cleopatra*, Octavius Caesar praises Mark Antony's name:

> The death of Antony
> Is not a single doom; in the name lay
> A moiety of the world. (JC, V:1)

The difference between Cassius's dismissal of Caesar's name as insignificant and Octavius Caesar's praise is due to the fact that certain names and titles carry in themselves some specific senses and thus are no more arbitrary than designations like other proper names. Take away the definite description, "the King of England" from Richard and he considers himself bereft of everything, he feels he has lost his own identity:

> What must the king do now? Must he submit?
> The king shall do it: must he be deposed?
> The king shall be contented: must he lose
> The name of King? O, God's name, let it go. (R2, III:3)

When Bolingbroke is seeking Richard's crown he says, "my ancestor is Lancaster and I come to seek that name in England." The title, "King of England" was given to Richard at his coronation, Richard thinks, that on losing his title he is losing his name, which was bestowed at his birth.

> I have no name, no title,
> No, no! That name was given me at the font
> But 'tis usurped, alack, the heavy day
> That I have born so many winters out
> And know not now what name I call myself. (R2, IV:1)

Richard regards his title as an extension of himself and his army as a part of his title.

> Is not the king's name
> Twenty thousand names.
> Arm, arm my name! (R2, III:1)

And when his army disappears and his title is taken away from him he considers himself to be a naked corpse even before his death.

The semantic distinction between the name Richard and his title, the King of England, which is the definite description of him, lies in that a personal name that is given to him by the bestower is in the logician's vernacular "a rigid designator," a peg on which may hang or from which may be taken away many descriptions. While his title, "the King of England" could be taken away from him and given to another name-seeker like Bolingbroke, his name cannot be.

Not only titles or definite descriptions, but also some proper names such as "Cassius" or "Falstaff" have retained their specific senses, although they were once just arbitrary designations, as is recognized by casting directors in their choice of players fitting their descriptions that Cassius "has a lean and hungry look" and Falstaff has "a white beard, a decreasing leg, and increasing belly." In Desdemona's forbidden name there is a signal for death and disaster. "Her name that was as fresh as Diana's visage" laments Othello, "is now begrimed and black as mine own face."

The disastrous consequence of confusing proper names is exemplified in *Romeo and Juliet*, *Richard III*, and also in *Julius Caesar* when Cinna the poet was taken wrongly to be Cinna a conspirator, "It is no matter, his name's Cinna, pluck his name out of his heart." However, there are examples of the beneficial power of names in moving soldiers, masses, and lovers. In *Henry VI*, part 1:

> Alarm: Enter an English soldier, crying, "A Talbot! A Talbot!"
> They fly, leaving their clothes behind.
> Sold.: The *cry* of *Talbot* serves me for a sword,
> For I have loaden me with many spoils
> Using no other weapon but his name. (1H6, II:1)

In *Henry VI*, part 2, Cabe states,

> Was ever feather so lightly blown to and fro as this multitude? The name of Henry the Fifth hales them to hundred mischiefs.... (2H4, IV:8)

We hear in *Richard III*:

> Besides the king's name is a tower of strength. (R3, V:3)

In *King Lear*, the Duke of Albany says,

> Trust to thy single virtue; for thy soldiers,
> All levied in *my name,* have in my name
> Took their discharge. (LR, V:3)

In *Antony and Cleopatra* there occurs a happy marriage between a name and its bearer. For Cleopatra the name Antony is so much intermingled with Antony that the mere sound of that name vibrates waves of images in the body and the soul of "The serpent of the Nile." Her maid Mardian tells Antony:

> ... the last she spake
> "Antony! Most noble Antony!"
> Then in the midst a tearing groan did break
> The name of *Antony*; it was divided
> Between her heart and lips. She rendered life,
> Thy name so buried in her. (ANT, IV:12)

Hear the queen's last words on her heavenly mating:

> Husband, I come:
> Now to that name my courage prove my title!
> I am fire, and air; my other elements
> I give to baser life. (ANT, V:2)

Of the four ancient substances of Empedecles, earth, water, air, and fire, she has chosen air and fire, pure and moving elements that are near kin to her soul rather than the dusty earth and tainted water that are elements of her body.

In *Twelfth Night*, in the short dialogue between Feste the clown and Viola, there are certain significant semantic remarks on the usage of words and sentences, on the meaning of proper names and on the paradox of reasoning against reason, all in jest. It begins when Viola points to the clown's careless manner of using words. The clown responds by using a metaphor when he likens a sentence to a glove.

> A sentence is but a cheveril glove to a good Wit . . .
> How quickly the wrong side may be turned outward
>
> (TN, III:1)

In his view a sentence is a mere artifact that in the hands of its maker may produce a rich tapestry or pierce a skin, having no unalterable essence or objective meaning since words are often used ambiguously. Viola agrees and says that "they that dally nicely with words may quickly make them wanton." The clown then speaks of words as rebels, "Words are very rascals." They are unwilling to accept any bondage that is a rigid and exact definition. Words are metamorphosed into unruly rascals where "Bonds disgrace them." He then says that her sister's name is a word and therefore to dally with that word may also harm the bearer of that word. "I would therefore that my sister had no name." The clown's last words are also significant. He points to a paradoxical feature of reasoning against reason, and his unwillingness to fall into a liarlike paradox. On being asked by Viola for the reason for his thesis, he answers that he can provide no reason without using words, and words are "grown so false" (TN, III:1).

Finally, consider the pragmatic aspect of language on the issue of the connotation, that is, the relationship of the speaker to the words and the issue of the punning of names. Connotation is a psycholinguistic concept having to do with the association of a name with persons or places that the hearer makes upon hearing a name and as such should not be confused as is often done by critics with the semantic aspect of sign, namely, its sense, that is the objective property of words. We may notice many examples of name connotation. While Jacques says that he does not like Rosalinda's name, Isabella says of Mariana's name, "I have heard of the lady, and good words went with her name" (AYL, III:1).

In *A Midsummer Night's Dream* charming names such as "Pease-Blossom," "Mustard-seed," and "Moth" were given to fairies for their connotative power. In *Henry IV*, part 2, to mock the wisdom of country judges they are named "Shallow," "Silence," and "Mouldy." Thus a pun is created when Falstaff says, "I do see the bottom of Justice Shallow" and Shallow says, "Ha, ha, ha, most excellent in faith! Things that are mouldy lack use." Professional madams are named "Quickly," and "Mistress Overdone." We hear the audience laughing when puns are used such as when Polonius says that once in a play he performed the role of Julius Caesar. A Brutus killed me," and Hamlet comments, "It was a brute part of him to kill so capital a calf." However, not every pun is so obviously transparent. Consider Caliban's, name which is an anagram of cannibal and ban meaning a curse. Caliban drunkenly sings his name, "Ban, Ban, Ca, Caliban," which is a perfect fit of its denotation (TMP, II:2).

Chapter 6

SUBJECTIVITY

INWARDNESS OR CONSCIOUSNESS

> "But I have that within which passeth show."
> —Hamlet (I:2)

Hamlet claims that there is something within him besides the "dejected haviour of the visage," the bones and marrow, the blood and sinews under his skin and inside his skull that is the core of his being. Call that entity "the soul" or "the spirit" in commonplace language and in Augustine, or a thinking substance in Cartesian ontology, or "consciousness" or "for-itself," in the Hegelian conceptual scheme. In the Shakespearean world of words, phrases such as "the inward man," "the inward service of the mind," something within that truly denotes Hamlet, the inmost part of Gertrude, "the grief that lies within," such phrases are employed that are semantically equivalent within the context of the word "consciousness" although that word itself is absent from the text, which is replaced with equivalent words such as conscience or awareness or being virtuous or vicious or feeling morally damned and remorseful or guiltless and blessed. Consciousness, unlike the overt behavior of a person, is said to be entirely private and subjective like conscience, its moral component. However, there seems to be a philosophical link between these two. Gilbert Ryle has noted that the old theological concept of privacy of the conscience became the new philosophical idea of privacy of consciousness, in the Cartesian ontology of two substances, matter and mind. Descartes believed that thought is the essence of mind as extension is of matter, that mind always thinks and thinking is indubitable proof that he exists.

The new Cartesian idea of separation of mind and matter and of thought as the essence of mind reminds us of the old Socratic notion of mind as a divine element in the soul and of self-knowledge as being aware of ourselves when we are awake and not out of our minds. In Hamlet there are at least three direct references to the idea of awareness or what is later called consciousness. In *Hamlet,* the king speaks of Hamlet's strange behavior and his opaque mind.

> Something, have you heard
> Of Hamlet's transformation; so I call it,
> Since nor the exterior nor the inward man
> Resembles that it was. What it should be
> More than his father's death, that thus hath should
>   have put him
> So much from the understanding of himself,
> I cannot dream of (HAM, II:2)

Laertes warns Ophelia, his sister,

> As this temple waxes,
> The inward service of the mind and soul
> Grows wild withal. (HAM, I:3)

The overused metaphor of mirror as a symbol of self-revelation appears in *Hamlet* in Hamlet's conversation with his mother. "You go not, till I set up a glass/ Where you may see the inmost part of you" (HAM, III:4). Hamlet himself reveals the inwardness that, as he says, truly denotes him and that lies behind his "seeming" manner. He is emphatic that what "can denote [him] truly" is his inner self and not all the "trappings and suits of woes" when he explains to his mother the difference between "seems" and "is."

> Seems, madam! Nay, it is;
> I know not "seems."
> 'Tis not alone my inky cloak, good mother,
> Nor customary suits of solemn black
> Nor windy suspiration of forc'd breath
> No, nor the fruitful river in the eye,
> Nor the dejected haviour of the visage,
> Together with all forms, moods, shapes of grief,
> *That can denote me truly*; these indeed seem,
> For they are actions that a man might play:
> But I have that within which passeth show;
> These but the trappings and the suits of woe. (HAM, I:2)

The old philosophical dichotomy between the illusory appearance and the robust reality is spoken by Hamlet's simple words, "seems," and "it is," which seem like "let be" in the final scene. Wallace Stevens surely points to this semantic distinction in saying, "Let be, be final of seem" as noted by Harold Bloom.

Using the new idiom of "point of view"[1] in place of the old subjective-objective dichotomy, we may look at the two aspects of Hamlet: the outward actions and the inward processes of his mind. His behavior, which includes his speech acts, is accessible to all points of view among his audience and readers, whereas his inner life, his doubt and anxiety, his melancholy are all private since they are accessible to him alone and real only from his point of view.

To him Denmark is a prison, but not so to his two Danish classmates. His inner thought and emotion, his fancies, are not accessible to others unless he expresses them in words that are not in his private possession but are in the public domain, like gold in the treasury or coins in the market place. The truth value of his statement, however, should be taken at its face value until his future behavior proves otherwise. In the graveyard scene, for example, he does claim that he loves Ophelia,

> I lov'd Ophelia; forty thousand brothers
> Could not, with all their quantity of love,
>   Make up my sum. (HAM, V:1)

though in an earlier scene he rebukes her bitterly on the suspicion that she is spying for the court.

> [B]e thou as chaste as ice, as pure as snow, thou shall not
>   escape calumny.
> Get thee to nunnery; go. (HAM, III:1)

What is entirely inaccessible is not his speech act about his inner life, but the quality of his feelings, which is phenomenologically private and hence is not shareable. Hamlet wishes that his mother would understand the depth of his feelings. He is not demanding, however, that Gertrude share the quality of his feeling since no word is a substitute for its denotation. We do observe with Polonius all the overt moving behavior of a player who speaks of Priam's slaughter, "Look! wh'er he has not turned his colour and has tears in's eyes. Prithee, no more" (HAM, II:2). But we do not grasp, despite all our sympathy, the quality of his feelings. In speaking of the quality of the so-called ineffability of his feelings, we might quote the oracular statement of Wittgenstein at the end of the *Tractatus*, even though that statement is about metaphysical subjects that, according to his picture theory of language, are unsayable, "Whereof one cannot speak, thereof one must be silent."[2] Hamlet, speaking to his mother about his strange behavior and the secrets of his mind, makes use of public language that he has learned from "good mother" and has mastered in Wittenberg University. In his speech act he did in fact conceptualize his raw feelings when he conveyed his crystallized word out of the material of language and thus made his private secret a public affair. Hamlet, or a deaf-mute, or a Helen Keller prior to her understanding of words, or a child reared alone by a wolf, is beyond his own reach; he would not be aware of himself as a person without language. Our knowledge of Hamlet's mind and his inwardness much praised by literary critics is due to the use of language, a gift of Prometheus to humankind, according to Shelley in his *Prometheus Unbound*; Asia says in act 2, scene 4: "He gave man speech and speech created thought which is the measure of the universe."[3]

The discussion about the relationship between feeling and its expression in language is taken up by Immanuel Kant whose epistemological thought held that without language there cannot be concepts, without concepts experience is blind, and without experience concepts are empty, which is as modern as the Wittgensteinian dictum in his later work: "The inner processes stand in need of outer criteria." There has been a persistent frustration about the failure of language to express thought and feeling and hence about the existence of an unbridgeable gap between these inward phenomena and their expression in language. Nietzsche exalted subjectivity and the phenomenon of inward feeling while slighting action and the speech act. Harold Bloom, enchanted by Hamlet's inwardness, quotes Nietzsche in the epigraph of his book, *Shakespeare: The*

Invention of the Human: "That for which we find words is something already dead in our hearts. There is always a kind of contempt in the act of speaking."[4]

Almost everyone has had the feeling that words could not adequately express his or her feelings on some occasions. Thus Cordelia, unwilling to enter into a love-swearing contest with her hypocritic sisters, answers her father who demands to know which of his daughters loves him most,

> Unhappy that I am, I cannot heave
> My heart into my mouth. (LR, I:1)

The psychological disparity between feeling and language appears in Macduff's words after seeing the bloody body of Duncan,

> O horror! horror! horror!
> Tongue, nor heart
> Cannot conceive nor name thee! (HAM, II:3)

Richard II, like Hamlet, speaks of the privacy of his inner life—his subjectivity—and his outward visage and behavior; like Hamlet he uses the glass metaphor for self-revelation. Richard asks for a glass in order to look at himself. The glass, however, does not reveal any physical change that he expected. The sorrow-struck king shatters the glass and looks inside, where he finds with his inner eye his tormented soul, his "substance."

> Rich.: Give me the glass and there I read.
> No deeper wrinkles, yet? Hath sorrow struck
> So many blows upon this face of mine
> And made no deeper wound? O, flattering glass

>   Like to my followers in prosperity,
>   Thou dost beguile me
>   . . .
>   Was this the face
>   That like the sun did make beholders wink?
>   Was this the face that fac'd so many follies,
>   And was at last out-faced by Bolingbroke?
>   [dashes the glass against the ground]
>   For there it is crack'd in a hundred shivers.
>   Mark, silent king, the moral of this sport,
>   How soon my sorrow hath destroy'd my face.
> Bol.:   The shadow of your sorrow hath destroy'd your face.
> Rich.:   Say that again
>   The shadow of my sorrow! Ha! Let's see:
>   'Tis very true, my grief lies all within;
>   And these external motions of my lament
>   Are merely shadows to the unseen grief
>   That swells with silence in the tortur'd soul;
>   There lies the substance. (HAM, IV:1)

The metaphor of shadow-substance appears also in *Henry VI*, part 1, when Talbot, the hero, is abducted by a French countess who says to Talbot, "long time, thy shadow hath been thrall to me for in my gallery thy picture hangs, but now the substance shall endure the light, and I will chain these legs and arms of thine."

> Tal.:   I laugh to see your ladyship so fond
>   To think that you have aught but Talbot's
>   shadow . . .
> Countess: Why, aren't not thou the man?
> Tal.:   I am indeed.

> Then have I substance too.
> No, no. I am but shadow of myself;
> You are deceived; my substance is not here.
> [The gate being forced, enter Soldiers]
> How say you, madam! Are you not presumed
> That Talbot is but shadow of himself?
> These are his substance, sinews, arms, and strength,
> With which he yoketh your rebellious necks . . .
>
> (1H6, II:3)

Talbot, unlike Richard II, identifies his substance not as a subjective self hidden behind his action, but as the objective action of his soldiers. Richard II, like Hamlet, reveals the subjectivity that lies behind his actions and the show of his emotions. Talbot's perspective has been in fact adopted by the new behaviorists and their philosophical kin in holding that in the long run we are what we do, while rejecting the old tenets of mentalism as a belief in *The Ghost in the Machine* (Ryle). Shakespeare in effect presents both the old tenets of mentalism and the new philosophy of behaviorism. Hamlet, notwithstanding his tortured mind, "thinking too precisely in the event" but doing nothing at the end, takes arms and "drinks hot blood." Similarly Macbeth when he concludes, "Words to the heat of deeds to cold comfort breath gives" and proudly announces that he is ready to fight: "I'll fight till from my bones my flesh be hacked" (MAC, V:3). On occasion a well-performed act may even speak louder than words. "Action is eloquence," says Voluminia, "and the eyes of the ignorant/More learned than their ears" (COR, III:2).

As action is eloquent, so, too, is a bodily gesture of the player. Ulysses speaks of Cressida's nonverbal behavior that like a sign language may convey messages to her lover.

> Fie, fie upon her!
> There's language in her eyes, her cheeks, her lips
> Nay, her foot speaks; her wanton spirits look out
> At every joint and motion of her body. (TRO, IV:5)

CONSCIENCE OR MORAL AWARENESS

> "Conscience is but a word that cowards use."
> —Richard III (V:3)

The concept of subjectivity, inwardness, or consciousness that we have dealt here includes moral awareness, or conscience, an aspect of the mind that, according to American philosopher John Dewey, reflects and debates and responds to problematic situations. Conscience is considered to be the private possession of a person; by some it is believed to be the theological voice of God. Immanuel Kant called it "the court of justice" within a person's mind; Sigmund Freud called it the "superego." Richard III, in Falstaff's footsteps, tried hard to turn off the voice of his conscience by reducing it to mere words, a senseless sign while he proudly echoes Thrasymachus's words in the *Republic* that justice is nothing but the disguised interest of the strong. "Conscience is but a word that cowards use, devised at first to keep the strong in awe. Our strong arm be our conscience, sword, or laws." Nonetheless it is conscience, not his name, that eventually brings havoc into Richard's mind. It is an irony that that "bottled spider" that "foul hunchback toad," the one who makes conscience and empathy words, now fears its invisible sword. If a villainous Richard early in the play debunks conscience and then at the end laments that he is afflicted by its voice, Hamlet from the outset is unable to end his life because of that very voice.

> Thus conscience doth make cowards of us all
> And thus the naked hue of resolution is sicklied o'er the
>   pale cast of thought
> And lose the name of action. (HAM, III:1)

The great king Henry VIII likewise was conscience-stricken when he tells Cardinal Wolsey,

> My Wolsey, see it furnished, O my lord . . .
> But conscience, conscience!
> O 't is a tender place; and I must leave her. (H8, II:2)

The king's courtier Suffolk hints to the Lord Chamberlin at the sexual source of the king's moral struggle over the divorce from Catherine, and his passionate desire for Anne Boleyn.

> Cham.: It seems the marriage with his brother's wife
>   Has crept too near his conscience.
> Suf.: No, his conscience
>   Has crept too near another lady. (H8, II:2)

Not only kings and princes but even the hired murderer of Richard was momentarily conscience-stricken:

> Second
> murderer: That word, "judgement" had breathed a kind of
>   remorse in me (though upon hearing
>   a reward he changes his mind).
> First
> murderer: Where's your conscience now?
> Second
> murderer: In the Duke of Gloucester's purse

> First
> murderer: So when he opens his purse to give us reward, thy conscience flies out. (R3, I:4)

In *The Tempest*, Antonio, like Richard III, dismisses that moral authority as a fiction in Falstaff's manner. Here he speaks to Sebastian:

> Seb.: But, for your conscience?
> Ant.: Aye, where lies that? If it were a kibe
> 'Twould put me to my slipper;
> But I feel not
> This Deity in my bosom; twenty consciences
> That stand twixt me and Milan, candid be,
> And melt ere they molest! (TMP, II:1)

KNOWLEDGE OF OTHER MINDS

> "There's no art to find the mind's construction in the face."
> —Macbeth (I:4)

Some idealist philosophers do question that we may truly understand our own minds let alone know others'; and some psychologists believe that unless a person is analyzed, he lives in darkness. Such a skeptical view has no privileged place in Shakespeare's plays, where a player speaks with all candor about his mind, even if that mind is "full of scorpions" (Macbeth) and another player not only confesses his wickedness but also provides a reason for his murderous intent: "Since I can't prove a lover I am determined to prove a villain" (R3, I:1).

The problem of knowing the thoughts of other minds affects a number of characters in various plays. When King Duncan acknowledges the opacity of other minds, he regrets that he had not been able to read the mind of the general he had trusted, the Thane of Cawdor. "There is no art/ To find the mind's construction in the face: He was a gentleman on whom I built an absolute trust" (MAC, I:4). His second failure in reading another mind had an even more dire consequence: he was murdered in his sleep by another trusted general, the second Thane of Cawdor, his host, Macbeth. Not all minds are opaque to others since some keen observers may be able to read the hidden secret of the mind in the face. So says Lady Macbeth when she rebukes her husband's transparency.

> Your face, my thane, is as a book where men
> May read strange matters. To beguile the time,
> Look like the time; bear welcome in your eye,
> Your hand, your tongue: look like the innocent flower
> But be the serpent under't. (MAC, I:5)

Beginning with Adam and Eve the serpent has been the symbol of deception in the Western world. Macbeth has already spoken of masking his deed by forcing all feeling from his face. "False faith must fight what the false heart doth know" (MAC, I:7), and so he is attentive to his wife's warning that he must dissemble. In Henry V's conversation with his courtier, the king speaks of other minds: "I daresay you love him not to wish him here alone, however you speak thus to feel other men's minds" (H5, IV:1).

In *Measure for Measure* the venerable duke wants to know all about the sickness of Angelo's mind.

> Twice terrible shame on Angelo,
> To weed my vice and let his grow!
> O, what may men within him hide
> Though angels on the outward side! (MM, III:2)

In *Othello* we find an example of this philosophical problem where one character hides his thoughts and emotions while another demands to have access to the contents of that mind. Note this exchange between Othello and Iago:

> Oth.: If thou dost love me, show me thy thought.
> Iag.: My lord, you know I love you.
> . . .
> Oth.: I think thou dost;
> And, for I know thou art full of love and honesty,
> Weigh'st thy words before thou giv'st thou breath,
> Therefore these stops of thine fright me the more;
> . . .
> I pray thee, speak to me as to thy thinkings.
>
> (OTH, III:3)

Iago whets Othello's fearful desire to know what he senses Iago is hiding:

> Iag.: I am not bound to all that slaves are free to. Utter my thoughts?
> . . .
> Oth.: By heaven I'll know thy thoughts.
> Iag.: You cannot, if my heart were in your hand;
> Nor shall not, whilst 'tis in my custody.
>
> (OTH, III:3)

While indirect access to other minds is achievable by making inferences from the overt and public behavior of a person as to the contents of his mind, that inductive inference can be either mistaken or correct. Had Othello some indirect access to Iago's opaque mind by observing the pattern of his actions or by suspecting his racial bigotry, his envy of Othello's rank as general, his sexual jealousy, he could have been saved.

In *The Comedy of Errors,* a player speaks of access to other minds by simply listening to his spoken words though not without questioning their veracity. Note the exchange between Adriana, Dromio, and Luciana.

> Adr.: Say, did'st thou speak with him? Know'st his mind?
> Dre.: Aye, aye, he told his mind upon mine ear
> Beshrew his heart, I scarce could understand.
> Luc.: Spake he so doubtfully, thou could'st not feel his meaning? (ERR, II:1)

Chapter Seven

THE PRAGMATIC DIMENSION
SHAKESPEARE'S PRESENTATION OF MORAL AND POLITICAL VALUES

VIRTUE AND VICE

> "But value dwells not in particular will; It holds its
>   estimate and dignity
> As well wherein 'tis precious of itself
> As in the prizer. 'Tis mad idolatry
> To make the service greater than the god"
> —Hector (TRO, II:3)

The title of this chapter must be explained in the light of contemporary debate among literary critics on the subject of literary work and authorship. Jacques Derrida's claim that "There is nothing beyond the text" and the deconstructionists' claim about "the death of the author" are true only if literary critics accept the plea that they must concentrate on the semantic aspect of the text and not on its pragmatic dimension.[1] We shall argue that the study of the pragmatic dimension of the text is not to be dismissed since knowledge of the author's social and political background is an indispensable asset for a close reading of the text.

Shakespeare's presentation of moral and political values falls squarely within the pragmatics of his writing. Our detailed inquiry into the semantic aspects of his writing wherein the author is absent nevertheless reveals certain salient and undeniable facts about the author's mind. It reveals without a shadow of doubt Shakespeare's extensive knowledge of classical literature and philosophic ideas that he skillfully incorporated within the contest of the poems and plays. The author is fully present when he enters into philosophical dialogue on moral and political values and when he displays on the stage models of "devils incarnate" or paradigms of victimized women and children, or the great-souled nobleman in the throes of an agonizing moral dilemma. Occasionally the author lets the players engage in an abstract meta-ethical dialogue on the meaning and usage of words such as "virtue," "vice," "mercy," "justice," "honor," and "conscience." We shall argue that the playwright's view of values, despite his deliberate impartiality and in particular his avoidance of engaging in political and religious controversy, falls roughly within the category called "objective relativism," namely, belief in the objectivity of our basic values and interests relative to human needs and external conditions and the recognition of conflict among those values. The objectivity of certain values, we know now, is grounded by our biological makeup. Love, altruism, and sociability that we share with some animals are triggered by our genes, even though culture reinforces what nature has already provided. In *Troilus and Cressida*, Paris and Pandarus discuss the geneaology of love and its relation to thought and action.

Par.: He eats nothing but doves, love; and that breeds hot blood, and hot blood begets hot thoughts, hot thoughts beget hot deeds, and hot deed is love.
Pan.: Is this the generation of love? Hot blood? Hot thoughts, and hot deeds? Why, they are vipers: is love a generation of vipers? (TRO, III:1)

Here there is an oblique mockery of the Platonic-Christian notion of Divine Love, and perhaps of the bard's own romance with the sublimated and lustless love that is expressed in some of his sonnets.

In *All's Well that Ends Well* a clown gives a simple answer for "generation of love." In answer to the Countess's question "Tell me thy reason why thou wilt marry?" the clown answers, "My poor body, Madam, requires it: I am driven on by the flesh" (AWW, I:3). The clown's biological explanation, while true as far it goes, does not take into account the cultural forces that created the moral perception that love is a value. We shall discuss Shakespeare's presentation of models of vice and virtue and then the abstract argument on the meaning of moral concepts.

Søren Kierkegaard holds that rather than listening passively to abstract moral systems and religious sermons in churches, the most effective way to moral enlightenment is in the observation of the actions and speeches of players when they display their thoughts and actions on the stage as Shakespeare has done, for example, in the presentation of Richard: "That horrible demonic, the most demonic figure Shakespeare has depicted, Richard III. . . . What made him into a 'demonic'? Apparently his inability to bear the sympathy heaped upon him from childhood. His monologue in the first act of *Richard III* has more value than all systems of morality, which have no intimation of the nightmares of existence or their exploitation."[2] Kierkegaard holds that Richard's conscious choice for evil makes him fully responsible for his actions, even if we accept a Nietzschean explanation of Richard's actions in terms of his inborn deformity. At the outset of the play Richard declares his evil intentions:

> But I, that am not shap'd for sportive tricks,
> Nor made to court an amorous looking-glass;
> I, that am rudely stamp'd, and want love's majesty
> To strut before a wanton ambling nymph
> . . .
> Deform'd, unfinished, sent before my time
> Into this breathing world, scarce half-made up,
> And that so lamely and unfashionable
> That dogs bark at me, as I halt by them;
> Why, I, in this weak piping time of peace,
> Have no delight to pass away the time,
> Unless to see my shadow in the sun
> And descant on mine own deformity:
> And therefore, *since I cannot prove a lover,*
> . . .
> *I am determined to prove a villain.* (R3, I:1)

Richard exercised his villainy by murdering his own family. In the play we hear the outraged voice of Queen Margaret, widow of King Henry VI, when she curses Richard: "that fowl defacer of God's handiwork":

> O! Upright, just, and true-dispensing God,
> How do I thank thee that this carnal core
> Preys on the issue of his mother's body,
> And makes her pew-fellow with others' moan. (R3, IV:4)

Shakespeare's live models of unrelenting cruelty and moral depravity as Kierkegaard observed in his discussion of *Richard III*, and in the plays with the occasional appearance of characters who are examples of unflinching loyalty and sincerity, are the most effective way of teaching moral enlightenment. They constitute effectively disguised sermons on virtues and vices. Apart from portraying these models there are also direct discourses on values. However, in only one play, *Troilus and Cressida,* Shakespeare lets players engage in a philosophical dialogue on objectivity or relativity of values and on the subject of extrinsic means in pursuit of those ends.

We shall provide an analysis of those arguments after considering the nonethical uses of the words "good" and "bad" in certain plays, for example, in Hamlet's famous expression about life in Denmark, where there appears an undertone of meta-ethical language about the meaning of words like "good" and "bad" when he engages in a scholarly debate with his two university fellows, Rosencrantz and Guildenstern, whom he suspects of spying.

> Ham.: What have you, my good friends, deserved at the hands of Fortune, that she sends you to prison hither?
>
> Guild.: Prison, my lord!
>
> Ham.: Denmark's a prison.
>
> Ros.: Then is the world one.
>
> Ham.: A goodly one in which there are many confines, wards, and dungeons, Denmark being one o' the worst.
>
> Ros.: We think not so, my lord.
>
> Ham.: Why, then, 'tis not to you, for there is nothing good or bad, but thinking makes it so: to me it is a prison.
>
> Ros.: Why then, your ambition makes it one; 'tis too narrow for your mind. (HAM, II:2)

Hamlet refers in this passage to the title of the Montaigne essay, "That Taste of Good and Evil Depends in Large Part on the Opinion We Have of Them."[3] The content of Montaigne's essay reveals that the author is admiring the stoical response to natural happenings such as death and disease, and is not concerned with morality as such. Hamlet likewise does the same. He does not advocate moral nihilism in the line of Iago's "Virtue! A fig! 'Tis in ourselves that we are thus or thus" (OTH, I:3), nor in *Richard III* who says, "Conscience is but a word that cowards use" (R3, V:3). It has been suggested by some ethical theorists that Hamlet here is propounding an emotive theory of ethics, to wit, that ethical pronouncements are subjective expressions of one's emotions (a theory which is named by its critics "the Boos-Hurray theory of ethics"). That old misinterpretation of Hamlet's words is still in vogue. Professor A. D. Nuttall in his recent book *Shakespeare the Thinker* writes, "Hamlet, lost in a new subjective darkness, sees in Horatio an innocent Stoic, but when Hamlet appropriates Stoic language to himself, all else is gone. 'There is nothing either good or bad but thinking makes it so.' Harold Jenkins, in his note on this line . . . is clear that the sentiment expressed is a Stoic commonplace and that there is no suggestion at all of ethical relativism, but Jenkins's confidence is misplaced."[4] We maintain, on the contrary, that Jenkins's interpretation is correct.

Hamlet's pronouncement, though it seems to convey a metaethical view about the meaning of ethical words, is merely an expression of his disgust and claustrophobic feeling about Denmark. "Denmark's a prison," he declares to Rosencrantz and Guildenstern, who answer, "We think not so, my lord." "Why then, 'tis none to you; for there is nothing either good or bad but thinking makes it so: to me it is a prison." This exchange is a clear indication of Hamlet's subjective mode saying in effect, *De gustibus non est disputatum* ("In matters of taste, there can be no disputes."); it is a matter of perception whether Denmark is a prison. Portia echoes that thought when in *The Merchant of Venice* she says, "Nothing is good, I see, without respect: Methinks it sounds much sweeter than by day" (MV, V:1). Had Hamlet believed in ethical relativism he would not have said that his uncle committed a heinous crime and his mother adultery, the wrongs that his whole life was set to make right. Hamlet says to his mother about his unintentional killing of Polonius,

> A bloody deed! almost as bad, good mother,
> As kill a king, and marry with his brother. (HAM, III:4)

Here Hamlet uses good and bad in ethical terms. Hamlet regrets killing Polonius. "He weeps for what is done," says his mother (HAM, IV:2), while he is sorry that the victim was not Claudius.

Now consider what a number of writers have seen as the first serious moral and political argument in Shakespeare's plays, which occurs in *Troilus and Cressida* between Troilus and Hector.

> Tro.: Nay if we talk of *reason*,
> Let's shut our gates and sleep: manhood and honour
> Should have hare-hearts, would they but fat their thoughts
> With this cramm'd reason: reason and respect
> Make lovers pale, and lustihood reject.
> Hec.: Brother, she is not worth what she doth cost
> The holding.
> Tro.: What is aught but as 'tis valu'd?
> But value dwells not in particular will;
> It holds his estimate and dignity
> As well wherein 'tis precious of itself

> As in the prizer. 'Tis mad idolatry
> To make the service greater than the god.
>
> (TRO, II:2)

In these speeches there are three meta-ethical points. First, anything may have a value; second, but values are not mere expressions of a particular individual's sentiment. Thus we hear Albany's words, "Wisdom and goodness to the vile seem vile—Filths savour but themselves" (LR, IV:2). They are good in themselves. "Good alone is good without the name," said the king (AWW, II:3). Thus life is, for example, regarded as a universal value all through the ages from the code of Hammurabi, the Ten Commandments according to the Christian ethic, and the declaration of Independence, so we may say it is good in itself; it has intrinsic value. In addition, we do praise life. This love is in essence natural although it superficially seems to be cultural. The innate endeavor for survival is the trait of mouse and man. Third, some values are instrumental or extrinsic, they are means to an end and as such are dispensable when they are detrimental to end-values. Hector, in effect, is questioning the worth of an annihilating and no-win war for the sake of Helen and taking revenge at any cost. He questions the dogmatic pursuit of an absolute value, such as the absolute stand of the Chorus in Sophocles' *Antigone: Fiat justitia, Pereat mundus* (Let justice be done and may the world perish).

Hector's view is expressed by Coriolanus who denies that all values are time-dependent and so are absolutes; our virtues lie in the interpretation of Time.

> And Power! unto itself most commendable
> Hath not a tomb so evident as a chair
> To extol what it hath done. (COR, IV:7)

Shakespeare's presentation of Hector's philosophical idea is expressed a century later by David Hume: "When a man denominates another his enemy, his *rival*, his antagonist... he is understood to speak the language of self-love, and to express sentiments peculiar to himself.... But when he bestows on any man the epithets of *vicious*, or *odious*, or *depraved*, he then speaks another language and expresses sentiments in which he expects all his audience are to concur with him... he must move some universal principle of the human frame, and touch a string to which all mankind have an accord and symphony."[5]

There are indeed many expressions of moral sentiments through the Folio that speak of "some universal principal of the human frame that touch a string to which all mankind have an accord." The sin of ingratitude is such a heinous crime that in the eyes of Albany, Lear's two elder daughters are tigers in disguise. "Tigers, not daughters... most barbarous and degenerate" (LR, II:2). Albany expresses his utter disgust:

> If that the heavens do not their visible spirits
> Send quickly down to tame these vile offenses,
> It will come,
> Humanity must perforce prey on itself,
> Like monsters of the deep.

King Lear himself, using a powerful simile in the strongest terms, condemns ingratitude, the sin which goes against our natural love for our own parents:

> Filial ingratitude!
> Is it not as this mouth should tear this hand
> For lifting food to 't! (LR, III:4)

He denounces certain religious norms such as the Puritan verdict of death for adultery:

> Thou shalt not die for adultery! No.
> The wren goes to't and the small glided fly
> Does lecher in my sight.
> Let copulation thrive; for Gloucester's bastard son
> Was kinder to his father than my daughters
> Got 'tween the lawful sheets. (LR, IV:6)

Lear's opinion of adultery is expressed also in the Sonnets. Helen Vendler writes, "he [the Speaker] condones adultery throughout the 'Will' sonnets and elsewhere, and sees adultery as less criminal than adulterated discourse. For Shakespeare (the master of language) miscalling is the greater sin. The speaker is a rebel against received ideas."[6]

Consider also the relativity aspects of values, the conflict between loyalty and liberty, revolt against tyranny and the pledge of allegiance to a sovereign. Take Brutus's tortuous decision to do away with his beloved father-figure Caesar for fear that he would become a tyrant and his own love of liberty. Plutarch, the Roman historian, praises Brutus as a self-sacrificing defender of the Republic[7] while Dante damned him as an ungrateful traitor committing a sin.[8] For that sin Dante places him at the bottom of hell where a three-headed Satan is slowly chewing him. Brutus sacrificed his life and his family for the sake of the liberty of the Republic. Here between Dante and Plutarch we have a clear example of conflict between two irreconcilable value systems, the system of the Roman Republic and that of the Italian Catholic Church.

Shakespeare, who used Plutarch's *Lives* as a source for *Julius Caesar*, meticulously depicts the conflict in Brutus's mind, which leads to the assassination of Caesar, and the conflict between two camps, the Republicans who stood for liberty as a supreme value and those who stood for loyalty, the hero worshipers of the great conqueror, without showing his own preference, leaving the audience to make up their minds. At the end it is the loyal Antony who praises Brutus before burying him: this was the noblest Roman of them all. His life was gentle, and the elements so mixed in him that nature might stand up and say to all the world, "This was a man."

We shall return to Hector's speeches, which now touch upon both ethics and politics.

> Paris and Troilus you both said well,
> Unlike young men whom Aristotle thought
> Unfit to hear moral philosophy. (TRO, II:2)

Hector speaks about the idea of justice which appears in Plato's *Republic*, where Polemarchus, an interlocutor, quotes Simonides (a famous elegiac poet) on justice: "It is just to give to each what is owed to him"[9] and then he alludes to Plato's main concept of justice in the state as the harmonious well-ordered organization and to the soul as a working of the three parts in unison, which makes the citizen just and virtuous. The Stoic concept of a macro-cosmos and a micro-cosmos, which is adopted from Plato, appears many times in the folios. In *Troilus and Cressida*, Hector speaks:

> The reasons you alleged do more conduce
> To the hot passion of distemper'd blood
> Than to make up a free determination
> 'Twixt *right and wrong*; for pleasure and revenge
> Have ears more deaf than adders to the voice
> Of any true decision. Nature craves
> All dues be render'd to their owners; now

> What nearer debt in all humanity
> Wife is to the husband? . . .
> There is a law in each well-order'd nation
> To curb those raging appetites that are
> Most disobedient and refractory.
> If Helen then be wife to Sparta's king,
> As it is known she is, these moral laws
> Of nature, and of nations, speak aloud
> To have her back return'd: thus to persist
> In doing wrong extenuates not wrong,
> But makes it much more heavy. (TRO, II:4)

The question of genetic influence on character, for good or ill, appears in a number of Shakespeare's plays. In *The Tempest* Miranda says, "Good wombs have born bad sons." In *King Lear* Edmund and Edgar are both sons of Gloucester, yet Edmund is a villain while the second is a loyal offspring. Kent points out that "it is the star . . . Else one self mate and make could not beget such different issues" (LR, IV:3). In *All's Well that Ends Well* the First Lord speaks of one's life metaphorically as a web of "mingled yarn, good and ill together: our virtues would be proud if our faults whipped them not; and our crimes would despair if they were not cherished by our virtues" (AWW, IV:3). The King of France argues that a poor physician's daughter, without a title or property, could be virtuous and that heredity has nothing to do with virtue, a critique of the ideas held by the aristocracy and the belief in inherited nobility. He castigates Bertram's snobbery.

> 'Tis only title thou disdain'st in her, the which
> I can build up. Strange it is that our bloods,
> Of colour, weight, and heat, poured all together,
> Would quite confound distinction, yet stand off

> In differences so mighty. If she be
> All that is virtuous, save what thou dislik'st
> A poor physician's daughter, thou dislik'st
> Of virtue for the name; but do not so:
> From lowest place when virtuous things proceed,
> The place is dignified by the doer's deed:
>
> . . .
>
> Good alone
> Is good without name; vileness is so;
> The property by what it is should go,
> Not by the title.
>
> . . .
>
> honours thrive
> When rather from our acts we them drive
> Than our foregoers. (AWW, II:3)

The King's belief is familiar to us, although it was unusual in his time when it was generally believed that children of the nobility inherit their characters like their genes. Only a few years after Shakespeare's death, Sir Robert Filmer, upholder of the divine right of kings, argued in his *Patriarcha*, or *The Natural Power of Kings*, that the king should be obeyed since he was the direct heir of Adam in the male line, having his noble blood.[10] That book was severely criticized by the philosopher John Locke, the great defender of political rights and government by the consent of the people who inspired the America's Declaration of Independence. There are many echoes from Aristotle's philosophy as we have already observed as well as to other systems of morality such as the Stoic, the Epicurean, and the Cynic. Some players speak favorably of the Epicurean ethics in pursuit of pleasure and others unfavorably. Cassius says, "You know that I held Epicurus strong, and his opinion" (JC, V:4). Macbeth, however, calls his enemies "the English Epicures" (MAC, V:2), and Master Ford speaks of Falstaff saying, "What a damn Epicurean rascal is this?" (MWW, II:2).

JUSTICE AND MERCY

> "There is a law in each
> Well-order'd nation"
> —Hector (TRO, II:2)

In the final scene of *Henry IV*, part 1, Hotspur, the surname of Henry Percy, makes a significant philosophical statement just before he is killed by Prince Hal: "But thought's a slave of life and life time's fool" (1H4, V:4). We shall thereby sketch the political, social, and religious life that governed thought in Shakespeare's time.

There are many references in the Folio, direct and oblique, to catastrophic upheavals and revolutionary events of an age that Hume called rude and Samuel Johnson described as barbarous. Indeed to understand this very "rude" age is to understand some aspects of the plays that were unfairly criticized by those critics who paid attention only to the semantics of the text and were unmindful of the pragmatic dimension of the text in relation to the author and his audience. Roland Frye, in his careful study of *Hamlet*, shows the parallels between the events surrounding Mary Queen of Scots, her hasty marriage to the murderer of her husband, and many events from adultery to political intrigues to arson that were committed in her Scottish court. "My concern here," Frye writes, "is to establish the patterns of reactions to killing a king and marrying with his widow, so that we may judge how people in 1600 would most probably have approved Hamlet's reaction to Gertrude and Claudius. . . . Hamlet's . . . response was essentially the same as that which everyone in Europe (from king and pope and lord to pamphleteer and peasant) had to Mary Queen of Scots . . . no one in the sixteenth century would have argued, as T. S. Eliot did in the twentieth, that Hamlet had no objective correlative to justify and explain the strength of his aversion. Within the context of the audience and the time for which Shakespeare wrote, Hamlet's reaction to Gertrude's behavior simply would not have been regarded as either excessive or neurotic."[11]

Shakespeare was born in the period that saw the beginning of the modern world. Dramatic changes had already taken place and the heroes and villains of his plays became the stuff of his art. In his plays we see humanized the political power and economic rule of the feudal aristocracy that had passed to the new commercial interests that created the middle class with the consequent change in the class structure of British society. In a greater-than-life portrait we meet the magician who would no longer need magic or miracles to create new wonders that colonization and exploration would bring into European consciousness bringing thus a new vision of the world geographically. In his plays references to the scientific discoveries in Copernican astronomy and Galilean physics—and the New World—must have been thrilling for his audience to hear. Aided by the development of her great navy, England had become a European power in the age of science. It was the period of transition of the political and economic power of feudal aristocracy to the commercial middle class. We know that Hamlet had seen the closing of the gap between the classes, and the groundlings that stood to watch and listen together with the more affluent in the audience who sat each must have had differing reactions as they heard the prince exclaim, "By lord Horatio. These three years I have taken note of it. The age is grown so pickl'd that the toe of the peasant comes so near the heel of the courtier, he galls his kibe" (HAM, V:1). The world was very much in the bard's compass: there are references to America, the Indies, Spanish plunder of the Indians' gold, the defeat of the great Spanish Armada by the English in 1588, and to the voyage of the Shirley brothers to Persia and to "the Sophy," Shah Abbas I who had become an important trading partner in England's new international trade interests.[12]

A long-enduring issue in British public life centered on Catholicism, which gave rise to the Gunpowder Plot. Catholic protests had been unsuccessful against the severe penalties of the laws against the practice of their religion. Hoping to incite a general uprising of Catholics, a group of conspirators hid a huge store of gunpowder under the House of Lords sufficient to wipe out the entire government when Parliament met on November 5, 1605; fortunately for the Lords, the plot was discovered a week before the intended explosion. There are allusions to that plot and to the false oath of conspirators—the "Equivocators" in *Macbeth* when Macbeth states,

> If thou speak's false,
> Upon the next tree shalt thou hang alive
> Till famine cling thee; if thy speech by sooth,
> I care not if thy dost as much for me.
> I pull in resolution and begin
> To doubt the equivocation if the fiend
> That lies like truth; (MAC, V:5)

and in *Hamlet*,

> How absolute the knave is!
> We must speak by the card or equivocation will undo us.
> (HAM, V:1)

A Catholic manuscript that showed the way to confess without lying—to equivocate—was published during that time. Many Catholic conspirators were brutally tortured, hanged, and quartered. There are references to those killings in *Timon of Athens* in which Timon rages at Alcibiades for his pitilessness, "Nor sign of priests in holy vestments bleeding, Shall pierce a jot. There's gold to pay thy soldiers" (TIM, IV:3), and in *Measure for Measure,* in which a description of methods of torture is revealed by the evil Escalus, "To the rack with him! We'll touse you joint by joint, / But we will know his purpose" (MM, V:1). Those cruel punishments were continued for many years. Thus the *raison d'etre* for reform of the penal laws in England and for Article VIII of the American *Bill of Rights* against such cruel and unusual punishments.

Some Puritans who held strong anti-establishment beliefs against any form of state or church left their homes for the Massachusetts Bay Colony aboard a ship with John Harvard among them. They are the Pilgrim fathers of American history. Although, as we have said, it is highly problematic to ascribe a particular religious or political bias drawn from the dialogue in Shakespeare's plays, we can be certain that Shakespeare would have had no sympathy for the vicious hatred that led to the torture of Catholic priests. There are various condescending references to Puritans although nothing as harsh as Jonson's in his play *The Alchemist.* There Jonson writes, for example, "that she would make a puritan of the devil if he should cheapen a kiss of her."

Puritans who carried the Bible with them constantly indoors and out were referred to as Gospelers. There are also scornful references to Catholic rituals practiced by the head of the state such as Queen Margaret's on her husband's religiosity:

> I thought King Henry had resembled thee
> In courage, courtship, and proportion
> But all his mind is bent to holiness,
> To number Ave-Maries on his beads;
> His champions are the prophets and apostles;
> His weapons holy saws of sacred writ;
> His study is his tilt-yard, and his loves
> Are brazen images of canoniz'd saints.
> I would the college of the cardinals
> Would choose him pope, and carry him to Rome.
>
> (2H6, I:3)

There appears in *All's Well that Ends Well* a mocking of both Catholic and Puritan religious sanctions. Charbon, the Puritan, eats meat on Friday while Poysam eats fish! The Clown (Clo) points out that "For young Charbon the puritan, and old Poysam the papist, how some'er their hearts are severed in religion, their heads art both one" (AWW, I:3).

Shakespeare refers to Cicero's *Natura Deorum* in which he argues against the Epicurean idea of chance in the universe in favor of the Aristotelian theory that the cosmos, like an artifact, reveals order and purpose and thus should the human world be governed.[13] In *Julius Caesar*, Casca, one of the conspirators, asks Cicero's advice. He speaks of "civil strife in heaven" such as the sudden appearance of a storm, lightening, just before the appearance of Caesar in the Capitol. Cicero responds to Casca's superstitious beliefs saying, "they are portentous things." Cicero continues: "Indeed, it is a strange-disposed time; but men may construe things after their fashion, / Clean from the purpose of the things themselves" (JC, 1:3). In *Troilus and Cressida*, Ulysses says,

> Degree being vizarded,
> The unworthiest shows as fairly in the mask.
> The heavens themselves, the planets, and this centre
> Observe degree, priority, and place. (TRO, 1:3)

And Hector, in the same play, observes,

> There is a law in each well-order'd nation
> To curb those raging apetities
> That are most disobedient and refactory. (TRO, 2:2)

Henry VIII and his two daughters, one of whom was "bloody Mary," and her half sister Queen Elizabeth and her successor, King James, were all absolute monarchs. However, there was an appearance of justice. There was a Parliament, the House of Lords, and the Church, with a monarch at its head and trials by appointed judges. The two houses were summoned by the order of the sovereign from time to time and their members were directly chosen by the sovereign, and indirectly selected by clan-lords.

Magna Carta (1215), which was established during the reign of King John, was meant to limit the absolute power of the monarch and protect the liberties of feudal magnates. It declares, "No freeman shall be taken, or imprisoned—or exiled, or any otherwise destroyed—but by the lawful judgement of his Peers, or the Law of the Land." The charter was upheld and sworn to by every monarch although it was neglected by the Tudors. It was an ancestor of the law of *habeus corpus* and of the American slogan, "no taxation without representation."

There are, however, no references in the Folio to that law or its intent, or to the idea of natural rights except perhaps in Cade's speech, "I thought ye would never have given out these arms till you did recover your ancient freedom" (2H6, IV:8).

Neither is there any reference to the divine right of kings except an indirect reference in *Richard II* in which Bishop Carlisle consoles Richard saying, "Fear not my lord: that power that made you King hath power to keep you King in spite of all" (R2, III:2). He then defends Richard's right to the throne on the ground that he is "the figure of God's majesty, his captain, steward, deputy elect, anointed, crowned," and may not "be judg'd by subjects of inferior birth" (R2, IV:1).

Contrary to Dr. Johnson's opinion, the defense of Richard's right to kingship by the bishop is by no means an indicator of Shakespeare's support of the Divine Right of Kings. In the same play Bolingbroke claims that he, too, is "a prince by fortune of my birth, near to the King in blood" (R2, III:1). Shakespeare, who was for a time connected to the king's court, is only indirectly critical of that right and of the idea of the inherent virtues of blood. He neither defends the right of the people to govern themselves, which at any rate was not a political issue, or the right of kings to rule over their subjects because of their blood. Though he is severely critical of tyrannous kings, princes, and cardinals, his critical remarks in general are restrained compared to Marlow who lets a player ask, "What right had Caesar to the empire?" in *Jew of Malta*. In *Julius Caesar*, Brutus speculates on the danger of allowing Caesar to be crowned king:

> How that might change his nature, there's the question:
> It is the bright day that brings forth the adder:
>
> . . .
>
> Fashion it thus: that what he is, augmented,
> Would run to these and these extremes;
> And therefore think him as a serpent's egg
> Which, hatched, would, as his kind, grow mischievous
> And kill him in his shell. (JC, II:1)

We should remember also that freedom of playwrights was curtailed by an office called "Stationer's Register" with the warning that no playwright could express opinions against the monarch or "representing any modern Christian king." In 1606, Chapman's *Byron* was suppressed, following other suppressions, and a general prohibition of plays was ordered.

In 1595 the Bard was aware of the censorship of plays, including his own *Richard II*. Written in 1595 it was lightly censored when it reached the stage with the elimination of the playing of the scene in which Richard abdicates the throne: according to a number of Shakespearean scholars, this censorship was provoked because the scene was associated with public agitation on the part of supporters of Essex, Queen Elizabeth's lover, for Elizabeth to abdicate the throne in favor of Essex. Essex became a national hero in 1596 when he led the expedition against Spain that conquered Cadiz. In *Henry V* there is a reference to Essex's public acclaim. Here the Chorus proclaims:

> But now behold
> In the quick forge and working-house of thought,
> How London doth pour out her citizens.
> The mayor and all his brethren in best sort
> Like to the senators of the antique Rome,
> With the plebeians swarming at their heels.
> Go and fetch their conquering Caesar in. (H5, V:1)

Shakespeare included censorship in his list of the state's villainies in Sonnet 66: the Speaker says he is

> Tir'd with all these, for restful death I cry
> As to behold desert a beggar born
> And needy nothing trimm'd in jollity,

And purest faith unhappily forsworn,
And gilded honour shamefully misplac'd,
And maiden virtue rudely strumpeted,
And right perfection wrongfully disgraced,
And strength by limping away disabled,
And art made tongue-tied by authority . . .

Shakespeare, while attacking tyrannous kings, lords, and priests, was unsympathetic to the rule of the masses, to a revolt of citizens against the state and to attempts to eliminate the right to hold private property. In this he follows Aristotle's criticism of direct democracy and the abolition of private property. In *Henry VI*, part 2, the mob leader Jack Cade revolts against the state and property:

> Cade: There shall be
> in England seven halfpenny loaves sole for a
> penny; . . . and I will make
> it felony to drink small beer. All the realm shall be
> in common . . .
> Dick: The first thing we do, let's kill all the lawyers.
>
> (2H4, IV:2)

Shakespeare's reference to a sort of primitive communism, an egalitarian community without private property is intended as a criticism of Sir Thomas More's *Utopia* (translated in 1551), Montaigne's fictional picture of the happy primitive life of Brazilian Indians, and of Plato's propertyless-guardian-ruled *Republic*, their ancestor. He describes the "ideal" society in the words of the inept Gonzalo to Sebastian and Antonio in *The Tempest*:

> Gon.: I' the commonweath I would by contraries
> Execute all things; For no kind of traffic

>   Would I admit; no name of magistrate;
>   Letters should not be known; Riches poverty,
>   And use of service, none; contract, succession,
>   Bourn, bund of land, tithe, vineyard, none;
>   No use of metal, corn, or wine or oil;
>   No occupation; all men idle, all;
>   And women too, but innocent and pure;
>   No sovereignity . . .
>   All things in common nature should produce
>   Without sweat or endeavor; treason, felony
>   Sword, pike, knife, gun, or need of any engine,
>   Would I not have. But nature should bring forth
>   Of its own kind, all folson, all abundance,
>   To feed my innocent people.
> Seb.:   No marrying among his subjects?
> Ant.:   None, man; all idle, whores and knaves.
> Gon.:   I would with such perfection, govern, sir,
>   To excel the golden age. (TMP, II:1)

The entire passage conveys a mockery of More's *Utopia*, which like Erasmus's *The Praise of Folly* [14] was a serious joke in the form of a thought experiment, and not a serious discourse like Plato's *Republic* for the construction of an ideal state. In that book a tale is told by a sailor, Hythloday, about an island in the southern hemisphere called *Utopia*. In Utopia ("utopia" literally means "nowhere"), all things are held in common, as Plato prescribed for the state ruled by guardians who were the educated citizens.

The idea of the Golden Age as described by Gonzalo suggests Shakespeare's reading of Montaigne who imagines life among South American Indians, although the phrase was current among Renaissance historians who referred to the period of Marcus

Aurelius, the Stoic philosopher-king, as the time when the condition of the human race was most happy and prosperous.

So much on the players' mocking words about the Golden Age with its abolition of private property, the wisdom of the mob, and anarchy. Now let us consider the positive passages on the necessity of law and order in civil society and on justice and mercy. In *Troilus and Cressida* we find this exchange between Ulysses and Hector:

> Ulyss.: Degree being vizarded,
> The heavens themselves, the planets, and the centre
> Observe degree.
> Hect.: There is a law in each well-order'd nation
> To curb those raging appetites that are
> Most disobedient and refractory. (TRO, II:2)

Here again we note the Stoic concept of macrocosm, an ordered universe (degree in heaven) and a microcosm, the inner world of the person, which also should be ruled by the dictates of reason.

We have noted above Shakespeare's awareness of Cicero's *De Natura Deorum*, that the universe, like a book, exhibits a certain order.[15] That book, like the clockwork cosmos of scientists, became the argument of design with God as the author of the universe. Plato in the *Republic* speaks of cosmic order, which for him is the model of justice and of the harmonious working of the three parts of his ideal state.

In *Henry V* a similar metaphor is used by the Duke of Exeter speaking to the king, the Archbishop of Canterbury, and to others:

> For government, though, high and low and lower,
> Put into parts, doth keep in one consent,
> Congreeing in a full and natural close,
> Like music.

Cant.: Therefore doth heaven divide
       The state of man in diverse functions.
       For so work the honey bees,
       Creatures that by rule in nature
       Teach the act of order to a peopled kingdom.
                                               (H5, I:-2)

At the end of *Richard III* Richmond sums up the civil war:

England hath long been mad, an scarr'd herself;
The brother blindly shed the brother's blood,
The father rashly slaughter'd his own son,
The son, compell'd, been butcher to the sire:
All this divide York and Lancaster,
. . .
Now civil wounds are stopp'd, peace lives again. (R3, V:4)

Henry VI also laments civil dissension "a viperous worm that gnaws the bowls of the commonwealth"(1H6, III:1), and John of Gaunt, eulogizing "This earth of majesty. . . . That England, that was wont to conquer others" nevertheless laments that England "Hath made a shameful conquest of itself" (R2, II:1). That a government of law and order governed by a just, compassionate, and fair sovereign is a necessary condition for survival of civil society recurs often in the plays. In *Henry IV*, part 2, King Henry boasts of the rule of law and justice in his domain. His concept of impartiality and fairness is reminiscent of Plato's dialogue *Euthyphro* in which Euthyphro is under a sacred obligation to prosecute homicide even when the accused is his own father. King Henry speaks to the chief justice like Euthyphro when he mocks the court and the absolute monarchy of the Turkish sultan, the *Amurath,* a commander of a territory who wins power and holds it by force.

Henry: This is the English, not the Turkish court;
Not Amurath an Amurath succeeds
But Harry, Harry.
. . .
You all look strangely on me:
[to the chief justice] and you most;
You are, I think, assur'd I love you not.
. . .
How might a prince of my great hopes forget
So great indignities you laid upon me?
What! rate, rebuke, and roughly send to prison
The immediate heir of England!
. . .

Ch. Just.: I then did use the person of your father;
The image of his power lay then in me:
And, in the administration of his law,
While I was busy for the commonwealth,
Your highness pleased to forget my place
The majesty and power of law and justice,
The image of the king whom I presented,
And struck me in my very seat of judgement
Whereupon, as an offender to your father
I gave bold way to my authority
And did commit you.
. . .

Henry: You are right, Justice; and you weight this well;
Therefore still bear the lance and sword
And I do wish your honours may increase
Till you do live to see a son of mine
Offend you and obey you as I did.
So shall I live to speak my father's words:

> "Happy am I that have a man so bold
> That dare do justice on my proper son." (2H4, V:2)

In the context of justice and law there are further references to the Ottoman dynasty, and to other kingdoms such as the Persian as well as the monarchically governed Islamic sects, the Sunni and the Shia, and in fictions such as Thomas Preston's play, *Cambyses, King of Persia*. In *Henry IV*, part 1, Falstaff alludes to Cambyses who, according to Herodotus, lashed the sea in arrogant fury when he lost a sea battle to the Greeks.

> I must speak in passion, and I will do it
> in King Cambyses' vein. (1H4, II:4)

The strong ruler Henry V proclaims:

> We are not tyrant, but a Christian king unto whose
> Grace our passion is as subject
> As our wretches fetter'd in our prisons. (1H4, I:2)

In Sonnet 107 there is a reference to the tyrant Queen Elizabeth and her monument:

> And thou in this shalt find thy monument
> When tyrants' crests and tombs of brass are spent.

Shakespeare, who knew of the beheading of young queens and princes and lovers, and the corruption of the English and the Scottish courts, is alluding to these institutions when a player in Hamlet says, "Something is rotten in the state of Denmark."

In *Troilus and Cressida,* Ulysses argues philosophically like

Socrates in the *Republic*. Socrates argues against Thrasymachus's belief that "Justice is nothing but the interest of the strong," that pursuit of power alone would destroy the social order and eventually destroys those who use power without justice, and, he says, "there is justice even among a gang of thieves." He describes what goes on the soul of a tyrant who is afraid of his own shadow.

"All his life he is beset with fear and is full of compulsion and distraction" (Bk 11), "the tyrannical man is the most miserable of all" (Bk 9). In *Pericles: Prince of Tyre,* Pericles repeats that description:

> . . . tyrants' fears
> Decrease not, but grow faster than the years.
> . . .
> How many worthy princes' blood were shed,
> To keep his bed of blackness unlaid ope. (PER I:2)

Ulysses also speaks about the misuse of power.

> Force should be right; or rather, right and wrong—
> Between whose endless jar justice resides—
> Should lose their names, and so should justice too
> Then every thing includes itself in power,
> Power into will, will into appetite;
> And appetite, a universal wolf,
> So doubly seconded with will and power,
> Must make perforce a universal prey,
> And last eat up himself. (TRO, I:3)

The philosophical issue of justice is in the foreground of *The Merchant of Venice.* It is evident that Shakespeare chose Venice, the foremost business and maritime trading center of Europe, as a fitting context for the story he wanted to tell, of business transactions tragically affected by a loss of cargo at sea, and the theme he wanted to embody, the nature of justice tempered by mercy. In this play, justice is subjected to severe inquiry as it raises the question of abstract ideas related to human experience in real life. It is Shylock who pleas for justice: he bitterly complains of insults heaped upon him because of his religion, and particularly focuses on Antonio who has asked him for help by lending him money to save his friend's business. Now that Antonio must forfeit the bond, Shylock demands retributory justice under the law governing his contract with Antonio, which requires that Antonio forfeit a pound of flesh from his own body. He further argues that he is *human* although he has been subjected to treatment that assumes he is different from the Christian Venetians among whom he lives, different and somehow less human than they are and thus deserves less than human treatment from them. In what way different? "I am a Jew. Hath not a Jew Eyes? Hath not a Jew hands, organs, dimensions, senses, affections, passions? fed with the same food, hurt with the same weapons . . . as a Christian is? If you prick us do we not bleed?" Then suddenly Shylock's plea becomes more specific: he wants justice interpreted as measure for measure, which, in this case could mean Antonio's death: "and if you wrong us shall we not revenge? If we are like you in the rest, we will resemble you in that. . . . The villany you teach me I will execute" (MV, III:1).

The key Shakespeare uses to open justice to argument is the issue of mercy. Portia's description of mercy as a *quality* puts it into a metaphorical context that echoes the third of Aristotle's ten categories. As a quality, mercy is a natural attribute of emotions—"The quality of mercy is not strain'd/ It droppeth as the gentle rain from heaven"—just as the quality of hardness in a rock is a natural attribute of a substance, the first of Aristotle's categories. Furthermore, it cannot be forced ("strain'd," constrained). Shakespeare treats it, again in Aristotelian terms, as an "*affective quality*" since, as Portia argues, it is perceptible in its consequences: "It blesseth him that gives and him who takes." At the end of the play Shakespeare reminds the audience that mercy cannot be compelled: When Shylock has lost everything and has been forced to become a Christian, Gratiano, a bona fide Venetian Christian, not satisfied with the verdict and not moved by the quality of mercy any more than Shylock was, delivers his own vengeful verdict:

> Had I been a judge, thou shouldst have had ten more
> [godfathers]
> To bring thee to the gallows, not to the font. (MV, IV:1)

The theme of justice contending with mercy also drives the plot of *Measure for Measure*. In both plays, as in others, there are allusions to both the Old Testament and the New Testament. Portia, in response to Shylock's plea for justice, pleads for mercy. She points out that mercy is "an attribute of God himself" (MM, IV:1), a reference to a passage in the Sermon on the Mount, "Be compassionate as your Father is compassionate" (Luke 6:36). When Shylock demands interest on his loan to Antonio, he cites biblical precedence, recalling the story of Jacob who managed to get interest indirectly by using a stratagem that added to his wealth measured in the number of his ewes and lambs (Gen. 30: 25–43). Antonio asks, "is your gold and silver ewes and rams?" and Shylock replies, "I cannot tell; I make it breed as fast as I can," to which Antonio remarks, "The devil can cite scripture for his purpose" (MV, I:3).

In *Measure for Measure* the title and theme have two sources. Mark, in explaining the parables to the Chosen Twelve, quotes

Jesus saying, "Take notice of what you are hearing. The amount you measure out is the amount you will be given" (Mark 4: 24-25). In Matthew's account of "The Sermon on the Mount" he quotes Christ's words, "Do not judge, and you will not be judged; because the judgements you give are the judgements you will get, and the amount you measure out is the amount you will be given" (Matt.7:1-3). Thus, with exquisite Shakespearean irony, the duke declares,

> The very mercy of the law cries out
> Most audible, even from his proper tongue
> "An Angelo for Claudio, death for death!"
> Haste still pays haste, and leisure answers leisure,
> Like doth quit like, and Measure still for Measure.
>
> (MM, V:1)

The villainous character of the ironically named Angelo, who has sentenced Claudio for a sin of which he himself is guilty, is drawn from the following lines in Matthew, "Hypocrite! Take the plank [splinter] out of your own eye first, and then you will see clearly enough to take the splinter out of your brother's eye" (Matt. 7:5-6).

Shakespeare was aware of the current interpretation of Machiavelli's theory that justified the ruler in all matters in terms of protecting his own power, which was identical with the state, for the purpose of establishing a stable society. Various playwrights of that time, such as Ben Jonson in *Volpone* and George Chapman in *All Fools*, ridiculed the popular conception of Machiavellian political ideology. In *Timon of Athens* there is a reference to "real politics," the Machiavellian justification of force for "Reasons of State," where one of the three strangers says,

> But I perceive
> Men must learn now with pity to dispense
> For policy sits above conscience. (TIM, III:2)

Shakespeare in *Henry IV* (V:4) shows that the name Machiavelli connotes an evil person. "You! Alecon! that notorious Michievel." The fullest expression of a Machiavellian character is Iago, who frankly boasts of his duplicity.

We will observe in our discussion of morality that Shakespeare's presentation of moral discourses falls under a philosophical view called Objective-Relativism. The same is true of his political views. This is the view that underlies the many speeches condemning tyranny, authority over the arts, anarchy, mockery of mob rule, as well as the pleas for justice and a well-ordered society along with mercy and tolerance; it is the view that presents objective values while recognizing the relativity of values when ultimate values are in conflict, exemplified by his impartial representation of Brutus's and Antony's actions where liberty stands in opposition to loyalty.

Finally, we must look from a wider perspective where Shakespeare lets his great tragic and comic personae, Hamlet and Falstaff, speak their minds against wanton war. First Hamlet:

> Even for an eggshell.
> . . .
> When honour's at the stake.
> . . .
> I see
> The imminent death of twenty thousand men,
> That, for a fantasy and trick of fame,
> Go to their graves like beds. (HAM, IV:4)

Falstaff in his famous soliloquy on honor mocks the aristocratic code that demands fighting to death for honor: "What is honour?" he asks rhetorically and concludes, "Therefore, I'll have none of it." (See also chapter 2 on "Falstaff: A Parody of Socrates.")

Along with antiwar speeches in Shakespeare's plays we also hear the echoes of the Stoics who are pleading for peace among nations and within man's soul. "One touch of nature makes the whole world kin," says Ulysses. "Men must endure their going here, as their coming hither. Ripeness is all," says Edgar (LR, V:2).

NOTES

PREFACE

1. Text citations to plays and sonnets are in parentheses.Semantics and pragmatics refer to two of the three divisions of semiotics, the science of signs; the third division is syntax, which considers the formal problems of language.

2. M. M. Bakhtin, *Speech Genres and Other Late Essays*, V. W. McGee, trans. (Austin: University of Texas Press, 1986).

INTRODUCTION

1. Abbreviations of Shakespeare's works are standard, as is the order in which the works appear, that of the Folio. Citations follow *Shakespeare: Complete* Works, edited by W. J. Craig (London: Oxford University. Press, 1969). All italics in quotations are mine.

2. Benson Mates, *Stoic Logic* (Berkeley: University of California Press, 1960).

3. Farhang Zabeeh, *What Is in a Name?* (The Hague, Netherlands: Martinus Nijhoff, 1960).

4. John Dryden, "To My Honored Friends," first published, 1666, from *Essay of Dramatic Poesy,* 1668.

5. Francis Bacon, *The New Organon*, from *The Essays of Francis Bacon*, John Pitcher, ed. (London: Penguin Books, 1985), pp. 48–49.

6. Francis Bacon, *The Advancement of Learning*, from *The Essays of Francis Bacon*, John Pitcher, ed. (London: Penguin Books, 1985), p. 118.

7. For details see C. Clark, *Shakespeare and Science* (New York: Haskell House, 1970), p. 16. "Many believe that Shakespeare was referring to the early telescope in *All's Well that Ends Well* when he uses the word "perspective": "His scornful perspective did learn me" (V:3). The same word is also used in *Twelfth*

Night: "Same face, one voice and two persons. A natural perspective, that is and is not" (V:2).

8. Friedrich Nietzsche, *Thus Spake Zarathustra*, A. W. Kaufman, trans. (New York: Vantage Press, 1971).

9. Jonathan Bates, *The Genius of Shakespeare*. (New York: Picador, 1997).

10. Frank Kermode, ed., *Four Centuries of Shakespearean Criticism* (The Avon Library, 1965), p. 33. "To the Memory of My Beloved, The Author Mr. William Shakespeare," from the preface reprinted in the first folio, 1673.

11. George Santayana, *Interpretations of Poetry and Religion* (Ann Arbor: University of Michigan Press, 1921). In "Three Philosophical Poets." Santayana writes that "Shakespeare is remarkable among the greater poets for being without a philosophy and without a religion."

12. Jan Kott, Trans. *Shakespeare Our Contemporary* (New York: W. W. Norton, 1966), pp. 26–27.

13. A. C. Bradley, *Shakespeare's Tragedies*, 2nd ed. (New York: C. Fadiman, 1966), p. 253.

14. Henry James, "The Birthplace," in *The Short Story of Henry James*, edited by C. Fadiman (New York: Random House, 1945).

15. Approximate dates according to the *Columbia Encyclopedia*, 6th ed. (New York: Columbia University Press, 2000).

16. Erasmus, *The Education of a Christian Prince*, L. K. Born, trans. (New York: W. W. Norton, 1936).

CHAPTER ONE: PHILOSOPHY AND POETRY

1. Friedrich Nietzsche, *The Birth of Tragedy*, Walter Kaufmann, trans. (New York: Vantage, 1974).

2. Gilbert Ryle, private letter.

3. Plato, *Apology, Phaedrus*, and *Phaedo*, in *The Dialogues of Plato* Benjamin Jowett, trans. (New York: Random House, 1932).

4. *Ion* is the title of Euripedes' trag-comedy; the name is also used by Plato for one of his dialogues.

5. Virgil, *Aeneid*, book 2, pp. 671–75.

6. Plato, *Phaedrus*, 244. Bk7, p. 180.

7. Jonson, Ben, "Ode" in *Works*, H. Herferd, ed. (Oxford, UK: Clarendon Press, 1926).

8. Peter Ackroyd, *Shakespeare's Biography* (New York: Talese, 2005), p. 292.

9. Francis Bacon, *The Advancement of Learning*, from *The Essays of Francis Bacon*, John Pitcher, ed. (London: Penguin Books, 1985), bk. 7, p. 180.

10. Francis Bacon, *The Essays of Francis Bacon*, John Pitcher, ed. (London: Penguin Books, 1985), p. 49.

11. John Hale, *The Civilization of Europe in the Renaissance*, "On Civility" (New York: Atheneum, 1994); Shulwod, ed. *William Shakespeare* (1778), p. 13.

12. Thomas Hobbes, *Leviathon*, 1651.

13. David Hume, *A Treatise of Human Nature* (Oxford: Oxford University Press, 1961), p. 45. See Farhang Zabeeh, *Hume Precursor of Modern Empiricism* (The Hague, Netherlands: Martinus Nijhoff, 1965).

14. See Pico della Mirandola, *The Renaissance*, Peter Walter, trans. (New York: Modern Library, 1954).

15. Frank Kermode ed., *Four Centuries of Shakespearean Criticism* (The Avon Library, 1965), includes Ernest Jones, "Hamlet and Oedipus" In Jones's essay titled "Hamlet Diagnosed," he writes, "two explanations, therefore, of the delay . . . to fulfill his father's demand for vengeance is that to Hamlet the thought of incest and patricide combined is intolerable to be born," p. 451.

16. John Donne, "The First Anniversary," in *Selected Poems*, N. A. Sharrby, ed. (New York: Appleton Century, 1958). Donne's poem is a response to the Copernican Revolution, which was supported by Giordano Bruno who visited England in 1580. He argued on mathematical grounds that the infinity of the universe is incompatible with the geocentric theory. The Copernican hypothesis was strengthened when Galileo discovered four new planets through the use of the telescope in 1510. The "new philosophy" refers to the Copernican System; the treatise as published in 1543.

17. William Blake, *The Complete Poems*, W. H. Stevenson, ed. (London: Longman Group, 1980).

18. Quoted in the *International Philosophical Quarterly* 3:2 (May 1963), p. 315.

CHAPTER TWO: FALSTAFF: A PARODY OF SOCRATES

1. Harold Bloom, *Shakespeare: The Invention of Human* (New York: Riverside Books, 1998), p. 298.

2. M. M. Philips, *In the Adages of Erasmus* (Cambridge, UK: Cambridge University Press, 1943).

3. This description of Socrates' death is also recounted by E. M. Moore, *Shakespeare's Henry V* (Mirror Press, 1956).

4. Plato, *Phaedo*, p. 117, *Dialogues*, section 252.

5. Plato, *Symposium*.

6. Heraclitus, *Fragments*, p. 103.

7. Plutarch, *Lives of the Noble Grecian and Roman*.

8. Bloom, *Shakespeare*, p. 66.

9. Naseeb Shaheen, *Biblical References in Shakespeare* (Newark: University of Delaware Press, 1993), pp. 3–4.

10. According to W. C. Chew, the author of *The Crescent and the Rose* (New York: Oxford University Press, 1937), in a section called "Moslems on the London Stage," pp. 497–546, a play under the title of *Three English Brothers* by Anthony Nixon, circulated in London and was published in 1608. It was based on a report written by the Sherley brothers about travel to Persia (1564–1568).

11. Guilder was the name of a Dutch coin that circulated in the coastal cities of the Persian gulf. The "Sophy" refers to Shah Abbass of the Safavi Dynasty who paid guilders to the British mercenaries for the use of their artillery.

12. Aristophanes, *The Clouds,* in *Aristophanes: The Acharniaus, the Clouds, the Knights, the Wasps*, trans. and ed. by B. B. Rogers (Cambridge, MA: Harvard University Press, 1986).

13. Plato, *Symposium*, p. 208.

14. Erasmus, "The Praise of Folly," in *Adages: A Collection of Proverbial Wisdom* (New York: W. W. Norton, 1936).

15. Leszak, Kolakowski, "The Priest and the Jester" in *Towards Marxist Humanism* (New York: Grove Press, 1968), p. 35.

16. Plato, *Republic*, bk 1, 344c.

CHAPTER THREE: PLATO'S VOICE

1. "Ficino's translations were an immediate best-seller. The first edition, 1484, was furnished in 1025 copies." *The Cambridge History of Renaissance Philosophy*, Charles B. Schmitt and Quentin Skinner, eds. (Cambridge, UK: Cambridge University Press, 1990).

2. T. W. Baldwin, *William Shakespeare's Small Latin and Less Greek* (Urbana, IL: University of Illinois Press, 1949), p. 348.

3. Lewis Wyndham, *The Lion and the Fox: The Role of Heroes in the Plays of Shakespeare* (New York: University Paperback Press, 1930).

4. Stephen Kegel, *Imagining in Shakespeare: A History of Taste and Vision* (New York: Macmillan, 2005), pp. 113–29.

5. Plato, *Symposium*.

6. Plato, *Republic*, 506.

7. Aristotle, *Metaphysics*, in Richard McKeon, ed., *The Basic Works of Aristotle* (New York: Random House, 1971), p. 1094.

8. Helen Vendler, *The Art of Shakespeare's Sonnets* (Cambridge, UK: Cambridge University Press, 1997), p. 446.

9. Plato, *Republic*, bk. 7, 517.

10. Ibid., bk. 10.

11. Plato, *Symposium*, 103.

12. *Phaedrus*, 252

13. Plato, *Symposium*, 13.

14. Ibid.

15. Ibid

16. The verse in Horace is rendered in English by Aaron Kunin in *Publications of the Modern Languages Association of America*, 1124 (January 2009). "I have finished a monument more lasting than bronze and loftier than the pyramid's royal pile. One that no wasting rain, no furious north wind can destroy, or the countless chain of the ages' flight. I shall not altogether die, but a mighty part of me shall escape the death-goddess. On and on I shall grow fresh with the glory of aftertime."

17. Plato, *Charmides*, 4.

18. Plato, *Alcibiades*, 1, 133.

19. Chriton Collins, J.D (1862-1918).

20. Plato, *Phaedo*, 90-96.

21. Sophocles, *Oedipus Rex*, 49.

22. Fyodor Dostoyevsky quoted in B. F. Skinner, *Beyond Freedom and Dignity* (New York: Alfred Knopf, 1971).

23. Genesis, 3:3.

24. John Hale, *The Civilization of Europe in the Renaissance* (New York: Atheneum, 1994), p. 567. Hale questions the intentions of the playwright concerning astrology, overlooking Shakespeare's mockery in his plays and poems, when he writes, "Whether the intention was to put the audience on the side of Edmund in *King Lear* or, more probably, condemn his disbelief is unclear. . . ."

25. Dante, *Purgatory*, canto X5, 58-72.

26. Plato, *Apology*.

27. See the chapter on Aristotle on "shuffle off this mortal coil." See *The Aeneid*, Allan Mandelbaum, trans. (New York: Macmillan, 1971), "when death has once dissolv'd her mortal frame." Shakespeare used the *Aeneid* when Hamlet in act II, scene 2, as the director of the play asks the players to enact a passage from the *Aeneid*, book 2, p. 670.

28. Hans Reichenbach, *Philosophy of Science* (Berkeley: University of California Press, 1948).

29. Stephen Greenblatt, *Hamlet in Purgatory* (Princeton, NJ: Princeton University Press, 2002).

30. Peter Ackroyd, *Shakespeare: The Biography* (New York: Nan A. Talese, 2005), p. 430.

31. John Donne, The poem appears in "Divine Poems."

32. Helen Vendler, *The Art of Shakespeare's Sonnets*, p. 25.

33. Samuel Taylor Coleridge, *Shakespearean Criticism* (London: Middletown, 1931).

34. Thomas Acquinas, "On Soul," in *Summa Theologica*.

35. Lucretius, *"The Folly of Fear of Death,"* in *Of the Nature of Things*.

36. Dante, "Inferno," canto 3.

37. From a different perspective Nutall, in his *Shakespeare the Thinker*, sees certain allusions to Christianity when he writes, "Shakespeare probably did think of Christ when he conceived the character of Cordelia. Christian love is an evident reality in that dread pre-Christian world of *King Lear,*" p. 316; in his discussion of *Measure for Measure* he writes, "Is there a Christ figure in this play? There is, but it is not the sort of person we might expect to see in such a part. The answer is Angelo," p. 200.

38. Søren Kierkegaard, *Fear and Trembling*, Walter Lowrie, trans. (Princeton, NJ: Princeton University Press, 1974), p. 132.

39. Quoted in Gabriel Rabe, "The Question about Faculties," *Kant's Critical Essays*, M. M. Knox, trans. (Oxford, UK: Clarendon Press, 1966), p. 334.

CHAPTER FOUR: ARISTOTLE: POETRY AND HISTORY

1. Aristotle, *Poetics*, 105, *The Basic Works of Aristotle*, Richard McKeon, ed. (New York: Random House, 1971). All references to Aristotle are drawn from this work.
2. Ibid., pp. 1448-1.
3. Ibid., p. 1461.
4. Gottlob Frege, "On Sense and Reference." In Farhanq Zabeeh, E. D. Klemke, and Arthur Jacobson, ed., *Readings in Semantics* (Champaign: University of Illinois Press, 1985).
5. Jonathan Bates, *The Genius of Shakespeare* (New York: Oxford University Press, 1997).
6. Ann Barton, *Essays, Mostly Shakespearean* Cambridge, UK: Cambridge University Press, 1996.
7. Aristotle, *Categories*, part 1, chapter 5, 1451–1460.
8. Aristotle, *Poetics*, chapter 6.
9. Jonathan Bates, "The Mirror of Life." *Harpers* (April 2007).
10. Aristotle, *Ethics*, bk. 3
11. There is an interesting footnote to these lines in Hardin Craig's *The Complete Works of Shakespeare*, where Craig notes that "Aristotle says this of political philosophy in the *Nichomachean Ethics*." Shakespeare's line is paralleled by a sentence in Bacon's *Advancement of Learning* (bk. 2): "Is not the opinion of Aristotle worthy to be regarded wherein he saith that young men are not fit auditors of moral philosophy?" Sir Sidney Lee, in his *Life of Shakespeare,* App. 2, points out that both Bacon and Shakespeare relied in all probability on a summary paraphrase of Aristotle's *Ethics* translated from Italian and published in 1547, in which *political*, as referring to civil society, is made the equivalent of *moral* as understood in the Renaissance period. Sidney Lee, *Life of Shakespeare* (New York: Macmillan, 1923), p. 876, note to page 165.
12. Stephen Booth, *Shakespeare's Sonnets* (New Haven, CT: Yale University Press, 1969), p. 306.

13. George Santayana, "The Absence of Religion in Shakespeare," in *Essays in Literary Criticism* (New York: George Scribner's Sons, 1956), p. 137.

CHAPTER FIVE: ON THINKING AND SPEAKING

1. Plato, *Sophist*, 164.
2. Michel Montaigne, *The Complete Works of Michel Montaigne*, D. M. Frame, trans. (New York: Knopf, 1959). I quote two passages from Montaigne that clearly indicate his belief in what is now called Perspectivism. In the essay, "Apology for Raymond Sebon," he writes, "When I play with my cat, who knows if I am not a pastime to the cat more than she is to me." In "On Experience," he writes, "Upon the highest throne in the world we are seated still upon our arses," p. 196. Perspectivism also appears in Shakespeare's *Hamlet* when Hamlet speaks of Denmark as a prison; his perspective is not shared by his two classmates and in his mocking conversation with Polonius about a cloud, Hamlet asks the Lord Chamberlain, "Do you see yonder cloud that's almost in shape of a camel?" Polonius agrees, "By the mass, and 'tis like a camel, indeed." Hamlet continues to expose the servile character of Polonius, willing to agree with anything his prince says:

   Ham.: Methinks it is like a weasel
   Pol.: It is backed like a weasel.
   Ham.: Or like a whale?
   Pol.: Very like a whale. (HAM, III:2)

The same view is expressed in Hamlet's conversation with the messenger Osric about the weather, whether it is cold or hot.
3. Aristotle, *Poetics*, 20, 145, 146.
4. E. H. Gombrich, *Art and Illusion* (Princeton, NJ: Princeton University Press, 1972).
5. Harold Bloom, *Modern Critical Interpretation of Shakespeare* (New York: Riverside Press, 2000).
6. Aristotle, *Physics*, Vol 3-5.
7. Frederick Turner, *Shakespeare and the Nature of Time* (Oxford, UK: Clarendon Press, 1977).

8. Plato, *Timaeus*.
9. Martin Heidegger, *Being and Time*, John Marquarrie and Edward Robinson, trans. (New York: Harper & Brothers, 1962), p. 469.
10. Bertrand Russell, *A History of Western Philosophy* (New York: Simon and Schuster, 1948), pp. 44–47.
11. Matthew 6:34.
12. Rudolph Carnap, *Reading in Semantics*, Farhang Zabeeh et al, ed. (Urbana, IL: University of Illinois Press, 1974).
13. Northrup Frye, *Shakespeare's Richard II* (New Haven, CT: Yale University Press, 1986). The same view is expressed in Hamlet's conversation with the messenger Osric about the weather, whether it is cold or hot.
14. Gilles Deleuze, *Kant's Critical Studies* (Minneapolis: University of Minnesota Press, 1985).
15. Augustine, *Confessions*, chapter 20.
16. Ludwig Wittgenstein, *Tractatus Logico-Philosophicus*, C. K. Ogden, trans. (London: Routledge & Kegan Paul, 1935).

CHAPTER SIX: SUBJECTIVITY

1. Thomas Nagel, *The View from Nowhere* (Oxford, UK: Oxford University Press, 1986), chapter 5.
2. Ludwig Wittgenstein, *Tractatus Logico-Philosophicus*, C. K. Ogden., trans. (London: Routledge & Kegan Paul, 1935).
3. In standard reference works on Greek mythology Prometheus's gifts to humankind do not include speech or language. See Henry Nettleship, J. E. Sandy's Oskar, and Oscar Seyffert, *Dictionary of Classical Antiquities* (Meridian Library, 1957) and Edward Tripp, *The Meridian Handbook of Classical Mythology* (New York: New American Library, 1970).
4. Harold Bloom, *Shakespeare: The Invention of the Human* (New York: Riverside Books, 1998).

CHAPTER SEVEN: THE PRAGMATIC DIMENSION

1. A. D. Nuttall, *Shakespeare the Thinker* (New Haven, CT: Yale University Press, 2007) quotes Derrida.

2. Søren Kierkegaard, "Eulogy of Shakespeare," in *Fear and Trembling*, H. Herford, ed. and trans. (Princeton, NJ: Princeton University Press, 1945), p. 105.

3. Michel Montaigne, *The Complete Works of Michel Montaigne*, D. M. Frame, trans. (New York: Knopf, 1959).

4. See Nuttall, *Shakespeare the Thinker*.

5. David Hume, *Inquiry concerning Human Understanding*, Selby Bigg, ed. (Oxford, UK: Oxford University Press, 1960), p. 277.

6. Vendler, Helen, *The Art of Shakespeare's Sonnets* (Cambridge, UK: Cambridge University Press, 1997).

7. Plutarch, *Lives* (London: Everyman Library, 1910).

8. Alighieri Dante, *The Divine Comedy*. Allen Mandelbaum, trans. Berkeley: University of California Press, 1982).

9. Plato, *Republic*, bk. 1, Benjamin Jowett, trans. (New York: Random House, 1932).

10. Robert Filmer, *Patriarcha or The Natural Power of Kings*, 1686.

11. Roland M. Frye, *The Renaissance Hamlet* (Princeton, NJ: Princeton University Press, 1984), p. 110.

12. Wyndham Lewis, *The Lion and the Fox: The Role of the Hero in the Plays of Shakespeare* (New York: Harper & Row, 1929).

13. Cicero, *De Natura Deorum*, H. Rackham, trans. (Cambridge, MA: Harvard University Press, Loeb Classical Library Editions, 1961), number 268.

14. Erasmus, *The Praise of Folly*, quoted in Bertram Russell, *A History of Western Philosophy* (London: Allen & Unwin, 1961).

SELECTED BIBLIOGRAPHY

Ackroyd, Peter. *Shakespeare: The Biography.* New York: Nan A. Talese, 2005.

Aristophanes, *The Clouds*, B. B. Rogers, trans., in *An Anthology of Greek Drama*, Charles Alexander Robinson, ed., Holt, Rinehart & Winston, 1964.

Aristotle. *The Basic Works of Aristotle.* Richard McKeon, ed., Place: Publisher, 1941.

Auden, W. H. *Lectures on Shakespeare.* Arthur Kusch, ed., Princeton, NJ: Princeton University Press, 2000.

Bacon, Francis. *The Essays of Francis Bacon.* John Pitcher, ed., London: Penguin Books, 1985.

Baldwin, T. W. *William Shakespeare's Small Latin and Less Greek.* Urbana: University of Illinois Press, 1944.

Barton, Ann. *Essays, Mostly Shakespearean.* Cambridge, UK: Cambridge University Press, 1996.

Bate, Jonathan. *The Genius of Shakespeare.* New York: Picador, 1997.

Bloom, Harold. *Shakespeare: The Invention of the Human.* New York: Riverside Books, 1998.

Booth, Stephen. *Shakespeare's Sonnets.* New Haven, CT: Yale University Press, 1969.

Bradley, A. C. *Shakespearean Tragedy.* 2nd ed. New York: F. Fadiman, 1966.

Chew, W. C. *The Crescent and the Rose.* New York: Oxford University Press, 1937.

Cicero, *De Natura Deorum*, H. Rackham, trans. Harvard: Harvard University Press, (Loeb Classical Library Editions, no 268), 1961.

Clark, C. W. *Shakespeare and Science.* New York: Haskell House, 1970.

Craig, Hardin, ed. *The Complete Works of Shakespeare.* Chicago: Scott Foresman and Company, 1951.

Craig, W. J., ed. *Shakespeare: The Complete Works.* London: Oxford University Press, 1974.

Dante, Alighieri. *The Divine Comedy*, Allen Mandelbaum, trans. Berkeley: University of California Press, 1982.

Deleuze, Gill. *Kant's Critical Philosophy.* Minneapolis: University of Minnesota Press, 1985.

Donne, John. *Selected Poems*. N. A. Sharby, ed. New York: Publisher, 1958.

Erasmus. *Adages*. Cambridge, UK: Cambridge University Press, 1979.

———. *The Education of a Christian Prince*. L. K. Born, trans. New York, W. W. Norton, 1936.

Filmer, Robert. *Patriarcha or The Natural Power of Kings*. Published posthumously, 1680.

Frye, Northrup. *Shakespeare's Richard II*. New Haven, CT: Yale University Press, 1986.

Frye, Roland M. *The Renaissance Hamlet*. Princeton, NJ: Princeton University Press, 1984.

Gibbon, Edward. *The History of the Decline and Fall of the Roman Empire*. New York: The Book Club Associates, 1972.

Goddard, Harold A. *The Meaning of Shakespeare*, 2 vols. Chicago: The University of Chicago Press, 1951.

Greenblatt, Stephen. *Hamlet in Purgatory*. Princeton, NJ: Princeton University Press, 2002.

———. *Will in the World*. New York: W. W. Norton, 2004.

Heidegger, Martin. *Being and Time*. John Macquarrie and Edward Robinson, eds. New York: Harper & Row, 1962.

The Holy Bible (King James Version).

Homer. *The Iliad*. L.V. Rieu, trans. West Drayton, UK: Penguin Classics, 1949.

Hume, David. *History of England*, vol. 5. Philadelphia: Levis & Weaver, 1810.

———. *Inquiries*. Selby-Bigg, ed. Oxford, UK: Oxford University Press, 1960.

———. *A Treatise of Human Nature*. Oxford: Oxford University Press, 1961.

Jones, Katherine Duncon, ed. *Miscellaneous Prose, Philip Sydney {Sidney}*. Oxford: Oxford University Press, 1973.

Jonson, Ben. *Works*, H. Herford, ed. 11 vols. Oxford: Clarendon Press, 1925.

Kermode, Frank, ed. *Four Centuries of Shakespearean Criticism*. The Avon Library, 1965.

Kierkegaard, Søren. *Fear and Trembling*, H. V. Houd, ed. and trans. Princeton, NJ: Princeton University Press, 1945.

Kott, Jan. *Shakespeare Our Contemporary*. New York: W. W. Norton, 1966.

Lee, Sidney. *Life of Shakespeare*, rev. ed. New York: Macmillan, 1924.

Lewis, Wyndham. *The Lion and the Fox: The Role of the Hero in the Plays of Shakespeare*. New York: University Paperback Press, 1930.

McGinn, Colin. *Shakespeare's Philosophy: Discovering the Meaning Behind the Plays.* New York: Harper's Perennial, 2006.

Mirandola, Pico della. see Peter Walter, *The Renaissance.* New York: New American Library, 1959.

Montaigne, Michel. *The Complete Works of Michel Montaigne,* D. M. Frame, trans. New York: Everyman's Library, 1959.

Nietzsche, Friedrich. *Thus Spake Zarathustra.* A. W. Kaufman, trans. New York: Vantage Press, 1971.

Nuttall, A. D. *Shakespeare the Thinker.* New Haven, CT: Yale University Press, 2007.

Plato. *The Dialogues of Plato (Apology, Ion, Phaedrus, Phaedo, The Republic, Symposium),* Benjamin Jowett, trans. New York: Random House, 1932.

Plutarch. *Lives.* London: Everyman Library, 1910.

Reichenbach, Hans. *Philosophy of Science.* Berkeley: University of California Press, 1957.

Santayana, George, *Interpretations of Poetry and Religion.* Ann Arbor: University of Michigan Press, 1921.

Spevack, M., ed. *The Harvard Concordance to Shakespeare.* Cambridge, MA: Harvard University Press, 1973.

Tripp, Edward. *The Meridian Handbook of Classical Mythology.* New York: Penguin, 1974.

Turner, Frederick, *Shakespeare and the Nature of Time.* Oxford: Clarendon Press, 1971.

Vendler, Helen, *The Art of Shakespeare's Sonnets.* Cambridge, UK: Cambridge University Press, 1997.

Virgil. *Aeneid*, 2:671-675.

Wittgenstein, Ludwig. *Tractatus Logico-Philosophicus.* C. K. Ogden, trans. London: Routledge & Kegan Paul, 1935.

Zabeeh, Farhang. *Hume: Precursor of Modern Empiricism.* The Hague: Nijoff, 1963.

———. *What Is in a Name? An Inquiry into the Semantics and Pragmatics of Proper Names.* The Hague: Nijhoff, 1968.

———, ed. *Readings in Semantics.* Champaign: University of Illinois Press, 1974.

INDEX

abbreviations of Shakespearean titles, 10
Abraham, 129–30
"Absence of Religion in Shakespeare, The," 27
"abstract," 135
abstract knowledge, 135
Academus (demigod), 24
Achilles, 35, 63, 88, 92, 96, 124
Ackroyd, Peter, 119
Adages, 77
Adages of Erasmus, The, 56
Adam and Eve, 220
Adriana, 192, 222
adultery, 232
Aeneid, 35, 117
afterlife, Christian belief in, 119
afterlife in heaven, 122
Agathon, 91–92, 149
Aguecheek, Sir Andrew, 167
Ahreman, the god of darkness, 72
Ahura-Mazda, the god of light, 72
air, 205
Albany, 230–31
Alchemist, The, 239

Alcibiades, 66, 67, 79, 239
Alcibiades I, 95–97
All Fools, 253
All's Well that Ends Well, 21–23, 167, 188
American *Bill of Rights*, 239
Amores, 45
Amurath, 247
anatomy, 37
Anaxagoras, 99
Andogynous, 93–94
animals compared to humans, 156
anthropomorphism, mockery of, 134
Antigone, 42
antischolastic views, 12
Antonio, 165
Antony, Mark, 59, 170
Antony and Cleopatra, 20–21, 170, 202, 205
Apemantus, 78–79
Apollo, 32, 100
Apologia for Poetry, 40
Apology, 33, 60, 110
Aquinas, Thomas (Saint), 52–53
Ariel, the spirit, 28

Aristophanes, 32, 93–94
Aristotle
    authority of, 19
    "Categories" of, 136
    definition of courage, 145
    Ethics, 49
    ideas of, 47
    influence on Shakespeare, 17
    natural philosophy of, 49–50
    philosophy of Christianity, 53
    "the philosopher," 33
    theory of tragedy, 139
    view of world in ten categories, 171
"Aristotle's checks," 144
"arrows of time, the," 170
Art of Love, The, 89
arts, dramatic, 132
As You Like It, 44, 49, 62, 98, 145, 188–90, 200
Asclepius, the god of health, 56–57
astrology, 101, 112
astrology, mockery of, 18, 110
astronomy, 37
ataraxia (contentment), 104
"Athenian Stranger, The," 78
Atlas, 100
Augustine, 52, 184, 209
Augustus, 89
Aurelius, Marcus, 245–46
Ausgezeichnete Moglichkeit (splendid possibility), 176
Austin, J. L., 17, 159, 161

Bacon, Francis
    called "the poet of science," 19
    and criticism of poetry and dramatic art, 40
    and heat caused by motion, 19
    and "word-play," 161
Bakhtin, M. M., 13
Banquo, 178
Banquo's ghost, 127
"Bard, the," *see* Shakespeare, William
Bardolph, 70
Barton, Ann, 135
base authority, 18–19
Bassanio, 164
Bassano, 18
bastard, 164
Bate, Jonathan, 24, 135, 140
behaviorism, 216
beheadings, 249
Being and Time, 176
beliefs, anti-establishment, 239
Benedick, 62
"Bergamo dance, the," 83
Berowne, 18, 51, 188, 194
Bertram, 188, 234
Bible, the, 70, 173, 239
Biblical References in Shakespeare, 70–71
Birch, W. J., 11
black magic of names, 17
Blake, William, 53
blasphemy, 196

blood, circulation of, 19
"bloody Mary," 241
Bloom, Harold, 12, 56, 170, 211
Boleyn, Anne, 218
Bolingbroke, 203, 242
bondage, 99
Book of Nature, The, 20, 37
Boyle, Robert, 19
Brabantio, 160–61
Brahe, Tycho, 51
"brute facts," 159, 166
Brutus, 49
Bucophlus, 136
Burgundy, Duke of, 22
"Buridan's Ass, the," 60
Byron, 243

Cade, Jack, 103, 244
Caesar, assassination of, 232
Caesar, Julius, 59
Caesar, Octavius, 202
Caliban, the devil, 28
Cambyses, King of Persia, 249
cannibals, 155
Cardo, 183
Carnap, Rudolf, 180
Cartesian ontology, 209–10
Cassius, 27, 49, 97, 103, 104, 135, 158, 202, 204, 235
Castiglione, 12
Catherine, 218
Catholic rituals, 239
Catholics, and censorship, 89

Celia, 98
censorship, 89, 243
Cephalus, 78–79, 173
Chamberlin, Lord, 218
Chapman, George, 253
character, genetic influence on, 234
Charles II, king, 19
Charmian, 20–21
Charmides, 95
Charon, 128
Chaucer, 70
chemistry, 19
Chiron, 93
Chosen Twelve, the, 252
Christian ethic, 230
Christianity, 53, 122
Church of England, 119
Cicero, 15, 172
Cinna, 204
"civil strife in heaven," 240
Clarence, Duke of, 128
Claudio, 124, 125, 253
Claudius, 36, 43, 229, 236–37
cloud forms, 169
Clouds, The, 32, 74–76
Coleridge, 123
Collins, Churton, 97
Columbus, Christopher, 19
Comedy of Errors, 72, 188, 192, 222
Concordance, 172
Confessions, 184

conscience, 12, 18, 117, 209–10, 217, 218, 224
"consciousness," 209–10
contemplation, 153
Copernican astronomy, 237
Copernican revolution, 50–51
Cordelia, 109, 214
Corin, 49
Coriolanus, 142
cosmic order, 246
cosmology, 132
Craig, Hardin, 97
Cressida, 63, 158, 161
Cupid, 61–62
"cut purses" (pickpockets), 66
Cymbeline, 190
Cynic philosophers, 52, 78–79, 235

Dante, 86, 110–11, 128
Dasein, 176
De hominis dignitato (*Oration on the Dignity of Man*), 41–42
De Natura Deorum (*On the Nature of the Gods*), 246
death
  as a blessing, 117
  fear of, 114
  imagery of, 114
  inevitability of, 107
Declaration of Independence, 230, 235
deconstructionists, 223

Deleuze, Gille, 183
della Mirandola, Pico, 12, 41, 52, 82
Delphi, inscription at, 95
Delphi, shrine of, 100
demonology, 113
Derrida, Jacques, 223
Descartes, 210
Desdemona, 29, 204
destiny, 100
determinism, 101
Dewey, John, 217
dialogue, meta-ethical, 224
Dimmesdale, Arthur, 197
Dionysus, 32
Diotima, 77, 90, 122
Divine Comedy, 111
Divine Love, 225
"Divine Poems," 120
Divine Right of Kings, 242
dogs, 156
Donne, John, 51, 119
doomsday, 176
Dostoyevsky, 101
Drake, Francis, 65
Dromio of Syracuse, 188, 222
Dryden, John, 19
duality, idea of, 86
Dumaine, 23–24
Duncan, 149, 168

earth, 205
Edgar, 78, 108–109, 234, 255

Edmund, 27, 52, 105, 108–10, 143, 234
elephants, 156
Eliot, T. S., 11, 27, 237
Elizabeth, queen, 39, 241
Elizabethan age, 32, 37, 53
Elizabethan culture, 15
Emilia, 29
emotions, 64, 228
Empedecles, four ancient substances of, 205
empiricism, 40
End of Time, 174
England, penal laws in, 239
English Renaissance, 26
Epictetus, 29, 104
Erasmus, 12
Eros, the Greek god of love, 61
Escalus, 239
Esperimentum Crucible, 118
Essex, Earl of, 120
Eternity, 176–77
eternity, Christian belief in, 119
ethical relativism, 228
ethics, 132
Ethics: The Book of Kings, 93–94
"Eulogy of Shakespeare," 130
Euripides, 34, 134
Euthyphro, 58, 247
Euthyphro, 247
expectation (future), 184
extrinsic values, 230
eyes, as mirror of the soul, 96

fairies, 207
Falstaff
  death of, 56
  as the "Elizabethan Socrates," 56
  nickname "bare-bones," 196
  and Puritans, 70
Farsi, 71
fatalism, 27, 99, 108
feelings and language, 213
Ferdinand, 158, 165
Ferdosi, 93
Feste, 78, 162, 205–206
Ficino, Marsilio, 81–82, 172
Fideism, 77–78
Filmer, Sir Robert, 235
fire, 205
First Book of the Republic, 173
First Folio (Jonson's), 24–25
Folio, the, 27, 55, 236
Folly of Fear and Death, The, 126
"Forms of life," 30
Fortinbras, 60
free will, 99
Frege, Gottlob, 84, 134–35, 159
Freud, Sigmund, 43, 217
Frye, Northrup, 180
Frye, Roland, 236

Galilean physics, 237
Galileo, 25, 46–47
Gargrave, Thomas, 29–30
Garnet, Henry, 163
Gaunt, John of, 247

Genesis, 173
Geneva Bible, 70–71
Genius of Shakespeare, The, 24
geography, 37
geometry, 85
Gertrude, 142, 209, 212, 236–37
Ghost in the Machine, The, 216
ghosts, 50, 118, 126–27
Gide, André, 11
Gilbert, William, 19
Glendower, 113
Gloucester, Earl of, 108
Goethe, 169–70, 198
Golden Age, the, 245
Golden Mean, 140
Gombrich, E. H., 170
Gospelers, 239
Gratiano, 252
Great-Souled Man, 140
Greenblatt, Stephen, 26, 119
Grey, Queen Lady, 200
Griffith, 127–28
"groundlings," 26, 237
Guildenstern, 154, 227–28
"Gunpowder Plot, The," 163

habeus corpus, 241
Hades, 128
Hale, John, 39, 110
Hamlet
　and cloud shapes, 169
　eulogy of man, 12, 41
　and the ghost, 50
　and the "mouse-trap," 26, 37, 106
　and Plato's faculty of psychology, 43
　skepticism of old natural philosophy, 51
　soliloquy ("Now I am alone . . ."), 35
　soliloquy about man, 42
　thoughts on paranormal events, 50
Hamlet, 22, 50
Hamlet in Purgatory, 119
Hammurabi, code of, 230
Harvard, John, 239
Harvey, William, 19
Hawthorne, 197
Heaven, 74
Hector, 35, 146, 229, 230, 233
Hecuba, 35, 63
Heidegger's metaphor, 176
Helen, 46
Hell, 128
hemlock, 55, 77, 101, 116
Henry IV, 55, 122, 175, 188, 207
Henry V, 22–23, 56, 138
Henry V, 46
Henry VI, 138, 154, 204
Henry VIII, 98, 127–28
Henry VIII, 218, 241
Heraclitus, 150
Hercules, 69
Herodotus, 133
Hesiod, 173

Hester, 197
Hippolyta, 37, 185
Hobbes, Thomas, 39
Holefernes, 45
Holingshed's Chronicles, 139
Homer, 34
Homeric tragedies, 37
homicides, prosecution of, 247
Horace, 93
Horatio, 22, 37, 50, 52, 118, 166, 228
Hotspur, 59, 113
Howard, Luke, 169–70
human autonomy, 99
human power of choice, 106
humanism, 18
humanists, Renaissance, 12
Hume, David, 32, 40, 59, 123, 152, 153, 231, 236
Hythloday, 245

Iago, 52, 192, 221
idealists, 96, 219
ideas, theory of, 85
Idols, 20
Ignoratio Elenchi (irrelevant conclusion), 40
illusions, 211
imagination, 24, 37, 38, 40, 41, 45, 46, 133, 153
imagination versus reason, 39
immortality, idea of, 91, 92, 114, 119, 121

Imogen, 190
In Praise of Folly, 77–78
Indians, American, 155
inductive inference, 222
Inferno, 128
ingratitude, 231
instinct, 69, 142, 143, 144
"institutional facts," 159, 166
intrinsic values, 230
introspection, 96
inwardness, 217
Ion, 34
Isaac, 129
Islamic sects, 249
Italian Catholic Church, 232
Italian Renaissance, 81–82
Italianita, 82

Jacob, 252
Jacques, 200–201
Jaffe, Irma B., 9
James, King, 39
Jenkins, Harold, 228
Jesus Christ, 253
Jew of Malta, The, 18
Jocastra, 100
Johnson, Samuel, 236
Jones, Ernest, 43
Jonson, Ben, 24–25, 30, 82, 253
judgment, 13, 45, 64, 73, 78, 130, 148, 179
judges, country, 207
Julius Caesar, 139, 193, 204, 232

justice, 80, 174, 233, 250–51
justice tempered by mercy, 251

Kant, Immanuel, 130, 184, 213, 217
Kantian Philosophy, 183
Kant's Critical Philosophy, 183
Katherine, 127–28
Kegell, Stephen, 83
Keller, Helen, 213
Kent, Earl of, 108
Kierkegaard, Søren, 129, 225
King John, 164
King Lear, 21–22, 61, 143, 205, 234
King's Men, the, 39

Laertes, 210
Lafeu, 21
language, Semantic Dimension of, 160
Lavinia, 152
Lawrence, Friar, 49
Lazarus, 70
Leibniz, 177
Leigh, Irvin, 147
Leonato, 49
Lesser Hippias, 79
Lewis, Wyndham, 11
life, themes of, 92
Lincentio, 145
Lincoln's Inn, 120
Lives, 232

Locke, John, 235
logic, 132, 145, 154
logic, laws of, 177
logic, syllogistic, 160
Lone, G. G., 147
Lorenz, Konrad, 142
Love as a noble madness, 37
Love's Labour's Lost, 18, 23, 45, 51, 162, 188
Lucentio, 46–47
Luciana, 222
Lucretius, 13, 26, 125, 126, 163
Luther, 53

Macbeth, 137, 149, 168, 216
Macbeth, Lady, 149
Macbeth , 122, 145, 149, 163, 178
Macduff, 144, 166, 180
Macduff, Lady, 144
Machiavelli, 12
Machiavelli's theory, 253
macrocosm, 246
macrouniverse, 18
Magna Carta, 241
magnetism, 19
magnets, 34
Malcolm, 166
Margaret, Lady, 154
Margaret, queen, 226, 239
Maria, 167
Marlow, 64
Marlowe, 18, 44
Martius, 152

Mary Queen of Scots, 236–37
Massachusetts Bay Colony, 239
materialism, 18, 125
mathematical axioms, 177
mathematics, 85, 177
matter and mind, 210
McGinn, Colin, 11
Measure for Measure, 124, 220, 239, 252
mechanistic theory, 99
mediaeval beliefs, 18
meditation, 41
memory (past), 184
mentalism, 216
Merchant of Venice, The, 18, 72, 149, 164, 229, 250–51
Merry Wives of Windsor, The, 55, 64
metalanguage, 193
metaphorical expressions, 168
metaphors, 60, 86, 95, 152, 167–70, 189
metaphysical expressions, 161
"metaphysics," 46
Metaphysics, 160
microcosm, 246
microhuman, 18
Midsummer Night's Dream, 22, 37, 45, 64, 83
miracles, 112
Miranda, 166, 234
mirror, as a symbol of self-revelation, 210
Montaigne, 18, 41, 77–78, 155

Moore, J. R., 56
moral awareness, 217
moral concepts, 225
moral enlightenment, 225
moral responsibility, 99
morality, systems of, 235
More, Thomas, 12, 82
Mowbray, Thomas, 158
Much Ado about Nothing, 49, 62
mystics, 177

names
  black magic of, 17
  clan, 199
  discussed, 58–59
  of fairies, 207
  functions of, 195
  and magicians, 196
  proper, 196
  and titles, 204
Natural Philosophy, 21, 46–47
Natural Power of Kings, The, 235
Nature/Nurture, 153
Navarre, King of, 23–24
Neo-Platonism, 12
Nerissa, 149
New Behaviorism, 101
New Testament, the, 252
Nicomachean Ethics, 17, 117, 132, 140
Nietzsche, 17, 24, 213
nobility, inherited, 234
"noble savage," 41

Nothing, discussed, 180–83
Novum Organum, 20
Nuttall, A. D., 11, 228

Objective-Relativism, 224, 254
Odysseus, 134–35
Oedipus, 99–100
Oedipus at Colonnus, 101
Oedipus Complex, 43
Oedipus Rex, 100
Old Testament, the, 252
Oldcastle, 71, 73
"On Sense and Reference," 134–35
On the Advancement of Learning, 135
On the Freedom of the Will, 102
Ophelia, 50–51, 82, 210
oracles of Western culture, 31
Oration on the Dignity of Man, 82
Orlando, 188, 190–91, 200–201
Othello, 29, 204
Othello, 160–61, 192, 221
Ottoman dynasty, 71, 249
Ovid, 44–45

Pandarus, 224
parables, 252
"paragon of animals, the," 82
parallel axiom, 21
Paris, 224
Parolles, 167
particulars, evaluation of, 85
passion, 64
Patriarcha, 235

Paudarus, 161
Pausanius, 91–92
Percy, Henry, 236
Pericles, 172
Pericles: Prince of Tyre, 173, 250
Persia, 71
Phaedo, 56
Phaedo, 99
Phaedrus, 37
Philebus, 196
Phillips, M. M., 56
philosopher-clowns, 78
philosophers, analytic, 32
philosophers, ancient, 12
philosophical issues, 12–13
philosophy, Western, 11–13
phoenix, 94
Phoenix and the Turtle, The, 90, 94
Phronisterion, 74
physics, 37, 132
Plato
  and the Allegory of the Cave, 83–84
  and criticism of poetry, 32
  dialogues of, 15–16
  Forms and shadows, 81
  ideas, theory of, 85
  Laws, 78
  trinity of ideas, 86
  view of censorship, 89
Platonic Academy, 28
plays, prohibition of, 243
Plotinus, 52–53

INDEX 281

Plutarch, 232
Poems, the, 55
poet laureate, 19
Poetics, 17, 132
poet-philosopher dispute, 53
"point of view," 211
Polemarchus, 233
political rights, 235
Polonius, 35–36, 50, 103, 123, 135, 138, 149, 162, 164, 207, 212, 229
Portia, 49, 72, 149, 150, 229, 252
pragmatics, 159
Praise of Folly, 18, 245
predestination, 99, 101
Preston, Thomas, 249
Priam, 35
priests, executions of, 90
primitivism, 156
Prometheus, 100
Prometheus Unbound, 213
Prospero, 28–29, 154, 155, 165
Protagoras, 52
Proust, Marcel, 195
providential design, 103
psychologists and analysis, 219
Ptolemaic universe, 22
Ptolomaic astronomy, 51–52
puns, 207
Purgatory, 118
Purgatory, 110
purification of the soul, 112
Puritans, 196, 239

Pyrrhonian ladder metaphor, 193
Pyrrhonic skepticism, 18
Pythagoras, 112
Pythagorean myth, 101

"quality of nothing," 182

Rape of Lucrece, The, 193
rationalism, mockery of, 53
real versus shadows, 83–84
reality, 211
reason, 40–41, 64, 193
Regan, 109
regicide, 137
Reichenbach, Hans, 117
religious sanctions, 240
Renaissance cultures, 32
"representations" in Shakespeare's plays, 135
Rhetoric, 145
Richard II, 39, 82–83
Richard III, 128, 139, 200, 204
Richardson, William, 11
Roman Republic, 232
Romeo and Juliet, 29, 49, 205, 197, 204
Roosevelt University in Chicago, 9
Rosalind, 62–63, 92, 112, 190–91
Rosencrantz, 48, 227–28
Ross, 144
Russell, Bertrand, 177
Ryle, Gilbert, 32, 209–10

sand clock, 186
Santayana, George, 11, 27
Scarlet Letter, The, 197
Scholastic theology, 172
Schopenhauer, 17, 102, 126
scientists, 32
Sebastian, 165
Sein-Zum-Tode, 176
self-knowledge, 95
self-mutilation, 101
self-revelation, 214
Semantic Dimension of language, 160
semantics, 12, 18, 134, 137, 159, 161, 236
semiotics, 159
Sermon on the Mount, 147, 252–53
sermons, religious, 225
serpents, as symbols of deception, 220
Sextus Empiricus, 156
sexuality, 65
shadows versus real, 83–84
shadow-substance, 215
"Shafalus," 174
Shaheen, Naseeb, 70
Shah-Nameh, 73
Shakespeare, William
  and Aristotle's influence, 17
  and belief in his own immortality, 92–93
  and biblical references, 70–71
  as a critic of spoken words, 157
  critics of, 27
  dedication to *Venus and Adonis*, 45
  eulogy of, 30, 39
  and extensive knowledge of classical literature, 224
  inscription on monument at grave site, 13
  mastery of language, 158
  and mathematics and science, 21
  mockery of astrology, 110
  on moral and political values, 224
  philosophic ideas, 224
  and Plato's faculty of psychology, 42
  and the privacy over our thoughts, 153
  and reason, will, and passion, 42
  as a secular humanist, 12
  and special uses of language, 166
  and Stoic philosophers, 17
  and superstitions, 197
  and themes of life, 92–93
  tragedies and comedies, 25
  vice and virtue, presentation of, 225
Shakespeare: The Invention of the Human, 56, 213–14
Shakespeare the Thinker, 228
Shakespearean titles, abbreviations of, 10
Shaw, Bernard, 11
Shelley, Percy Bysshe, 19, 213
Shia, the, 249

Shylock, 29, 30, 251, 252
Sibyl, 55
Sidney, Philip, 40
sight (present), 184
similes, 95, 168
Simonides, 173, 233
Siren Song, 133
Skinner, B. F., 101
skull, York's, 142
slavery, rejection of, 18, 29–30
Socrates
  and autonomy, 99
  criticism of poets, 34
  death scene, 56
  and philosophical issues, 15
  and presentation of poets, 33
  as a Sophist, 33
"Socratic dialogues," 15–16
Solomon, King, 20
Sophocles, 37, 42, 99–100, 134
soul, the, 33, 112, 120, 151, 209
"sovereign reason," 20
Spalding, K. J., 11
speech, verbal, 151
"Speech Act," the, 161
Spinoza, 26
"Spirit," 113
"Stationer's Register," 243
Stephano, 153–54
Stevens, Wallace, 169
Stoicism
  and cosmology, 18
  moral perceptions of, 29

Stoics' moral doctrine, 99
stone of time, 100
Strepsiades, 74–76
"string theory," 170
subjectivity, 217
Suffolk, 218
Sunni, the, 249
sun-worshipers, 71
"superego," 217
survival, 230
syllogism, 162
syllopsism, 96
Symposium, 64–65, 84
"Syntactics," the, 160
syntatics, 159
Sysiphus, 100

tabula rasa, 96
Talbot, 215–16
talking, act of, 151
Taming of the Shrew, The, 46, 55, 144
tautology, 117, 160, 163
Tehran, Iran, 9
Tempest, The, 28, 41
Ten Commandments, the, 230
Thane of Cawdor, 220
Theatatus, 85
Theogony, 173
Theseus, 37, 45
thinking, cognitive act of, 151
thought, identity of, 151
Thrasymachus, 12, 174

"Three Philosophical Poets," 27
Thus Spoke Zarathustra, 24
Timaeus, 172
time
   metaphors, 172
   natural, 171, 174
   objective, 174, 178, 185
   personal, 171
   subjective, 171, 174, 184
Timon of Athens, 17, 78, 239
Titus Andronicus, 93
Titus Andronicus, 152
Touchstone, 43–45, 49, 78, 145
Tractatus Logico-Philosophicus, 125–26
tragedy, 17
Tranio, 38, 46–47, 144–45
transmigration of souls, 112
Travels of the Three Sherley Brothers, 71
Treatise of Equivoation, A, 163
trinity, ideas of, 86
Troilus, 63, 158, 229
Troilus and Cressida, 21–22, 46, 145
Turner, Frederick, 172
turtle dove, 94
Twelfth Night, 78, 94, 112, 162, 163–64, 167
Two Gentlemen of Verona, 22
Two Noble Kinsmen, The, 120

Ulysses, 21–22, 96–97, 216, 240, 246, 249, 250, 255
universal values, 230
universe, creation of, 172–73
University of California at Berkeley, 9
Utopia, 133, 174
Utopia, 244

values, conflicting, 224
Vasari's Lives, 83
Vendler, Helen, 26, 87, 122, 232
Venetians, Christian, 251
Venus and Adonis, 91
Viola, 163–64, 205–206
Virgil, 35
visual metaphors, 189
Volpone, 253
Volumnia, (Coriolanus's mother), 26
Vulgate Bible, 70

water, 205
"Will" sonnets, the, 28
"willful suspension of disbelief," 160
Winter's Tale, The, 43–44, 83, 172
wisdom and self-knowledge, 95
witchcraft, 112
witches, 178
Wittenberg University, 213
Wittgenstein, Ludwig, 30, 125, 159, 181, 193, 213
Wolsey, Cardinal, 98, 218

Xanthippe, 55
Xenophanes, 134

Yeats, 140

Zend-Avesta, 73
Zeus, 93–94
Zoroastrianism (ancient Persian religion), 71